SEEING BABIES IN A NEW LIGHT

The Life of Hanuš Papoušek

SEEING BABIES IN A NEW LIGHT

The Life of Hanuš Papoušek

by

Lynne Sanford Koester
and
Otto Koester

LEA LAWRENCE ERLBAUM ASSOCIATES, PUBLISHERS
2005   Mahwah, New Jersey   London

Lawrence Erlbaum Associates, Inc., Publishers
10 Industrial Avenue
Mahwah, New Jersey 07430
www.erlbaum.com

Cover photographs by Dr. Mechthild Papoušek & Dr. Jennifer Waltz

Cover design by Kathryn Houghtaling Lacey

Library of Congress Cataloging-in-Publication Data

Koester, Lynne Sanford.
  Seeing babies in a new light : the life of Hanuš Papoušek / by Lynne Sanford Koester
and Otto Koester.
      p.   cm.
  Includes bibliographical references and index.
  ISBN 0-8058-4270-5
  1. Papoušek, Hanuš.   Psychologists—Biography.   I. Koester, Otto.   II. Title.
BF109.P35K64   2005
150'.92—dc22
                                                                    2005040104
                                                                            CIP

Books published by Lawrence Erlbaum Associates are printed on acid-free paper,
and their bindings are chosen for strength and durability.

Printed in the United States of America
10   9   8   7   6   5   4   3   2   1

We dedicate this to Torin and Reid,
who from infancy onward have enriched
our lives and been the source of immense
fulfillment and inspiration to us as parents

Contents

Foreword

Lewis P. Lipsitt
Brown University

On a sunny day in the mid-1960s I, my wife and young son and daughter drove in our VW squareback toward Cape Cod from our cottage in southeastern Massachusetts, intent on giving our esteemed visitor from Czechoslovakia the full Cape experience, through historic Hyannis and on to Provincetown. The pleasure of his company was palpable in all of us. As we arrived at the Bourne Bridge, I mentioned the origins of the Cape Cod Canal and the eventual completion of the project by the U.S. government. Then I noticed that Hanuš became uneasy.

By this date I had come to know Hanuš Papoušek rather well. We had been together at a conference of developmental psychologists, I had been asked to help with the editing of his manuscript that came from that conference, and we had had wonderful conversations about the field of infant learning and development and the scientists that we both knew. Moreover, he engaged Mark and Ann in marvelously memorable chats, and they, like Edna and myself, had come to be very fond of him. He had always been calm, measured in his speech, and even poetic in his use of the English language, which was still very much a foreign tongue for him. Now, however, as we drove alongside the beautiful canal toward the next bridge at the other end of the canal, I noticed in Hanuš an uncharacteristic incoherence and some discomfort as we chatted. When we came to the midway point on the canal road, I drove into a rest area, stopping in front of a sign which commemorated the opening of the bridge in the early 20th century, and honoring the US Army Corps of Engineers which had accomplished the construction. Hanuš read the sign and immediately said emphatically that he should not be there. He said something about international sensitivities and about constraints that Eastern Europeans must endure in visiting the US. While I did not believe that surveillance of us was a problem, Hanuš' concern was quite evident and we left the area, canceling our Cape Cod tour.

It was not until reading this book that I fully appreciated the extent to which, at that time, Hanuš probably felt distressed by the appearance of a governmental "facility," especially near the Atlantic coastline.

With the publication of this biography of Hanuš Papoušek, co-written by his colleague and friend, Lynne Koester, with her husband, Otto Koester, an expert in relationships among nations of the Cold War era, we are treated to the life of a brilliant person, an icon in the field of infant behavior and development studies, and a man of fascination for his scientific ingenuity and enormous breadth of knowledge. Papoušek had collegial connections with many peers in many countries over a long period of time, and thus his life history helps to illuminate the human consequences of the enduring global hostilities prevailing in the second half of the 20th century.

I was one of those who had the opportunity to know and admire Hanuš from the time he attended a conference in Stillwater, Minnesota in 1963 until his death in Munich in the year 2000. We talked in Stillwater about his pioneering work on infant learning, and especially about the sensory and learning capabilities of the newborn which I and my colleagues and students were studying at Brown University. One of his great contributions to the study of infant learning was his elaboration of the usual style of classical Pavlovian conditioning, to include as part of the process an "instrumental" component. He used unconditioned or congenital responses (head turning to a touch on the cheek, and sucking in the present of intra-oral stimulation), and he imposed conditioning stimuli (a buzzer or bell) which were to acquire, through training, the eliciting capabilities of the unconditioned stimulus. Elaborating on a typical Pavlovian procedure which would have terminated the trial if the subject did not respond, he "coached" the head-turning, moving the infant's head in the appropriate direction if the baby did not do it himself (that is, respond with a head turn to the peri-oral stimulation). In order to be reinforced, the baby had to turn its head appropriately. When the turn was made, milk was delivered. Thus the baby was required to engage in the response *in order to* receive the reward. That instrumentality of the required or to-be-learned response was the core of his innovation and, probably, the reason for his greater success in demonstrating infant learning than that of his Soviet predecessors and mentors.

Hanuš visited my laboratory and he lectured at Brown University. We were both participants in the program of the International Congress of Psychology in London in 1966, when I also visited his laboratory at the Institute for the Care of Mothers and Infants in Prague. While staying at his family apartment in Prague, Edna and our children had the excitement of Hanuš' fast driving on the narrow mountain roads from Prague to Brno, to meet his parents, while I was in Moscow for a Psychology Congress. We had numerous subsequent contacts in various places on the globe, and wonderful opportunities to talk about research and new developments in our fields of interest, often combined with memorable family interactions. Hanuš and his second wife Mechthild, her sister, and her mother stayed with us at our cottage, under less stressful conditions than on his first visit, and we toured museums together in the south of France, discovering in this way that Hanuš could probably have served as a docent in any museum in the world!

It would not be over-sentimentalizing a professional relationship to say that I and my family had in Hanuš an enduringly beloved friend. Those who have had close and lasting friendships will understand that Hanuš and I could write each other letters or have phone talks that were continuous, even after a rather large span of time had passed. He could do this with three different people in one day, in three different languages! The present volume on Hanuš' life captures beautifully this talent and enormous collegiality.

Yet, Hanuš was a man of some mystery as well. There were times when he could not be entirely candid, even with his close friends, and that becomes more understandable in view of the national and international political situation of his times. The canal event must be seen in that light. After reading the Koesters' treatment of his life, I have a clearer comprehension of Hanuš' need for vigilance.

This book, with all credit to the authors, is an excellent summation of and tribute to a remarkably generative man and innovative scientist, and a troubled time in the world of politics and human relationships across international boundaries. It is, moreover, an excellent commentary on the ways in which science and scientists overcome difficult times while doing their work. It is a striking exposition also of the way in which large-scale politics (as well as those of a more local nature) can provide impetus for, as well as interference with or suppression of, creative work.

Readers of this volume will have a good sense, by the end, of the man's remarkable sense of humor combined with an abiding cynicism. When Hanuš came to Brown to lecture on his infant behavior research in the late 1960s, the presentation was to be in a large auditorium of the new engineering building which had excellent projection equipment to accommodate his excellent photographic slides. When he entered the auditorium as the first lecturer to appear in that facility, we discovered there was no electric socket for the projector; none had been built into the walls of this room designed for modern projection equipment! Coming from a country which was known to be, as he put it, "somewhat retarded" in its technological advances, Hanuš was delighted to find some flaws in America. His pleasure was renewed the next day when he tried to patronize the new U.S. Post Office in Providence, the one that was celebrated on a U.S. postage stamp as the first completely automatic post office. He put his money in the machine, pushed the appropriate buttons, and nothing happened. Waiting in my car, I realized he was gone for a long time, so I went into the building— to find Hanuš banging on the machine like any American might do after losing his deposited coins. Later he teased me with: "Lew, are you sure it is completely automatic—maybe programmed to take people's money?"

Finally, reading here about Hanuš' second major research fascination, that having to do with his and Mechthild's notion of "intuitive parenting," I was impressed with the extent to which the methods of observation, the discussion of the underlying mechanisms, and the introduction of interventions match psychological processes and methodological techniques that have been identified with behavior analysis and behavior modification. The notions of stimulus control, capitalizing on congenital dispositions, keen observation of response occurrence and timing, shaping, and judicious administration of reinforcement following to-be-learned responses, are all there, in the context of a theory of response-reciprocity between mother and infant. I thought, as I became more acquainted with these instrumental elaborations of Hanuš' previous emendations of Pavlovian conditioning: How wonderfully ingenious. The linkage here between an essentially American kind of behaviorism with Pavlovian conditioning is, in words Hanuš Papoušek used frequently, "for sure."

Introduction

My own introduction to Hanuš Papoušek came in summer 1982. Otto and I, along with another faculty couple from North Carolina, were leading a student group to East and West Germany and I was coteaching a course on social policies affecting families and children—an East–West comparison during the time when the "Iron Curtain" was still very much in place. Our first stop was Munich. One of our goals was to expose the university students to social scientists and policymakers whenever possible during their 2-month stay, so I had contacted an American developmental psychologist, Peter Mangione, at the Max Planck Institute for Psychiatry for suggestions and assistance. It was our good fortune that Hanuš Papoušek was set to lecture the day after we arrived. Following his talk, Hanuš graciously invited me to meet with him the next afternoon to hear more about the history and current state of German developmental psychology, particularly infancy research. At that time, my knowledge of his research was based primarily on his early contributions to our understanding of infant learning, but that was sufficient to whet my appetite. Clearly, this was a person who had been on the cutting edge of infancy research at the very inception of that field of study, but also one who was continuing to offer exciting and provocative insights as he developed new interpretations of parenting behaviors.

The following day, I expected to meet with him for a brief discussion, perhaps a tour of his lab, and an opportunity to pick up some reprints of recent publications. Not only did the meeting far exceed these modest expectations, but it led to an opportunity to begin work with him as a Postdoctoral Fellow in 1983 and to continue that collaboration until his death 18 years later. He devoted most of the afternoon, a full 3 hours, to providing me with valuable information and personal observations, as well as "Kaffee und Kuchen" in his usual hospitable style. Topics ranged from the paucity of infancy research in Germany, to the advantages and disadvantages of socialism and its implementation in his own country of Czechoslovakia, and finally the possible risks to children of the "anti-authoritarian childrearing" movement popular at one time in Germany. It was obvious to me that this was a person from whom one could learn a tremendous amount simply by listening and asking the right questions. This thought was never far from my mind as I returned to my teaching at the end of the summer and planned for an upcoming sabbatical. My correspondence with Hanuš Papoušek during that year and his encouragement to apply for various fellowships stimulated this interest further, and eventually resulted in our moving to Munich in August 1983.

During the years of our collaboration, our families came to know each other quite well; we never tired of hearing fascinating anecdotes about Hanuš' life in Prague, wartime memories, his earlier visits to the United States, and the professional and political dilemmas he had experienced. All were told with humor, but also with a great deal of perceptiveness about human nature and the tensions between politics and science. Above all, the message that came through was one of a great humanitarian sensibility that motivated the life of this courageous but modest man. Many times, his recollections ended with a chuckle and the comment that "my friends tell me I should write a book about my life!" But this would quickly be followed by the statement that he would never write such a book, because it would focus too much on himself.

When I finally approached him with the question of whether or not he would be willing to let someone else write about Hanuš Papoušek, the response was hesitant but firm: "I would not agree to anything that might seem like a 'personality cult'—we have seen too much of what this can lead to in Eastern Europe already." The turning point was when he became convinced that the generations of younger (and future) scholars might benefit from understanding the life history of a researcher who managed, despite the Cold War and the severe restrictions that resulted, to be productive and successful in a career spanning from East to West. My own feeling was that discussion of this is largely omitted from textbooks and writings on the history of psychology, but it is important for students to be aware of the impact that government policies and practices can have on scientific endeavors both at the individual and at the institutional level. Of course, I was delighted when he and his wife, Mechthild, agreed to this project.

In the summer 1998, I was back in Munich again, this time for the purposes of conducting extensive interviews with Hanuš himself regarding his life's work, and of compiling a list with him of potential contacts for further interviews. It was evident during a phone call soon after my arrival that he was ill (a highly unusual occurrence), suffering from a sore throat from which he had been unable to recover. This came as a surprise because, in all of my years of working with him, I could not recall a time when he had been sick enough to complain or make others aware of any discomfort. Indeed, Hanuš visited a doctor 2 days later and Mechthild shared the diagnosis with me: acute leukemia. I was not the only one in shock. They hastily prepared to admit him to the hospital, with little idea of what the future might bring.

Ever optimistic, Hanuš insisted that I stay in Munich long enough to see how he responded to the first chemotherapy, and asked me to come to the hospital on his third day there to begin our discussions. Fortunately, he managed that first round of treatment extremely well, and I was able to spend the next several weeks interviewing him on an almost daily basis. Hanuš seemed to have decided he was not going to behave like a hospital patient at all: He described his daily routine of getting up early, preparing himself and dressing as if for work, making his bed, then spending the remainder of the day at his writing table—working, except for those annoying interruptions by nurses and doctors! Initially, I went with the expectation (as on the first day I had been introduced to him) that we might meet only briefly, perhaps to clarify a few things or brainstorm about colleagues to contact. Again I was surprised, this time by his stamina and enthusiasm and desire to talk about his life. This pattern continued throughout that first hospital stay, into many lengthy interviews, and resulted in much of the rich information we have been able to gather about his life for this book.

For the next 2 years he battled leukemia, which included remissions and hopefulness muted by relapses, and endured many difficult treatments. The experience was extremely challenging for Hanuš and his family, as well as for his numerous friends and colleagues around the world. For some of his contemporaries, there was a sense of disbelief that Hanuš—seemingly one of the healthiest and most resilient of them all—might be the first to go.

This biographical project thus became more intense and emotionally laden than we could ever have imagined: There were over 30 hours of tape-recorded discussions with Hanuš, reminiscing and reviewing his own life in great detail while knowing full well what his diagnosis likely would mean; there was also the sadness, the fear, the anticipated sense of profound loss as his family and friends also prepared themselves for the eventuality of his death. In fact, some of our interviews with his professional colleagues took place either shortly before or just after Hanuš Papoušek died on May 5, 2000. The notes and messages that followed provided ample testimony to the mark he made, the impact he had, and the many lives he deeply touched.

We feel extremely fortunate and grateful that Hanuš entrusted this project—his scientific biography—to us, so that the story of his courage, wit, intellect, and integrity can be preserved and passed on. We also feel a deep sense of loss knowing that he is no longer able to share these memories himself, with the flair and humor as only he could do. Although this book was not yet complete at the time of his death, we made an effort to emphasize to him the warmth and affection, the respect and admiration toward him that was evident from virtually every person we interviewed. In this small way, everyone who contributed to this volume also contributed to Hanuš Papoušek's awareness of the importance and significance of his life, even as he approached its end.

—*Lynne and Otto Koester*

Acknowledgments

Our gratitude is extended first and foremost to the Papoušek family, because without their agreement, cooperation, encouragement, and belief that this was a worthwhile endeavor, our efforts to uncover and understand Hanuš' life would never have begun. The timing of this project, coinciding as it did with the onset of his illness, led us to question more than once the advisability of continuing. Yet, the opportunity to share and be the recipients of Hanuš Papoušek's astute autobiographical memory led to a rich store of information that we hope will be as valuable and meaningful to his family as it has been to us.

Of course, such a book could not have been completed without the contributions of many individuals, mostly Hanuš' professional colleagues in North America, Germany, and the Czech Republic. We are extremely appreciative of the time, the reflections, and the deep fondness and respect for Hanuš that they shared so generously. A few in particular stand out for having also provided photographs, their early correspondence with Hanuš, hospitality during our travels, and personal support throughout the process. To these individuals we are deeply indebted: Mechthild Papoušek, Marc and Helen Bornstein, Jarka and Františík Dittrich, Lew and Edna Lipsitt, Darwin Muir, and Arnold Sameroff.

To our close friends Frances Hill, Shan Guisinger, David Schuldberg, Claire and Larry Morse, and our own two sons, we are especially grateful for their encouragement, motivation, editorial advice, and many helpful critiques. Two people who deserve special thanks for their hard work and ongoing assistance are Rose Marie Koester, who quickly and competently transcribed many hours of interviews during our sabbatical year, and Katarína

Guttmannová, whose careful reading, translating, and explaining of Hanuš' early Czech publications helped us immeasurably.

Bill Webber, our editor at Lawrence Erlbaum Publishers, was encouraging, enthusiastic, patient, and flexible as he guided us through this process; his assistance and good humor throughout were most appreciated!

Chapter 1

Hanuš Papoušek:
Youth, Education, and
Early Professional Years

In 1961 and 1962, at the height of the Cold War, a number of American psychologists traveled to Europe and the Soviet Union to familiarize themselves with research being conducted on learning in children and infants, a subject of growing attention in American developmental psychology. Working under the auspices of the Social Science Research Council's (SSRC) Committee on Intellective Processes, they visited well-known research centers such as the Pavlov Institute in Leningrad and the Rousseau Institute in Geneva headed by Jean Piaget. Two of the psychologists—William Kessen, of Yale University, and Frank Palmer, an SRCC staff member—also visited the newly established Institute for the Care of Mother and Child in Prague. Coincidentally, the person assigned as their guide was Hanuš Papoušek, a pediatrician and psychologist in charge of research on "higher nervous activities" in infants. Fortunately for the visitors, Papoušek spoke English proficiently.

By all accounts, the Americans were somewhat surprised by what they saw. The Institute was much larger and the experiments and observations much more extensive than they had expected. Moreover, the infants being studied were just 0 to 3 days old, much younger than those studied anywhere else in the United States or Western Europe. Most impressive of all were their interactions with Hanuš Papoušek, who not only answered all of Kessen's questions, but also showed him the laboratory, observation equipment, and data records (Dittrichová Interview, October 7, 1999). This openness stood in marked contrast to the reception that the American visitors had received at the Pavlov Institute in Leningrad, where the two visitors met with Institute directors in their offices, but were not allowed to meet any of the researchers or see the insides of the laboratories.

After returning to the United States, Kessen sent a report to the SSRC in which he called particular attention to the Institute for the Care of Mother and Child as a model of how infancy research might be undertaken in the United States if appropriate funding was made available. Soon after receiving this report, the SSRC extended an invitation to Hanuš Papoušek to visit the United States for a conference on comparative developmental processes and to spend 2 months (accompanied by Palmer) giving lectures and colloquia at Yale, New York University, the National Institute of Mental Health, UCLA, Stanford, and University of California–Berkeley. In short, by late summer 1963, Hanuš Papoušek, virtually unknown outside Czechoslovakia, suddenly found himself a "hot commodity" in the world of contemporary American psychology, and a rising "star" in the emerging international community of early developmental and infancy research.

But, who was this person with the name many Americans found hard to pronounce—Hanuš Papoušek? What was his background, what were his views on infancy, and what were some of his methods and preconceptions for studying newborns? If he was not a psychologist by training, then what was the scientific basis for his contention that infants were capable of performing many more tasks at birth than American psychologists previously had thought? And what about the Institute for the Care of Mother and Child? Was it not subject to the political controls of the Czech government and the dicta of the Communist Party? These kinds of questions likely were on the minds of at least some Americans who heard Papoušek speak, especially at a time when "speaker ban" laws existed on some U.S. campuses, and political tensions between East and West were at their height.

To explore these questions, this chapter first examines Hanuš Papoušek's background, beginning with his youth, education, and early professional training, and ending with his early years at the Institute for the Care of Mother and Child in Prague. It is argued that the direction of Papoušek's life was integrally related to larger events in the 20th-century history of Czechoslovakia, but that he also underwent an intellectual and personal development that was very much his own. Indeed, in the same way that much of 20th-century Czech history has been described as an effort by the Czechs to define their own path, so too can the life and scientific ideas of Hanuš Papoušek.

CHILDHOOD AND SCHOOL YEARS: 1922–1941

It is fair to say that Hanuš Papoušek's early life paralleled that of a new generation of Czechs born after World War I—a generation that grew up experiencing the hopes of a newly independent, democratic country, only to see their nation fall victim to a brutal Nazi occupation and the horrors of World War II. After the war, many members of this generation also joined in reconstructing Czechoslovakia for the purpose of building a more just and humane society under the leadership of the Communist Party. In the process of growing up and surviving the war, Hanuš Papoušek and many members of his generation also became involved in the political reform movement of Alexander Dubcek, which called for the creation of "socialism with a human face"; unfortunately, these dreams were harshly extinguished by the 1968 Soviet invasion. Hanuš Papoušek, working as a pediatrician and scientist, was one of this generation's best examples.

Knowledge of Papoušek's family background and early youth is based largely on anecdotes and stories that he told friends and colleagues later in life. To be sure, anyone who has worked with source materials consisting of recollections and retrospections understands that, by their very nature, such sources are the product of adulthood, and they may not reflect accurately the insights or lessons experienced during youth. At the same time, such materials offer interesting clues about formative youthful experiences that are perceived to be important for that person's later development. This is the case with the recollections of Hanuš Papoušek.

In a 1996 conversation with the Canadian psychologist Darwin Muir, for instance, Papoušek reminisced about his early life by saying that his formative experiences revolved around a combination of three basic themes: developmental psychology, biology, and medicine, and his desire to help prepare a new generation of postwar youth to deal more effectively with problems of conflict and peace (Muir Interview, October 26, 1996). As a broad summary, this retrospection undoubtedly is correct, but it also leaves many details and nuances unsaid. Indeed, as one examines recollections more closely, a more complicated picture of his early life begins to emerge.

Papoušek was born on September 9, 1922, in a small town of Moravia called Letovice. When still young, Hanuš' family moved to Brno, the Moravian capital. He lived there until 1949, when he was 28. By all accounts he was raised in a warm and caring environment. His immediate family consisted of his parents, himself, and a younger sister. Hanuš recalled being proud of the fact that both his parents were Moravians, and both came from educated families. His father was a teacher who came from a family of educators, biologists, and musicians (although it bears noting that he also was a military officer in World War I). His mother came from an educated family as well, and after marrying his father, became a housewife. As an adult, Hanuš liked to point out that his grandfather was a musician and colleague of the Czech composer Leo Janácek, and he himself grew up learning to play the piano. In old age, Hanuš enjoyed showing visitors to his home in Munich a life-size poster of his mother (photographed by himself, of course) leaning over the kitchen table and baking *Marillenknödel*, or apricot-filled dumplings, a Moravian delicacy that was Hanuš' favorite childhood dessert.

His family moved to Brno when his father, after several years as a small-town teacher, was offered a job as the director of a school. In addition to being the Moravian capital, Brno had a university and offered many intellectual and cultural opportunities for an intellectually gifted and multitalented child like Hanuš. The Papoušek family was happy living in Brno, a town to which Hanuš became very attached. The 1920s and early 1930s were also a good time for Czechoslovakia, which, thanks to a relatively speedy recovery from World War I, enjoyed one of the highest standards of living in all of Europe. In the political realm, enormous strides were also being made. To everyone's surprise, the end of World War I brought defeat to Germany and Austria–Hungary, but the Czechs received something they had been unable to attain for almost 300 years—independence achieved by peaceful means. For the first time since 1621, the destiny of these proud people lay in their own hands. Many Americans still hold the view that Czechoslovakia's independence was largely a gift from Woodrow Wilson under the terms of the Versailles Treaty. However, European historians tend to agree that Czechoslovakia's nationhood would not have come about without the political skills of several of the country's key leaders, or without the support for these leaders among the general Czech population (Korbel, 1977, pp. 25–38). With the patriarchal and stifling political and social order of the Habsburg Empire finally gone, the nation started to thrive under a democratic constitution and the humane leadership of its founding president, Thomas Masaryk.

It is significant to note that Papoušek mentioned the name of Thomas Masaryk quite frequently as an adult, and that Masaryk played an important role in his father's life. Hanuš' father was a great admirer of Masaryk. Like Hanuš' father, he was a native of Moravia and developed a moral vision of society that was firmly grounded in the tradition of Czech humanism; Hanuš' father shared Masaryk's commitment to a combination of nationalism, democracy, and socialism in building an independent Czechoslovakia. Toward the end of World War I, Hanuš' father and uncle were members of the "Masaryk Legion" in Russia at the time of the Russian Revolution. By the time the "Masaryk Legion" was disbanded (with aid from the Americans), Hanuš' father had risen to the rank of captain. In addition, when his father became the director of a school, it was at the newly built "Masaryk School" in Brno.

The Masaryk School was one of several educational experiments launched by the Ministry of Education for the purpose of overcoming socioeconomic and ethnic differences among young children, one of the major goals of the new Masaryk regime. The school in Brno was situated midway between the richest and poorest sections of town; Hanuš later remembered the impact of discussions with his father about the effect of education on children's attitudes, and the extent to which their attitudes were being changed. "The poor children came from the poorest possible part of Brno," he once said in an interview. "It was a slum area where you could really see terrible things, really at the bottom. . . . This had an effect on my thoughts" (Papoušek Interview, July 21, 1998). As an adult, Hanuš also became a great admirer of Masaryk who, together with the 17th-century educator and moral teacher Jan Amos Comenius, became one of several Moravians in his pantheon of heroes. (Papoušek liked to cite Comenius in his scientific publications. In 1965, for example, he introduced his first publication to appear in English with a tribute to Comenius for his early interest in child development. Similar tributes can be found in articles Papoušek wrote in the 1990s.)

At age 14, around 1936, Hanuš' interests began to focus more on school, reflecting his growing interest in the world of ideas. Interestingly, after completion of primary school, he did not enroll in the city's traditional *Gymnasium*, as might have been expected, but in Brno's 2nd *Realgymnasium*. It says a great deal about Hanuš and his educational background that he did not attend the more prestigious humanities-oriented *Gymnasium* with its emphasis on Latin, Greek, and classical philosophy, but instead chose the modern and "realistic" *Realgymnasium* with its emphasis on the natural sciences, mathematics, philosophy, and modern languages. His father, as an educator, must have known that the *Realgymnasium* was a better match for his son's talents. It appears to have been a good choice, because Hanuš was an excellent student in all subjects, and upon graduation stood near the top of his class.

During his *Realgymnasium* years, Papoušek also showed signs of becoming interested in foreign travel and making international contacts, a passion that continued throughout his adult life. (Professional colleagues who knew Hanuš well enough sometimes teased him about his seeming compulsion to attend yet another international conference or visit a new foreign country: "Hanuš, exactly which international meeting are you off to this time?") In late 1936, Hanuš, at his own initiative, found a boy his age in Yugoslavia who was interested in a student-to-student exchange. The agreement was that the Yugoslav boy would spend summer 1937 with Hanuš and his family in Brno, and Hanuš would spend summer 1938 in Yugoslavia. When the Yugoslav boy came to Brno, the two became fast friends, but when it came time for Hanuš to visit Yugoslavia, his parents refused to give him permission to go. Concerned about the growing danger of war with Germany, his parents preferred to keep him closer to home.

In 1938, the carefree days of Hanuš' childhood were coming to an end. His parents' refusal to allow him to go abroad was significant not so much as a missed opportunity to visit his first foreign country, but because, for the first time in his life, an inescapable political problem intervened in his personal plans. Masaryk died in 1937 and shortly thereafter Hitler threatened to invade Czechoslovakia in order to "bring home" the German minority living in the borderlands of the Sudetenland. Disregarding the Munich agreement of September 1938, Hitler ordered German tanks across the Czech border on October 1, 1938, and started a 6-year military occupation, one of the most ruthless and brutal imposed by the Nazis. The effect of these events was to confront Hanuš and every Czech adult and child with fundamental fears about the safety of their country and their personal lives, and force them to ask themselves what kind of action they would be prepared to take. Trauma and tumult entered everyone's life. Asked to reflect on these events, Papoušek later said:

> If I now compare my kids today, well, there's nothing comparable. There are no worries about war over here or there, and in practical terms there's just nothing—just questions about tactical moves, and some discussion afterwards

Hanuš with mother, Aloisie Papoušek, and sister, Véra.

Hanuš as infant.

Hanuš as a young boy.

Hanuš the Boy Scout.

Hanuš and young friends on bicycle trip near Brno, Czechoslovakia.

of those moves, but not about real, major problems. Whereas for us, it was
critical. . . . (Don't ask me) to write the history of Czechoslovakia, but I'm just
explaining that in practical terms, in everyday life, you were exposed to a mixture of philosophical, religious, scientific and political issues because it's difficult to separate those things from each other. . . . The mobilization meant
practically, for me, that our *Gymnasium* was taken by the Czech military forces
as a unit of a hospital. And we had to continue our studies at different schools
around town and share rooms in their facilities. So there was an engagement
which went through all parts of your present life. . . . From a political point of
view, these kinds of . . . things . . . actually pushed you away from politics. I
found scientific questions, and scientific interests and friends much more attractive than these political problems. Because, you know, . . . we were French-
oriented, tremendously French-oriented, so that this Munich agreement was
a great disaster—a moral disaster—for the young generation. So we had to
just somehow cope with it. (Papoušek Interview, July 14, 1998)

"Just somehow cope with it"? From a contemporary perspective, one is
tempted to say, how typically Czech! In many ways, Papoušek's response is
reminiscent of a recurring theme in Czechoslovakia's tortured history—an
example that the Czechs once again were holding back from defending their
personal liberty at any price. On the other hand, perhaps such a judgment is
made too readily. Then, as well as today, the question remains open whether
or not Edvard Beneš, Masaryk's successor as president of the First Republic,
was correct in calculating that military resistance against the Germans was fu-
tile and would cost too many Czech lives. For our purposes here, let it suffice
to note that the Nazi occupation posed a very real threat to Hanuš' father, his
uncle, and their families. By virtue of their service in the Masaryk Legion,
both his father and his uncle had extensive personal contacts among the underground network of democratic leaders, and both had fears of being

found out. When the Nazi troops came, Hanuš' uncle, living in a small southern Moravian town in the Sudetenland region, was reported to the German
authorities for turning around street signs to confuse the entering Nazi
troops and lead them in a different direction. (Czechs did the same thing
when Soviet troops invaded in 1968.) His uncle died during the early part of
the German occupation in a concentration camp.

From a different point of view, however, Papoušek's recollections about
the events of 1938 contain a very revealing insight about himself. Confronted by violence, oppression, and human disrespect, he felt "pushed"
away from the political world, while the world of science, scientific questions, and scientific friends drew him in. In comparing both worlds, he recognized that science and scientific inquiry "attracted" him more. It was a remarkable lesson for someone at that early age to learn, and one to which
later chapters return.

Toward the end of his *Gymnasium* years, Hanuš became increasingly interested in psychology and the natural sciences, particularly biology. His
philosophy teacher was a psychologist by training who left a lifelong impression on Hanuš by conducting psychological demonstrations and tests in
front of the class. This was very unusual for Czech schools at the time, and
Hanuš frequently was called on to help recruit young children from his father's school as subjects for the teacher's experiments. His interest in biology began as early as age 11, when he already had his own microscope and
started to conduct observations on algae. Beginning at age 14, his father's
brother, a professional biologist, began to take him under his wing. The uncle, Jan Kalášek, had been a university professor before the Nazi invasion,
but was reassigned to teach at a lower level in an agricultural vocational
school in Brno. As fortune would have it, the uncle's laboratory was within
sight of Hanuš' home, and the professor began spending many hours showing Hanuš how to set up systematic experiments. "I had my own microscope
at home," Hanuš remembered, "but I had an even better one at my uncle's
laboratory, and he acted like a consultant who was always available to me"
(Papoušek Interview, July 21, 1998).

In addition to Kalášek, another professional biologist also began teaching Hanuš. A friend of his father's, he often spent weeks with the Papoušek
family during their summer vacations in the countryside, and frequently
took Hanuš on long nature walks to study different kinds of plants and animals. "Long before becoming interested in medicine," Hanuš remembered, "issues like evolution, different comparative approaches to motives
in human behavior and animal behavior—I knew a lot about these things"
(Muir Interview, October 26, 1996). Guided by his biologist uncle and the
family friend, he recalled finding something in the world of science and nature of which he found less in the political world: "For me, it was that science was actually a potential piece of the world where you could find differ-

ent truths and different life conditions where truth means something. And if you are trying to find a little bit of truth in something, then you don't worry about your motivations. I don't know how easily the politicians are motivated for finding out the truth" (Papoušek Interview, July 14, 1998).

Not surprisingly, Hanuš chose biology as his field of concentration in preparation for his *Matura*, the examination required of all Czech students to graduate from *Gymnasium*. With the assistance of his biology mentors, he passed his *Matura* exams with flying colors. In spring 1941, at age 18, Hanuš graduated from *Gymnasium* with excellent marks.

SURVIVING THE WAR: 1942–1944

Unlike many Europeans his age, Hanuš was fortunate to survive the war without wearing a uniform, but he was not able to go to university either. After graduating from *Gymnasium*, Hanuš hoped to continue his studies, but the problem was, where? His goal was to study medicine, but after the German takeover, all Czech universities had been closed. In contrast to other countries, the students in Czechoslovakia had organized public demonstrations against the Nazi invasion, causing the Germans to fear that the universities would be ongoing centers of resistance. One option would have been to attend a university in Germany, but this was something neither he nor his classmates wanted. The Nazis were so despised that anyone seen even associating with a German was suspected of being a collaborator. Moreover, going to Germany would mean having to speak German, a language he wanted to avoid; he was too much of a patriot. Instead, waiting to see what might happen, he decided to enroll in a 4-month English language program in Brno. It was a short-term commitment and he had been interested in improving his English for quite some time. It also meant he could continue to live at home in Brno.

By the time his language program ended, however, the German war machine was in desperate need of labor, and in early 1942 Hanuš received notification to report for the Nazi's *Totaleinsatz*, or total mobilization effort. The Nazis never trusted the Czechs enough to recruit them for the German army's regular units, and instead drafted Czech youths from specific years to work in military-related industries. Hanuš decided he would report for the *Totaleinsatz*, and was lucky to get a local assignment:

Then came an incident in my life that's sometimes difficult to believe. I was sitting there waiting for these guys to make decisions—"you 15 guys go to the factories in Cologne, you 15 go to Vienna"—when someone comes along who says they were opening a new factory in my area, not very far from Brno where I was living. And they said, "Don't you have anybody whom we can employ in health service?" And the guy sitting there said to me, "Didn't you say that you want to study medicine?" I said, "yes," of course! (Papoušek Interview, July 14, 1998)

Fortunate enough to avoid military service, Hanuš was assigned to be a medical aid worker in the health services department of the *Ostmarkwerke*, a German manufacturer that built aircraft engines. With other plants already located in Germany and Austria, *Ostmark* had just finished building a new factory in Liesz, a town within commuting distance of Brno. He worked at the factory for the next 3 years, until late 1944. One week was spent working night shifts, the next week day shifts, 12 hours each day. Everyone was required to work 13 days, with the 14th day off. His commute to and from the factory was 2 hours each way, meaning his workday was a total of 16 hours a day. The days were tiring, but unlike many other classmates, he felt lucky not to be a soldier and to live at home.

After the war, Hanuš occasionally told friends and colleagues about some of his experiences at the factory. Because the majority of the workers were Czechs, a great deal of time was spent plotting, scheming, and organizing the daily routines in such a way that as little work as possible got done. In fact, large amounts of time were devoted to planning and carrying out small-scale acts of sabotage. Just as much as the Czechs constantly engaged in sabotage, the Nazi supervisors constantly were trying to find out who was responsible for the acts. "I think it's very difficult to imagine what it means for a young person," he once reflected. "You always felt like you had to do something—it was actually your patriotic duty. . . . You had to be tremendously careful, and always keep in mind that you might actually be detected by someone" (Papoušek Interview, July 14, 1998). Tragically, some of the distrust and suspicion experienced in the factory would recur again after the war.

Amidst the constant plotting and need to remain vigilant, Hanuš and the other workers in the health services unit also had a fair amount of unoccupied time during their work hours. Shortly after his arrival at the factory, a number of Czech medical students joined his unit, and the group soon began self-organized study sessions. It was his first introduction to the study of medicine. "They would invite me just to listen, since there was often not enough to do. There was enough time to study, and in those circumstances we came upon some textbooks. I could read and make my notes, and the time was not totally lost" (Papoušek Interview, July 14, 1998). It was an advantage for him that he already knew English, because the medical textbooks they used were mostly those left behind by American missionaries in Moravia.

By 1944, it was becoming clear to Hanuš that his days at the factory would come to an end, and as word of the Allied army successes traveled across the country, hopes began to emerge concerning Czechoslovakia's liberation. At that point it was still unclear whether Soviet or American soldiers would be the likely liberators, but with the end of the war in sight, air raids over major Czech industrial sites and large towns also began to occur. It was during one of these air raids, in late 1944, that Hanuš had a life-changing experience:

> When these armies approached my city, it also meant air raids, and I was caught by an air raid lasting four hours in the middle of the factory (field), with no shelter, just lying in the middle of everything. As a matter of fact, I thought that I was dying. I was hit by different things, and you know, the explosions, and all those things. It was a very significant experience. And I have to say, since that day, I have appreciated every single further day of my life as an unexpected blessing. And I really thought it was the end of my life in that air raid. So, I sort of changed in the sense that I made very serious decisions about my future life. I didn't want to spend any time on unimportant or irrelevant things. And my conviction became that something should be done against the danger of future wars and conflicts. It led me to the conclusion that we have to start very early in bringing up a new generation which will be, you know. . . . That it will be possible to change something, and be better prepared for eventual conflicts than our generation was. (Muir Interview with Hanuš Papoušek, October 26, 1996)

When the air raid was over, it was not at all certain that Hanuš would be able to carry out his life goals. However, he escaped with relatively minor shrapnel wounds. When the liberation finally came, he knew that, all things considered, fate had been relatively kind to him. Physically and mentally he was unharmed, and his parents and sister were alive. And yet, like most of his generation, he was totally unprepared for what awaited Czechoslovakia next. He recalled the end of the war:

> This was the Nazis. And then one day it (the war) is finished and you are happy that you survived, and that you are free. And then "Bang!", (the next thing you know) you are on the other side—you're within the Soviet bloc whether you like it or not. And again, you have the same situation, because you know that was "National Socialism," and now it was "International Socialism"—and the "social" in it was nowhere to be seen or to be found. (Papoušek Interview, July 14, 1998)

MEDICAL STUDIES AND EARLY PEDIATRIC TRAINING: 1944–1951

The preceding account leaves the impression that Hanuš Papoušek might have held a "Big Bang" view of history, although this most assuredly was not the case. In actuality, the change from National Socialism to Soviet-style Communism did not come overnight. Between the German defeat and the

Communist takeover were almost 3 years of freedom and social reform under the leadership of Edvard Beneš, whose government was brought back from exile. For Hanuš personally, these years became an opportunity to make up for lost time—to start his medical studies, begin a family and launch a career, and remain in touch with emerging political developments.

After getting hit in the air raid, Hanuš left the aircraft factory and almost immediately thereafter took up contact with a number of friends and associates in Brno, who by the end of 1944 started the first medical classes to be held since the closure of the university 6 years before. With the American armies approaching from the west, and the Soviet armies coming from the east, the German occupiers knew their days were numbered and started paying less attention to the activities of the local population, making it possible for university classes to resume. To be sure, large amounts of academic learning did not take place during these first months, because time and again the students were called on to help with service projects such as cleaning up the streets, restoring buildings, and repairing water and sewer lines. In addition, in late 1944 and 1945, items such as paper, pencils, and basic reading materials were very hard to find. In a very real sense, Papoušek was faced with having to start his medical studies from the ground up.

The end of the war came to Czechoslovakia in early April 1945, and was greeted by Hanuš, his fellow students, and the rest of the population with much jubilation and celebration by a popular uprising known as the "national revolution." Under an agreement reached by the major anti-fascist political parties, a government of "national unity" led by Beneš was created to lead the newly liberated country. One can well imagine the hopes that accompanied this happy occasion. Albert Pražák wrote that there seemed to be a logical link between the revolutions of 1918 and 1945. The goal of the first was for national liberation with a strong tendency toward social change; the goal of the second was to bring about both national and social liberation (Korbel, 1977, p. 218). Over the next 3 years, the Beneš government worked hard to pursue both liberations at the same time. Simultaneously, however, powerful postwar political conflicts began to emerge, making it clear that what promised to be the first invigorating experiment in the socialization of a democracy in an industrial society probably would not succeed. The Beneš experiment came to a tragic end in February 1948, when Jan Masaryk, Beneš' foreign minister, mysteriously "fell" out of an open window in Prague. Czechoslovakia became a one-party Communist state.

Hanuš was a medical student throughout the Beneš regime, and finished his studies in 1949. His university work was very demanding, although during these years he also devoted time to at least two other interests. One was his personal life. In early 1945, at age 23, he married his first wife, Draha, a fellow native of Brno. The other was Hanuš' involvement with various kinds of student groups and concerns about political issues of the day. Six years of occupation and war had left the country in ruins, albeit less than most other European countries. With many major political, economic, and social problems, not the least of which was the emergence of East–West hostilities between the Soviet Union and the United States, Czechoslovakia was caught geographically in the middle. In this new era of politics, many issues were hotly debated and discussed by Hanuš and his friends, despite the fact that with the Nazi invasion in 1938, Hanuš had felt "pushed away" from the political world.

Hanuš recalled that he studied medicine under conditions of academic independence but with minimal resources. Due to lack of basic supplies and instructional materials, students had to depend primarily on the notes of their professors, none of whom had taught since the universities had closed. As a result, he and his fellow students had to rely heavily on reading American medical textbooks sent by Czech-American associations, for which his knowledge of English again proved very helpful (Papoušek Interview, July 14, 1998). Academic autonomy came about largely because, like in Poland, Czech universities reopened in accordance with pre-Nazi policies that guaranteed a great deal of independence. Under the Beneš government, a concerted effort was made to reinvigorate the old academic structures and assure that qualified experts replaced those lost to the war, so that the reconstruction of the universities proved to be an almost apolitical task (Connelly, 1999). In addition, in contrast to Poland and the Soviet Union, Czech university officials disregarded the policy of favoring admission for children of workers and farmers, and continued the previous practice of basing entrance decisions primarily on high academic performance. Papoušek's own experience showed that admission of a student from a *bourgeois* family background was not a problem. Most of the professors, educated under the pre-Nazi system, continued to base their classroom expectations on students with a strong *Gymnasium* background. The emphasis on high standards for preparation and training was also reflected in the policies of the Czech Ministry of Health, which refused to follow the policy of sending underqualified "barefoot doctors" into the country. Despite pressing postwar needs, the Ministry insisted on completion of the full medical curriculum and all additional practical requirements before allowing physicians to practice (Papoušek Interview, October 15, 1999).

Consistent with decisions made following his life-changing wartime experience, Papoušek's interests focused on pediatrics. He came to admire the work of the chair of the pediatrics department, Otokar Teyschl. Teyschl was a kindly person who became an example for what Papoušek himself might do later in life. In addition to teaching students, he was something of a Moravian "Dr. Spock" who wrote books on childrearing (Papoušek Interviews, July 14, 1999, and October 15, 1999). Teyschl combined his knowledge of pediatric medicine with interests in education and psychology at a time when there was little interaction among the medical, educational, and psychological worlds. In Czechoslovakia, there was no one at the time who taught child psychology or early development from a psychological perspective, and parents encountering problems with children went to a pediatrician looking for answers. Papoušek came to think of Teyschl as a role model for pursuing a possible university career, although he knew such a career path might not be open to him. The problem, however, was not with his grades, but with his not being a member of the Communist Party.

For the most part, Papoušek followed the regular academic courses and internships, but because of his interest in psychology and "mental processes," he took the unusual step of signing up for an internship in psychiatry. Most of his fellow students considered psychiatry to be a waste of time. Later, when applying for a position at the Institute for the Care of Mother and Child, he found that this experience proved to be an advantage for him (Papoušek Interview, July 14, 1999).

Academic independence came with freedom of expression and the right to talk openly about political problems. In contrast to his viewpoints about politics under the Nazi occupation, Papoušek's retrospections from the years 1945–1948 were very different: "Here I was, this young guy, and with the first university students. We were hot (excited, fired up). The son of my uncle, you know the one who died under the Nazis, and myself, we were close friends. And all of us were sitting around and discussing what to do about this situation. As you can imagine, there were some wild ideas!" (Papoušek Interview, October 15, 1999).

What is it that could have made the two of them so "hot," especially in light of the country's newly acquired freedom? And what were those "wild ideas"? Hadn't Hanuš' more youthful sentiment been to say that the world of science attracted him more than politics? In light of the new situation, were his views changing?

As an adult, Hanuš generally was very reluctant to talk about the details of his political life, calling them personal and private. On one or two occasions, however, he talked more specifically about the postwar situation and about the major problems that concerned him, his cousin, and the other students. As he once explained in a quiet moment, the major problem at this time was the rising influence of the Soviet Union and the imminent Communist takeover of the Czech government. The question was what to do, if anything, to offer resistance:

> You know, my father was a captain in the Russian Czech Legions, led by Masaryk. . . . He was liberated by the American army . . . and he also fought against the Bolsheviks. . . . And then my father, because of this past, when the Nazis came, he acted as an under-officer in Beneš' illegal army. . . . He and my uncle had exactly the same history. And when the Communists came, it was

suspicious, because he was a Russian legionnaire but never joined the Red Army and eventually fought against the Red Army, and that was obviously known. So he was *persona non grata*. . . . My cousin, he tended to organize or enter some illegal organizations. But I was a member of a university committee that discussed such things very openly especially at the beginning. And then . . . there was the Iron Curtain, and the Czechs would be to the East of it. But we had contacts with the English people who were in Beneš' exiled government in London, and we also had contact with people in the American circle. . . . So we checked with all those sources to see what would be the best thing to do. And they actually discouraged us from doing illegal or underground activities, and said we should not offer resistance. They said we would get no support, either from Great Britain or from the United States, and it was going to be extremely dangerous because the Communists were known specialists in disclosing secret organizations. And so, you know, we were *discouraged* from doing anything, and I also told my cousin this, but he didn't obey. So he started boyish actions, decided to find an old printing machine and produce leaflets. And as you can imagine, a month later he was already arrested. (Just like his father, except that had been by the Nazis.) And so many of us at the university, or at least some of us, came up with the idea that we could do it the "Czech way." That means, we'll do what we are expected to do, but we'll add some of our own way to it. And I have to say that was quite effective. . . . There was a group of people who decided to join the Party, and carefully differentiate what to accept from the program and what not. . . . And this was my way to go. So, it led to unbelievable political activities. (Papoušek Interview, October 15, 1999)

In other words, faced with the threat of a Communist takeover, Hanuš gathered information, consulted with friends, and instead of offering overt resistance, came to the conclusion that doing it "the Czech way" would be more effective. His cousin, on the other hand, was cut of different cloth. He was the activist, political organizer, and uncompromising oppositionist. Hanuš discussed with student colleagues how to remain politically effective after a Communist takeover; his cousin landed in prison. Before long, however, more powerful political forces determined their fate. In September or October 1947, the Soviet-controlled Cominform revived the Leninist concept of class struggle and international class solidarity, and Klement Gottwald and the other Czech Communist Party leaders were ordered to stop supporting the democratic, multiparty parliamentary course of Beneš. In February 1948, the Czech party staged a successful coup with the assistance of Soviet agents who, among other crimes, murdered Jan Masaryk, Beneš' foreign minister and son of the former president. On February 25, 1948, Gottwald demanded from Beneš that he be allowed to form a Communist government. Beneš capitulated, as once before in 1938, and made a public announcement saying, "The state must be administered and led" (Korbel, 1977, p. 251).

Papoušek's American and English contacts had given him accurate information. Neither the Americans nor British made an effort to help, and on March 17, 1948, President Harry Truman persuaded Congress to approve the Marshall Plan, effectively sealing democratic Czechoslovakia's fate that it would not get any help from the West. Shortly after the coup, the Communist Party moved quickly to consolidate its power. Thousands of people were thrown out of their jobs, hundreds were arrested, and thousands more fled the country. An election was held in May 1948, showing "official" results that the Communist Party had won 86.01% of the popular vote. From then until the October revolution of 1989, Czechoslovakia remained a one-party Communist state. Although they had been forewarned, the coup was a major setback for Hanuš and his student friends.

Hanuš completed his medical classes and received a doctor of medicine degree from Purkinje University, previously named Masaryk University, in Brno, on September 9, 1949. Initially, he had dreams of going directly into pediatrics, preferably in Brno or in the nearby hospital where other colleagues were also interested in research. "But I was not allowed to go for political reasons. I was not 'reliable' enough," he recalled (Papoušek Interview, October 15, 1999). Instead, upon graduation, he was sent for regular medical training at a district hospital in the southern Moravian town of Kroměříž. In 1949, he moved with his wife Draha from Brno to Kroměříž, where they stayed until 1951. Their first child, Hanuš, had been born in Brno in 1949, just before the move. Hanuš Jr. was joined by a sister, Dagmar, who was born in Kroměříž in 1951. Kroměříž was also known as "Moravia's Rome," because it was the seat of the Catholic bishop and the home of several religious orders, some of whose members worked as nurses in the hospital.

Initially, his assignment in Kroměříž appeared to be an unhappy choice, because Hanuš spent the first year in regular medical training moving from one department to another. But, after the first year, a new children's ward was opened under the directorship of Jaroslav Sommer, a pediatrician from Prague, who was assembling a new team and was also interested in conducting research. "So they asked everybody, whether someone would be interested in doing pediatrics. And when Sommer came to me, I said yes of course. That was my dream" (Papoušek Interview, October 15, 1999). Sommer, a graduate of Charles University, hired Hanuš as one of his first coworkers and worked him endlessly. Hanuš explained, "But I didn't mind, you know. I was happy that I could do pediatrics. . . . We actually became good friends" (Papoušek Interview, October 15, 1999). He spent the second year of his stay in Kroměříž working in Sommer's department.

It was also while in Kroměříž, sometime in 1950, that Papoušek finally came to grips with whether or not to join the Communist Party. It was a difficult decision for him to make, and he was reluctant to do so. When asked later about his reasons for becoming a member, Papoušek gave several justifications for his decision. One of these, realistically, was to improve his chances for professional advancement. As some of his colleagues later confirmed, after 1948, it became almost impossible for medical school graduates to obtain good positions without Party membership. Papoušek himself had already received numerous indications to this effect himself, and extensive evidence is available to document how, with few exceptions, many professions were closed to anyone who was not a member. This was true for the medical profession, in particular, which in Czechoslovakia was considered very prestigious (Papoušek Interview, October 15, 1999).

Hanuš also hoped to increase the influence of intellectuals within the ranks of the party, and to create more room for exchange of ideas and debate. Politicians were more motivated by actions, he felt, whereas intellectuals tended to raise questions and look at evidence before taking a political stance. Finally, Papoušek thought that, as a member of the Party, he could be more effective in carrying out his work as a pediatrician to improve the well-being of children. He felt that many times, within the hospital and research environments where he worked, it was easier for him to obtain additional equipment or to introduce flexible policies that were to the benefit of his patients or to the quality of his research. For practical reasons, it was better to be an insider than an outsider.

A look at the Communist Party's membership rolls indicates that Hanuš was far from alone in coming to this decision. In June 1945, 2 months after the liberation, the party had 475,000 members. By January 1948, a month before the takeover, the number had risen to 1.3 million. And, by May 1949, more than a year after the coup, membership had increased to 2.3 million, or one third of the adult population. Josef Korbel, a Czech historian, says that of these 2.3 million members, "most of them were opportunists and careerists—a sad commentary on the moral fiber of the nation" (Korbel, 1977, pp. 223–254). In the case of Hanuš Papoušek, it is difficult to agree with Korbel's statement. Rather than rendering such global judgment, it would be more useful to look at the reasons why individual professionals joined the Communist Party on a case-by-case basis. Viewed in this way, one might arrive at a less moralistic and more balanced assessment.

Papoušek stayed in Kroměříž until late 1951, when Dr. Sommer, his supervisor, urged him to apply for a position at a new research institute that was being created in Prague, the Institute for the Care of Mother and Child. Sommer had heard from one of his medical school classmates that the Institute was looking for young researchers from different specialties and fields. Papoušek applied and was successful in getting hired. At the end of the year, he moved to Prague with his wife and two children. Their third child, Jirka, was born there in 1955.

BEGINNING A RESEARCH CAREER: 1951–1953

By coming to Prague and the Institute for the Care of Mother and Child, Hanuš Papoušek was introduced to a whole new world in at least two different ways. The first was in a physical, geographical, and cultural sense. Interested in music, art, and ideas, he had spent the first 29 years of his life in relatively provincial Moravia, whereas Prague was the intellectual, cultural, and political center of the entire country. It was a beautiful city, rich in architecture, art, and history, and a window to the wider professional and scientific world. The Institute for the Care of Mother and Child was to become Czechoslovakia's center for the study of pediatrics and maternal health throughout the entire country; within a few years after Hanuš arrived there, it had established a European-wide reputation as a research leader in its field. Befitting its importance, the site chosen for this Institute was an impressive turn-of-the-century building on the banks of the Moldau River with a view of Prague's castle and gentle hills on the opposite shore. The Institute's location and facilities were to become the envy of many scientists and researchers throughout the world.

The Institute was created in 1951 by converting an existing obstetric-gynecological and pediatric clinic of Charles University into a research center that reported directly to the Czech Ministry of Health. By all accounts, it was a unique creation. Communist Poland, Hungary, and the Soviet Union never managed to implement plans for such a specialized center at the national level. The Ministry of Health created the Institute for the purpose of improving the health and well-being of the nation's mothers and children, especially at the earliest stages of life, largely in response to very high postwar infant mortality rates and widespread illness among pregnant women and new mothers. It was established as both a research and clinical facility to study the major problems of maternal and child health. From the very outset, it was looked on as one of the government's favored institutions. When other research institutes were lacking for paper, equipment, or staff, the Institute for the Care of Mother and Child was always well supplied. Reflecting one of the ironies of the Czech bureaucratic system, it was classified—together with the military—as one of the "vital institutions" serving the country's national interests.

The person primarily responsible for the Institute's founding was Jiri Trapl, a highly respected gynecologist, author of medical textbooks, and professor of medicine at Charles University. Trapl also served as the first director of the Institute and was responsible for developing many of the policies and guidelines that have remained in place at the Institute to the present day. As an academic and non-Party member, Trapl's concerns were largely apolitical and were guided by the needs of science rather than the preferences of political leaders or administrative convenience. One of Trapl's main goals was to have research conducted on mothers and infants from multiple disciplinary viewpoints, stressing the importance of integrating clinical and research perspectives from obstetrics, gynecology, pediatrics, and psychology. To encourage greater cooperation and exchange of ideas, and more total understanding of particular problems, he instituted the practice of holding biweekly colloquia in which researchers were able to discuss their findings with colleagues in their own units as well as those in other departments.

A second idea of Trapl's was that the Institute's research should be dedicated as much to basic research as to practical applications, and it would be useful to study not only pathologies and abnormalities. Therefore, research at his Institute should include healthy subjects and practical measures for preventing the onset of debilitation or disease. Finally, from the very outset, he felt it was essential for researchers to observe patients or subjects in residence for longer periods of time, rather than dealing with them strictly on an "outpatient" basis. As is discussed in greater detail in chapter 2, many of Trapl's ideas about research and its organization would find a strong echo in the work of Hanuš Papoušek and his coworkers in the unit on "higher nervous system."

With the help of strong financial support from the Ministry of Health, the Institute was successful in assembling a relatively large research staff in a short period of time, and soon boasted of being one of the largest specialized residential research centers anywhere in Europe. By the end of the 1950s, for instance, the full-time professional research and clinical staff consisted of 24 obstetricians and gynecologists, 20 pediatricians, 3 psychologists, 2 biochemists, 1 chemist, 1 physiologist, 1 clinical physiologist, 1 pathomorphologist, 1 embryologist, 1 geneticist, 1 sociologist, 1 bacteriologist, 1 biologist, 1 immunologist, 3 archivists, and 1 statistician. In addition, the Institute employed a support staff of 55 technical assistants, 79 nurses, 2 rehabilitation workers, 110 administrative workers, and 42 custodial and other types of employees, for a total staff of 352 persons. A total of 98 beds were available for clinical and observational purposes (Institute for the Care of Mother and Child, 1961).

Significantly, despite the fact that Czechoslovakia was a one-party state, the Minister of Health was not a Communist. Rather, he was a Catholic priest named Josef Plojhar, leader of the Czech People's Party, a conservative political group that was rewarded with a cabinet post for its support of the Communists. Plojhar was also the leader of a conservative international peace movement, although some of his critics felt this was merely a front for the Party. In his capacity as minister, Plojhar sought to maintain an appreciation for the importance of high quality research, and helped to insulate the Institute from outside political pressures.

As numerous Institute researchers have attested, despite ebbs and flows, the atmosphere within the Institute always remained relatively free. Among the Institute's staff, most of the key administrators were members of the Party. There were several exceptions, however, and when Soviet-style hardliners were in those positions, tensions among researchers sometimes arose. Overall, the Institute was able to avoid the worst excesses of hard-line zealotry, and researchers were relatively free to pursue their scientific work. The predominant way for dealing with differences over major political events outside the Institute was to avoid such topics or treat them with silence. In a closed society, lack of trust among colleagues prevented speaking to each other about subject matter of a politically controversial nature.

In this regard, it is interesting to note that one of Papoušek's closest coworkers recalled having talked with him only once about a major issue of political controversy—the Hungarian Revolution of 1956—in their 16 years working side-by-side together in the same laboratory. (Although, chronologically, 1956 falls into the timeframe of later chapters, the point relates well to the problem discussed here.) The coworker, who was not a Party member and held strong religious convictions, made a comment indicating her support for the uprising, to which Papoušek is reported to have responded with a noncommittal, silent nod. The coworker knew very well that Papoušek was a Party member, and he easily could have reported her for having made such a remark. The fact that Papoušek did not do so was interpreted as a sign that he was not only trying to protect her, but he probably even concurred with her views. Such was the stifling nature of interpersonal communication among colleagues in a scientific institute whose coworkers felt that its political atmosphere was not relatively closed, but relatively free. One wonders what communications at the workplace were like at other research institutions where the atmosphere was relatively closed! This particular coworker never talked about political topics with Hanuš Papoušek again. "But I knew that he would do no harm to anyone" (Dittrichová Interview, October 7, 1999).

In his first years at the Institute, from 1951 to 1953, Hanuš Papoušek once again was put into a situation that required starting from the "bottom up." This time it also seemed to have its benefits. The advantage of working in a "start-up" operation is that the first employees often are given wideranging responsibilities that involve diverse problems and tasks, and in such a situation it often becomes an asset to the organization to be a "Jack-of-all-trades." This was also the case for Papoušek, who had a natural proclivity for many different tasks, whether scientific, theoretical, organizational, or mechanical in nature. Although assigned initially to the pediatrics department to do medical research, he was also assigned to work on projects that seemed to fall outside his expertise. For example, one of his early tasks was to study the size of baby cribs in state-run hospitals and infant nurseries, and to make recommendations to the Ministry of Health concerning standard dimensions and specifications. The problem was that a baby in one of the infancy units at a district hospital had died by getting its head caught between the bars of a crib, and no one in the Ministry of Health knew why crib bars were spaced in such a way. Other issues included the dissemination of research findings and free exchange of scientific information. As Papoušek recalled:

> When the research Institute opened, there was a confused period when the government didn't know how to treat the research institutes with medical services. . . . At first they wanted to apply the same criteria and the same regulations. So we weren't expected to publish our results and everything had to be kept secret. But then the medical authorities finally succeeded in convincing the bureaucrats that we had totally different problems and couldn't be compared with military facilities or something like that, and that publications were in fact the *sine qua non* for scientists. . . . Whatever you did, whatever you collected in your investigations, all of it was sensitive, confidential material and was not published without permission of the Ministry of Health. . . . The ideas of the politicians about how to organize a research institute were tremendously naïve and idiotic. (Papoušek Interviews, July 14, 1998, and October 15, 1999)

In addition to being a researcher/"Jack-of-all-trades," Papoušek spent the first 2 years finishing the requirements of his specialization in pediatrics at Charles University. After finishing his specialization, he was required under new guidelines adopted by the government to continue his studies in a further specialization that would ultimately lead to writing a dissertation and the award of a newly created "Candidate of Science" degree. For his specialization, Papoušek chose the field of developmental neurophysiology, which resulted in some of the pioneering infant conditioning and learning studies for which he first gained international attention (to be discussed in chap. 2). He received his Candidate of Science degree in 1959.

Looking further at his early Institute years, Papoušek became involved in other activities that quickly established him as one of the Institute's intellectual leaders. He soon gained respect for his intelligence, ingenuity, energy, dedication, and hard work. Equally important were his personality and social skills. Within a short time, he found himself the head of the Communist Party unit for his section of the Institute, a very important role. Fortunately, a variety of sources are available that help explain why, only 3 years after his arrival, he was given major responsibilities in the new unit that was being established for the study of psychological and mental processes of infants. This feat is particularly remarkable because at the time Papoušek had very little formal training in the field of psychology (although no one else in Czechoslovakia had started to study infancy behaviors and mental processes either). Obviously, he enjoyed the confidence of his superiors and coworkers to embark on this entirely new venture.

Several accounts from former Institute members give vivid insight into how Papoušek was perceived during these early years. One of the most illuminating of these accounts is a lengthy report from a pediatrician who shared an office with Papoušek for 7 years, and who knew him from his first day there:

> I came to the Institute in 1951. I was one of the first. And I think when I got there, Hanuš was also just joining our collective. You know, I'm a pediatrician, a medical doctor. And when he first got there, I knew Hanuš as a physiologist, not as a psychologist. . . . I was very, very fond of him. We shared this little office together for 7 years. And he always showed me new gadgets he was using. It was the first time I saw a *wingogram* (polygraph)! . . . There just never were any conflicts with him. He got along with everyone—even those strange Catholic nuns that he had known before in Moravia. You know, they were really religious, and nobody knew what to do with them. But they were really good workers, so we assigned them to him. We thought that if anyone could tolerate them, it would be Hanuš. . . . And you know something? They were infatuated with him. . . . (*Laughter*) In fact, all the young women in the Institute were infatuated with him. Even my wife. . . . (*Laughter*) I should tell you, I'm Jewish, and so was my wife. And I was one of only about 200 Jews left in Prague after the war. But Hanuš was someone I accepted. Hanuš used to come to our house, and he helped with the furniture when we moved in. . . . You know, there's a certain type of person where you know they come from a teacher's family. And those kids also had a certain social polish. Real social skills. Well, Hanuš, he was one of them. And he always worked so hard, and it was fun working with him. . . .
>
> I really have to say, he was a very intelligent, honorable young guy. He was a real model. . . . And at that time, shortly after the war, everybody was very friendly with one another. And Hanuš was the only one among us who was from Moravia. And one day, you know, I was so impressed with the guy, I went to my boss and asked him, "Where did you get this young fellow?" And he said, "Well, I went to a pediatric conference and told everybody I needed a really bright and talented young guy. And that's how I got him." . . .
>
> Yes, he was a Communist. [Otherwise], in 1951 he wouldn't have been hired in an institute such as this. They only looked for people who were in the Party. And you know, the only reason they hired me was because I was in the Party, too. It was only by accident that there were a few non-Party members. Most of them were holdovers from the days when this was still a children's hospital. And then some others came later. But in 1951 it was a condition *sine qua non* to be a Party member. . . .
>
> You know, he always helped all his colleagues. If one had a problem with one's research, he was always willing to talk about it. And even problems outside the realm of research. He was a very interesting, very intelligent man. And he was honest, too. Very fair and honest. . . .

And the thing was, well, our boss was a pediatrician, and he had just come back from Moscow. That was in 1951, and at first he expected something totally different from Hanuš. A pediatrician, mind you, and he said to everybody, "From now on all our research has to be based on a Pavlovian foundation." He just stated it as a proclamation. None of us knew what to say to him! Our colleagues in gynecology, they wanted to do endocrinology, not Pavlovian research. . . . But nobody among us knew what this new method was supposed to mean. Many of us laughed about it. I, for example, wanted to continue doing research on endocrinology, so I just did it "under the table." But what we then did, we sacrificed Hanuš for this Pavlovian business. And you know something? He didn't reject it out of hand, but tried to be as constructive as possible about it. . . . If he had stayed in Prague, I'm sure he would have become a professor at the university. Among all of us, nobody else was at his level. And when I left the Institute, that's what I told the head of pediatrics, too. You know, I left because I wanted to run away from all that research. I wanted to go to work in a real clinic. (Zeman Interview, October 7, 1999)

In addition to the perspective of a coworker and friend, accounts of Hanuš from two different supervisors help round out the picture during these years. As one of them said succinctly, "I knew Papoušek as a very hardworking scientist. He was one of the pillars of the Institute. And he was also the leader of the Communist Party in his section of the Institute. . . . But he was also one of those people who saw the bad sides of our government" (Horsky Interview, October 6, 1999). In contrast, the other supervisor's account is more extensive, perhaps because he worked closely with Papoušek from very early on:

I remember exactly when he arrived in Prague. He was hired as a pediatrician, because we needed someone to study hematology. But then very soon he changed course and became a member of the group for higher nervous activity. . . . And at that time, there was the group dealing with Pavlov. It was very theoretical and scholastic, all these sessions they did with us on Pavlov. And very Marxist, of course. Because you know, the Communists tried to *misapply* Pavlov to political goals. Of course the Pavlov people were saying, "It's all in the brain." The Communists tried to prove with Pavlov that everything is possible. That it's possible just to change the brain and what's going on in the mind. . . . It was just terrible. Theoretical genetics disappeared from our Institute entirely. Pathology, and the study of pathology in children disappeared. And suddenly pneumonia was no longer due to infection. And we had to get that every month. And we just didn't know what to do, and so Papoušek came and introduced some new ideas to that circle. It really helped us get out of all that. You know, I have to say, Hanuš Papoušek is one of the most intelligent people I ever met. (Poláček Interview, April 25, 2000)

In short, by late 1953, when the focus of his work shifted from physiology (hematology) to the study of behaviors and mental processes in newborns,

Papoušek was already perceived as "an important person" at the Institute (Dittrichová Interview, October 7, 1999). In his early 30s, he was part of a collective of young doctors and researchers who formed the nucleus of a growing new research setting that could count on relatively generous, on-going sources of governmental financial support. When the pediatrics department was told it needed to place its research on a "Pavlovian footing," whatever that meant, Papoušek saw it as an opportunity to pursue his long-standing interest in combining the study of pediatrics and psychology. The next chapter looks "inside the lab" of the research unit for "higher nervous activities" in infants, and the studies of infancy that Papoušek and his colleagues proceeded to undertake there.

Chapter 2

The Early Prague Years:
A Scientific Basis for Modern
Infancy Studies

When the Unit for the Study of Higher Nervous Activity was set up, Hanuš Papoušek and his colleagues were given a rare opportunity in the form of the mandate and resources to study an important phase of human development that had been virtually unexplored. Indeed, in the early 1950s, the field of infancy studies itself was still in its own infancy. Before then, most studies of human newborns were of a medical nature, with the exception of the occasional "baby diaries" popular in the earlier part of the 20th century and a few early Soviet studies of conditioning. Looking back on his early Prague years, Papoušek later was fond of saying that, from a scientific perspective, it was necessary to view the human newborn as if it were a new species altogether.

A look at his list of early publications reveals that Papoušek's first non-medical studies did not appear until the late 1950s, fully 8 years after his arrival at the Institute. In part, this undoubtedly was due to the fact that, like all other researchers at the Institute, his responsibilities consisted of far more than conducting scientific studies. As a pediatrician, he was also called on to spend considerable time making regular medical rounds and performing routine checkups of the infants and mothers on his ward. Indeed, Papoušek's first professional publication was a report that dealt with problems of the blood. Appearing in a Czech pediatric journal in 1954, this publication was titled "Hemorrhagic Diathesis in Toxic Diarrhoea in Infants." Moreover, his second scientific article (H. Papoušek & Janele, 1956) was "Factors of Hemocoagulation in the Pathogenesis of Birth Injury of the Central Nervous System in Full-Term Newborns." As the titles indicate, both publications reflected his medical training and ongoing interests in the biological aspects of medical practice.

Beginning in 1959, however, the results of Papoušek's investigations into the nonmedical aspects of infancy began to appear in a steady stream of ground-breaking conference reports, book chapters, and articles in key Czech journals. Over the next several years, the Unit for the Study of Higher Nervous Activity published studies that covered a host of new topics in infancy research, such as methods for studying higher nervous system functions in newborns, conditioned alimentary motor reflexes in newborns, the origins of voluntary activity, head rotation reflexes, sleeping patterns during the first 3 months, and so on. With their appearance, scholars in both the East and the West soon began to recognize that the old "paradigms" concerning our understanding of human newborns no longer applied. Far from viewing the infant's mind as a "blank slate" or a "blooming, buzzing" state of confusion, these new studies showed the newborn to be a remarkably dynamic organism from the moment of birth—from Day 1 possessing the capacity to learn, engage in simple social interactions, and perform a wide variety of tasks. It was a notable scientific achievement that remains largely unchallenged to the present day.

What were some of the sources for this new approach in infancy research, what new features of human newborns did they reveal, and what research methods did Papoušek and his team employ? Further, what were some of the problems encountered along the way, and why did this particular view of infancy develop in Prague rather than somewhere else? All of these questions deserve further exploration.

As sometimes happens in the history of science, a fundamental shift in thinking may be accompanied by considerable obstacles or frustrations, as was also the case with Papoušek and his colleagues in Prague. As H. Papoušek (1977) expressed it with characteristic mixture of understatement and irony:

Anyone who has studied infants for a longer period of time is aware that the researcher's appearance in public is greeted with mixed emotion. The [research] audience may acknowledge that infant research is concerned with important and interesting questions, and yet it remains skeptical regarding the ethical aspects of such research. Just what kinds of studies are in fact permissible with such a fragile, sensitive organism as a human infant, and to what extent is precise scientific analysis possible? When we began our studies of learning in infants twenty years ago, theories of learning were already highly developed. Experimental research had concentrated mainly on adult animals and humans, while the infant, at least until the 1950s, was relatively inaccessible and thus rarely the subject of research. However, those who once committed themselves to infant research remained remarkably loyal, and certainly not only because they were driven by messianic visions of conquering a totally new and unknown area of research. (p. 1)

Moreover, with regard to the question of why this particular research view emerged in Prague as opposed to elsewhere, Jerome Kagan responded by saying:

> In the end, every scientist is a partial opportunist. He is trying to see what niche there is, a good niche to fill, and is trying to make a new career. . . . Place is important. Pavlov, in 1900, there was only one laboratory in all of Europe that was equipped to do surgery for dogs. That was St. Petersburg. That is where Pavlov was. So if Pavlov had been in Moscow or Berlin, then Pavlov would not have discovered conditioning. It was the place. Mendel was sent to the only monastery that had a herbarium. So if his father knew an abbot from a different monastery, then Mendel doesn't discover the genetics of peas. Oh, place is absolutely critical. (Kagan Interview, November, 1999)

Indeed, as becomes clear in later chapters, it is difficult to imagine Papoušek's early infancy studies as having taken place other than in the Institute in Prague. And although "partial opportunism" undoubtedly played a role, a host of other contextual factors were influential as well.

PAVLOV, SOVIET PSYCHOLOGY, AND INFANCY RESEARCH

In looking at the theoretical and research foundations on which Papoušek's work was built, one of the most important factors was the role of Russian and Soviet psychology, particularly in the tradition of Ivan Pavlov. To be sure, pioneering nonmedical figures like Jean Piaget in Switzerland, G. S. Hall, Arnold Gesell, and other scholars from the early American "child development movement" had begun to describe various aspects of the young child's development, but they did not look at infancy in its earliest stages and were often lacking the rigorous methodology needed to support their claims.

Soviet psychology began to assume an increasingly important role in Czechoslovakia after the Communist takeover in 1948. To be sure, the Institute for the Care of Mother and Child reported to the Czech Ministry of Health, which throughout the 1950s was led by a minister who was not a member of the Communist Party. Thus, the Institute was able to maintain a reputation of a relatively high degree of autonomy in the scientific realm. On the other hand, its research staff could not ignore the growing influence of "the Soviet factor" in Czechoslovakian science. Indeed, one need merely point to the name of Papoušek's department, Unit for the Study of Higher Nervous Activity, to realize the extent to which official Soviet medical and psychological science impinged on the Institute's work. Although many Institute researchers were committed to doing things "the Czech way," by the early 1950s official Soviet scientific thinking, under the banner of "Pavlovian science," began to make its impact felt in many fields of Czech research, including not only physiology and psychology, but education ("pedology") and childrearing as well.

Riding a wave of nationalist sentiment with the defeat of fascism after World War II, many influential Soviet physiologists and psychologists during the 1940s had begun to promote "Pavlovian science" as the materialist opponent of bourgeois science with the goal of creating the "new socialist man." The "Pavlovianization" of Soviet science reached its high point at medical and psychological conferences in Moscow, also attended by a number of pro-Soviet researchers from Czechoslovakia in 1949 and 1950. The cult surrounding Pavlov, which had parallels to the Stalin cult in the political realm, lasted in the Soviet Union and several Eastern European countries until the late 1950s, when the "thaw" of Nikita Khrushchev brought a greater openness toward divergent scientific viewpoints. (Even the term *pedology* was dropped from the official Soviet vocabulary during the Khrushchev era, to be replaced by *pedagogy* or *educational science*.) (See also Valsiner, 1988.)

At the Institute for the Care of Mother and Child, the most vocal early advocate of "Pavlovian science" was M. Vojta, a Soviet-oriented Party member who had succeeded its founder (Trapl) as the Institute's director. After attending the All Union Congress of Soviet Psychologists in 1950, Vojta had returned to Prague with unquestioning enthusiasm for the latest Soviet trends and proceeded to organize mandatory seminars and discussions for Institute researchers and staff in all departments, regardless of whether they worked in obstetrics, gynecology, genetics, or higher nervous systems. (Vojta's influence was reinforced by the fact that his brother was an important member of the Central Committee of the Czech Communist Party. He was replaced as director of the Institute in the late 1950s, a process in which Papoušek claimed to have played an important role. Papoušek and others viewed Vojta as scientifically incompetent.) The political weight of Vojta's Soviet-inspired ideas provoked a great deal of controversy among the more independent-minded researchers in the Institute's ranks.

Based on interviews conducted with several Institute staff members after the demise of Communism in 1989, the application of "Pavlovian science" to human pediatrics and psychology was greeted with considerable skepticism by some of Papoušek's closest personal friends, who either were unfamiliar with or failed to see the relevance of Pavlov's studies to their own research. For example, the director of pediatrics, Karel Poláček, remembered that the monthly seminar sessions seemed to be an effort aimed not so much at interpreting Pavlov's studies in accordance with latest scientific thinking and ideas, but more of a Communist effort to "misapply Pavlov to political goals" (Poláček Interview, April 25, 1999). "Since Pavlov's research had been conducted on animals, how could it be applicable to humans?" Poláček asked. To Poláček, the central thrust behind Vojta's efforts seemed to be the desire for Pavlov's views on conditioning in animals to become established as the theoretical basis for creating the ideal Czech person in a Soviet-oriented collective society. Poláček concluded that "the Communists tried to prove by Pavlov that Communism is possible" (Poláček Interview, April 25, 1999).

Other critical comments about Vojta's efforts came from Jaroslava Dittrichová, a psychologist in the Unit for the Study of Higher Nervous Activity. Interviewed in 1999, Dittrichová recalled: "At that time they said that all medicine, pedagogy, and psychology, must be based on Pavlov's theory. It was a terrible time. For example, there was a physiological congress in Prague, and every paper had to have something with Pavlovian theory in it. It was terrible!" (Dittrichová Interview, October 7, 1999).

In contrast to some of his friends, however, Papoušek took a somewhat different approach to the debate over "Pavlovian science" and tried to make the best of a difficult situation. In November 1955, he published a lengthy article in *Československá Pediatrie*, at that time the major scientific journal read by practicing Czech medical doctors and pediatricians (translation provided by Katarína Guttmannová). "The Pavlovian Conception of Disease in Pediatrics" appeared in an issue dedicated to the theme of "Czechoslovak–Soviet Friendship." The article did not address the overarching theme of Soviet–Czech friendship or the general question of whether or not Pavlov served as an appropriate theoretical basis for all Czech science. Instead, because it was a medical journal, Papoušek limited himself to a description and explication of the physiological aspects of Pavlov's work. According to Papoušek, this article was never published in the Soviet Union (Papoušek Interview, October 19, 1999).

According to Papoušek, Pavlov's teachings were a revolutionary development in the understanding of the physiology of the nervous system and gave a scientific basis for the objective study of the primary role of the nervous system in disease and health. He contended that Pavlov's ideas provided objective evidence for the validity of the 19th-century Russian scientist Sechenov's view that trace stimuli are necessary for the creation of trace reflexes, which in turn are conditioned reflexes whose conditioned stimuli may be maintained in the nervous tissue at a later stage. Papoušek also suggested that Pavlov's teachings could be useful for understanding the pathologies of both animals and humans. Citing Soviet research indicating that even pathologies can occur due to trace stimuli, he contended that an understanding of these stimuli in pathologies can also provide a better understanding of the etiology and pathogenesis of disease. Trace stimuli can leave a residue in the nervous system even after their elimination, functioning somewhat like the ember of a fire that has the potential for flaring up again at some future point.

Interestingly, Papoušek also made a point of praising the Soviet Pavlov Conference of 1950, stating that several key presenters had helped to correct a number of previous scientific and medical misconceptions that the cortex was responsible for organizing and deciding pathological processes, and that the role of pathological agents was only a triggering mechanism for disease. Pointing out that quite the opposite is true, he argued that the cortex and central nervous system are not simply sources of disease, but also sources for defending against pathologies and getting well. Disease, he concluded, occurs only when the central nervous system is failing or not functioning properly. He proceeded to propose a "nervistic" notion of disease that defines illness as a "qualitatively new process of life functioning activity that develops as a result of the influence of an unusual stimulus or organisms" (H. Papoušek, 1955, p. 641; translation provided by Katarína Guttmannová). "Nervistic" disease, according to Papoušek, is characterized both by a functional disruption of the neuroregulatory apparatus, and by a reflexive switching on of defensive physiological mechanisms. Disease, he concluded, is the result of disequilibrium between the organism and the external environment, and the basic stages of infectious diseases illustrate how reflex processes play a part in the origins and development of pathologies and the defense of the organism against disease.

Viewed from today's perspective, it is fair to say that, with the exception of the discussion of trace stimuli and reflexes, much of what is contained in this article is a fairly standard explanation of Pavlov's ideas. By Czech and Soviet standards of the 1950s, however, it was a remarkably balanced and clear explanation of Pavlov's ideas from the perspective of medicine and physiology, while remaining silent about issues related to the applicability of Pavlovian science to psychology, childrearing, education, or the creation of the "socialist man." No wonder that, many years later, Papoušek's friends and colleagues still talked admiringly about his ability to find a fair way of dealing with even the most difficult scientific-theoretical and ideological problems—and why he came to be looked on as one of the Institute's "intellectual pillars" as the years progressed. Papoušek managed to explain the validity of Pavlov's scientific contribution, while simply treating the more troublesome aspects of the Pavlovian legacy with "benign neglect."

In addition to publishing this article, Papoušek found an opportunity in 1959 to travel to Leningrad and Moscow in order to further his understanding of the latest developments in Pavlovian and Soviet scientific research. In what proved to be his first and only trip to the Soviet Union, he spent a month visiting leading pediatric and psychological research institutes, and studying the Soviet system of infant and child day care. He visited N. I.

Krasnogorskii and N. Kasatkin, whom Papoušek characterized as "progressive" figures (Papoušek Interview, October 19, 1999). Papoušek was impressed especially with the research of Krasnogorskii, already an elderly man, who had been an assistant to Pavlov before the Russian Revolution. In 1907, Krasnogorskii (1967) published a paper reporting the successful conditioning of a 14-month-old human infant. Aware that he could not use the same salivary measurement technique with infants that Pavlov demonstrated so successfully with dogs (i.e., surgically diverting the salivation), Krasnogorskii developed a new procedure that involved observing the infant's swallowing to estimate amounts of salivary secretion. In later years, after Pavlov's death, he published other studies refuting the idea that infants less than 6 months old were unable to learn, and Krasnogorskii was one of the first to apply classical associative learning methods to the study of school-age children. Papoušek spent several days with Krasnogorskii in Leningrad learning more about some of the new procedures being used in his laboratory, and the two remained in personal contact after Papoušek's return to Prague.

Papoušek was equally impressed with the work of N. I. Kasatkin, who had conducted detailed studies of learning in early childhood and infancy since the 1930s, and was then director of the Laboratory for the Study of Higher Nervous Activity in Children, Sechenov Institute of Evolutionary Physiology. Kasatkin was not a pupil of Pavlov's, but instead studied with V. M. Bekhterev, Pavlov's main rival in Soviet psychology in the 1920s and 1930s. Bekhterev subsequently fell out of political favor and was virtually forgotten by the mid- to late-1940s when Pavlov's star began to rise. Bekhterev's students, however, continued to champion his "reflexological" research in humans that in many ways resembled the conditioning studies of Pavlov. During the 1920s and 1930s, two of Bekhterev's students, Denisova and Figurin, published a series of experimental studies on various aspects of conditioning reflexes in infants (Kasatkin, 1969).

After returning from the Soviet Union, Papoušek published two lengthy articles in Czech journals discussing the research ideas he had encountered in both Leningrad and Moscow. He was impressed with what he found, however, he also was not convinced that the view of infant learning emerging from these research labs was always correct. The relation of Papoušek's early studies to Soviet psychology is aptly characterized by Lewis Lipsitt, one of the first psychologists from the United States to visit him in Prague. Lipsitt explained:

> For sure, babies learn in different ways that nobody had thought of before, but what was most important back then was to establish that they in fact learned! We're going back 35 years and more. And during that time, the Soviets, the very ones whose research Hanuš had studied, were still saying babies cannot learn until they are 30 or 60 days of age. That's where Hanuš really

took off from them. He went back to his laboratory and, in effect, he said, "I don't believe that. They learn from the first day of life." And he implemented the technique to demonstrate it. (Lipsitt Interview, May 4, 2000)

PAPOUŠEK'S EARLY CONDITIONING STUDIES

The importance of Papoušek's early infant conditioning research is perhaps best explained by taking the work of Kasatkin as a point of departure. One of Kasatkin's innovations was the use of head movements, but again in a Pavlovian sense. In contrast to the strict Pavlovian and Soviet conditioning studies, however, in his own research Papoušek was more interested in what later became known as "goal-directed," or "purposive," behaviors, such as how the infant learns to repeat a movement that is adaptively significant (e.g., reaching for something). The new feature introduced by Papoušek to the study of conditioning was to combine elements of two different paradigms, a classical conditioning approach and an instrumental approach— something that had not yet been done with infants.

Clearly, there were few scholars in any country able to implement the repeated daily experimental sessions such as those undertaken at the unique research facility in Prague. Papoušek was motivated to explore this new frontier as he became increasingly aware of the lack of knowledge about early behavioral development and the adaptiveness of the human infant:

> As a pediatrician, I was amazed at the enormous discrepancy between general knowledge of the infant's biochemistry, morphology, and pathological deviations, and what was known about normal development, perception, learning, and cognitive processes. (H. Papoušek, 1977, p. 2)

> The chief advantage of studying neonates is that during this period of life different developing functions can be seen in their simplest forms—before they begin to interact or become complicated by the accumulation of experiences. There is also the advantage of being able to control a large number of external factors at this period of development. (H. Papoušek, 1967a, p. 260)

The conditionability of newborns had rarely been explored at the time of Papoušek's early studies, and this was the result of a variety of factors. First, there was a general lack of familiarity with how to deal with newborn babies as research subjects (the common refrain being, how does one "ask a research question" of a preverbal child?). Second, there were numerous logistical and organizational difficulties yet to be resolved when working with infants in a research laboratory, such as timing the experimental sessions when the infant is in an optimal state of alertness, working around unpredictable sleeping and feeding cycles, and coping with unexplained fussiness of the research subjects. And, third, there were few models or prior publications, and there was little support for researchers interested in studying these earliest forms of behaviors.

A handful of early studies had at least paved the way for what was still a newly emerging field of research. Denisova and Figurin (1929) and Ripin and Hetzer (1930) demonstrated the first natural "conditioned" sucking during the third week of life. Kasatkin and Leviková (1935) later succeeded in conditioning sucking to acoustic stimuli during the second and third months, and to visual stimuli during the third and fourth months. In 1931, Marquis reported even earlier conditioning, this time in newborns, using an oral response to a buzzer; Papoušek claimed, however, that results of this study were questionable due to methodological problems (H. Papoušek, 1967b). Kasatkin (1969) agreed with this critique, as indicated in his review of conditioned reflexes in early childhood in which he asserted that Marquis' criterion of reduced motor activity and fussing was not particularly promising. As Kasatkin noted, the infant's decreased amount of crying and moving might have simply made the sucking movements more apparent. Wenger (1936) was unable to establish a conditioned response in infants younger than 10 days old using either an appetitional or an aversive procedure. Subsequently, Wenger (1943) was able to condition the eyeblink reflex to a flash of light in newborns (4–8 days old), although the response remained highly unstable. Kasatkin reported that within the first few weeks after birth, being put to the mother's breast in a feeding position has become a conditioned stimulus, eliciting a conditioned reflex observed in rooting, searching, and sucking behaviors. (It is important to note that the terms *reflex* and *response* were being used interchangeably at the time when these studies were first being reported; Kasatkin, 1969.) By the ninth day, calming when placed in the feeding position can also be observed in infants who were fussy prior to feeding. By 16 to 18 days, infants were found to demonstrate a precise conditioned response when put into the position associated with feeding.

As Kasatkin (1969) concluded, the newborn is confronted with innumerable new stimuli during the transition after birth, so that the newborn's initial responses must rely on those forms of "nervous activity" that are innate. Research in various parts of the world was beginning to show that within the first few days after birth, signs of certain conditioned associations could already be observed (see both Kasatkin, 1969, and Papoušek, 1967b, for reviews of these early studies). It appears that during the 1950s at the Prague Institute, Papoušek was indeed at "the right place at the right time" to embark on his innovative new research investigating the processes of infant learning.

Institute for the Care of Mother and Child, Prague.

Entry hall, Institute for the Care of Mother and Child, Prague.

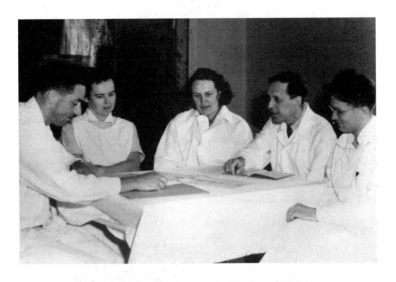

Research Unit of Higher Nervous Activity, Institute for the Care of Mother
and Child, Prague (l–r, Papoušek, Vlasta, Dittrichová, Janoš, Špála).

Papoušek at work, Institute for the Care of Mother and Child, Prague.

Papoušek as a young adult.

Indira Gandhi with Papoušek and infant from the Prague Institute.

Edna Lipsitt, Hanuš, and Draha Papoušek.

Hanuš swinging from rope at the Lipsitts' summer home.

Prague children: Hanuš, Jirka, and Dagmar Papoušek.

THE UNIQUENESS OF THE UNIT FOR THE STUDY
OF HIGHER NERVOUS ACTIVITY IN INFANTS

For research purposes, it was important to have reliable information on the health conditions and the psychological development of each child. The nursery environment was therefore kept fairly uniform, so that schedules for feeding, sleeping, waking activities, and general health checks by pediatricians and psychologists allowed the conditions to be comparable for infants involved in the variety of studies being carried out (see Table 2.1). On the other hand, Papoušek and his colleagues were extremely sensitive to the need to avoid any adverse social-emotional symptoms that might possibly be related to the "institutionalization" of these infants. He elaborated:

> Our infants first sleep, then eat, and then are exposed to social and emotional stimulation. This keeps the neonates awake for an adequate time. Naps in the fresh air throughout the whole year help to develop a very well fixed schedule by inducing deep, regular sleep. . . . Note that the infants are divided into two groups so that one-half of them are awake at any time, thus decreasing the nurse/awake-infant ratio. (H. Papoušek, 1967a, p. 261)

Papoušek (1967b) described the setting for these early studies:

> For our investigations, infants up to 6 months of age were reared in a special unit under relatively standard conditions. As far as possible, we tried to keep their life conditions comparable, at the same time meeting the demands of

TABLE 2.1
Schedule of Care for Infants at the Research Unit
at the Institute for Care of Mother and Child, Prague

Time	Group 1	Group 2
6:00 A.M.	Temperature and weight check Change of clothing and linen Experiments	Feeding
7:00 A.M.	Outdoor nap	Temperature and weight check Change of clothing and linen Experiments *Scheduled activities
8:00 A.M.		Outdoor nap
9:00 A.M.	Feeding Experiments Rounds by pediatrician and psychologist *Scheduled activities Fruit juice Outdoor nap	
10:00 A.M.		Feeding Experiments Rounds by pediatrician and psychologist Sun bath (natural or ultraviolet lamp) Outdoor nap
12:00 noon	Feeding Experiments *Scheduled activities Sun bath (natural or ultraviolet lamp) Outdoor nap	
2:00 P.M.		Feeding *Scheduled activities Fruit juice Outdoor nap
3:30 P.M. Or (3:30 P.M.)	Temperature check Bathing Feeding *Scheduled activities Or (Visits by the parents [with instruction in techniques of child care and in- fant gymnastics])	
5:00 P.M. Or (5:00 P.M.)	Indoor nap	Temperature check Bathing Feeding *Scheduled activities Or (Visits by the parents [with instruction in techniques of child care and in- fant gymnastics])
6:30 P.M.		Indoor naps

(Continued)

41

TABLE 2.1
(Continued)

Time	Group 1	Group 2
7:30 P.M.	Feeding	
	Putting to bed for the night	
9:00 P.M.		Feeding
		Putting to bed for the night
2:00 A.M.	Feeding	
3:30 A.M.		Feeding
5:30 A.M.	Feeding	

*Scheduled activities: Play with babies, stimulating sensory perception, exercises, hardening (exposure to fresh air, washing or shower with cold water), testing psychomotor abilities.

individual infants. Between 1956 and 1965, more than 130 infants were observed. They were healthy, full term, and without any evidence of pathology in the mothers' pregnancies or deliveries. The infants were cared for by their mothers and by specially trained nurses who could substitute for the mothers if necessary. Our team included a pediatrician who watched over the infants' health, nutrition, and somatic development, and a psychologist who was concerned with their mental development and educational care. If an occasional break in experimentation exceeded five days, the procedure being investigated during the period was eliminated from consideration. (pp. 252–253)

In comparison to other infant research settings around the world, the uniqueness of the Institute for the Care of Mother and Child was attributable to the fact that despite being housed in a "lying-in" obstetrical hospital, this unit was devoted to the care of healthy babies. (As Papoušek commented, incredulously, "I mean, who would come to the idea to open a department for healthy babies?" Papoušek Interview, October 19, 1999.) The implications for his research were enormous, but also brought up a number of problems, as clearly illustrated by one of his favorite anecdotes regarding battles with the Ministry of Health over certain policies generally implemented in the wards for sick children.

In particular, to reduce the risk of contagious illnesses, nurses and all other personnel were required to wear surgical masks whenever they were with their patients. Papoušek protested vehemently, pleading for an exception for his unit. Based on what he already understood about early development, he cited the importance of preverbal infants being able to see their caregivers' faces to detect oral-facial cues as they begin to learn to communicate. His training as a pediatrician notwithstanding, he held firm to this belief and ultimately prevailed:

And that was a very hard fight, between myself and the Ministry of Health, until they understood that if the baby would spend almost the entire preverbal stage this way, then the baby would miss a lot of information. But at that time, no one believed that we as parents display some models, you know, how to pronounce things, and so forth. And actually, the nonverbal, nonvocal, gestural communication just on the face, you know, would be lost! (Papoušek Interview, October 19, 1999)

A visit by Indira Gandhi put this decision into the spotlight, and caused some humorous but also time-consuming repercussions for Papoušek. The Indian politician Nehru was in Prague for a state visit, accompanied by his daughter. At the time, Indira was a young woman with no political aspirations, but she had studied abroad and had a keen interest in child care and social services. Ministry officials hosting the visitors came up with the idea of arranging for her to tour the Institute for the Care of Mother and Child, and asked Papoušek to be her host. He agreed willingly, but was not entirely prepared for the entourage of journalists that arrived with her, all eager for photo opportunities and quotable material. Papoušek agreed to bring one infant out for a photograph with their visitor from India, and the following events unfolded:

So here I was standing with a baby, one of our attractive babies on one arm, and Indira Gandhi next to me, and none of us is in a mask. As you can imagine, it went through all newspapers, even the Czech ones. And there was an avalanche of letters, asking "how is it that Czech parents are never allowed to visit their children, even if they are hospitalized for a long time, without masks? And here comes a woman from a country where they have all kinds of pests and tropical diseases, and she is allowed to enter the department without a mask!" So the Director of the Institute was furious, and he said "Papoušek, Papoušek!—that's what we get for your crazy ideas! Now you will answer all of the letters, and you will guarantee that they all will be answered, but you will not be using my secretary!" And I had something like 300 letters, and I had to answer them all, with more and more coming. (Papoušek Interview, October 19, 1999)

Jaroslavá Dittrichová, Papoušek's close colleague throughout their years at the Prague Institute, pointed to another unique feature of the Institute's infancy unit when she gave the following description of the variety of studies undertaken there during the 1950s and 1960s, some of which included infants with potential risk factors:

In the beginning, we concentrated on the study of healthy infants—to find some indicators of normal and abnormal development in early infancy. And that's why we came to study some high-risk infants, such as preterm infants and infants from mothers with diabetes. These were risk infants that were of interest to our pediatricians also. . . . This continued and later a new pediatrician came, a woman who also worked in the analyses of behavior—Dr.

Tautermanová—and she analyzed waking in infants. So we had the method of head-turn reflexes (Hanuš), of conditioned blink reflexes (Prof. Janos), analysis of sleep (Dittrichová), and then later came another pediatrician (Karel Paul) who was interested in EEG during sleep, and Dr. Tautermanová with waking. And then we compared our results and analyzed which indicators are important, which can show us very early that the development is not normal, in order to be able to start the rehabilitation or to take better care of these children. And besides that, we tried also to study some more general problems; for example it was the idea of Prof. Janos to see if we can describe when the infant's personality starts, and if we can recognize some traits in these small infants. And from the beginning, the research was interested also in the problems of individual differences—not only the development and how it is on average, but how the individual differs and which individual differences exist in development. So these were questions we tried to solve. (Dittrichová Interview, October 7, 1999)

One of the critical methodological problems to be solved before embarking on infant conditioning studies had to do with timing: At least several days are required to first establish a simple conditioned response; and more complex processes, such as extinction, can take weeks or even months to complete (H. Papoušek, 1967a). These were among the most compelling reasons for setting up a research unit where healthy infants would remain for the first several months of their lives. At the Institute for the Care of Mother and Child in Prague, most of their research subjects were born in the obstetrics unit and continued to live there with their mothers for the first 6 months. Mothers volunteered eagerly to participate, for a variety of social, economic, and medical reasons—one being the acute housing shortage in Prague at that time. Mothers then remained with their infants at the research unit, where they were housed and supplied with free meals, linens, and health care; in many cases, these young mothers were thus enabled to continue their schooling or jobs, knowing that their infants would receive the best of care during their absence (H. Papoušek, 1967a, p. 260).

NEW APPROACHES, RESEARCH METHODS, EQUIPMENT, AND PROCEDURES

There was little to go on in terms of developing reliable, effective methods and procedures for the study of early infant learning in the 1950s, as Papoušek acknowledged when he described his early observations as being "quasi-ethological." He viewed the usual experimental methods, especially those of learning psychology, as unsuitable for the delicate human neonatal organism: "Thus our first task was to develop our own methods, to determine appropriate parameters, and to observe and gain insight into the whole complex repertoire of infant behavior," he stated. "For this, a combination of quasi-ethological empirical observation and laboratory experimentation seemed the most suitable approach" (H. Papoušek, 1977, p. 3).

In addition, there were some important technological advances, particularly the development of polygraph equipment that allowed scientists for the first time to "communicate" with infants about their perceptual and learning capacities. Although the polygraph was initially used for physiological research, other developmental scientists began recording heart rates and noticing that "if we present stimuli to kids—if we do things to them— we can look at their heart rate and they can tell us whether they see them, hear them, and their responses to those stimuli" (Sameroff Interview, February 4, 2000).

Arnold Sameroff, one of the first Americans to go to Prague and study with Hanuš Papoušek, was initially taken aback by the paucity of research equipment at the Institute. Although Papoušek was willing to order what was needed, the process itself was markedly different from that to which Sameroff was accustomed in the United States:

> And the other thing was, there was no equipment! . . . in the States, you put in an order and within, well hopefully a month or so, you got your equipment . . . or these days, you can go to the corner store and buy it. There, you first had to have permission of the agency, the hospital, then the Ministry, and it was spending hard money because it was coming from West Germany . . . the electronic equipment. And then we had to wait. As it turned out, it was about a six-month waiting period before the equipment showed up! (Sameroff Interview, February 2000)

Of the several forms of conditioning that might be used with infants, Papoušek and his team found the appetitional procedure to be particularly appropriate "since the need to satiate hunger represents a very effective motivation in newborns" (H. Papoušek, 1967a, p. 263). Nevertheless, as Krasnogorskii pointed out earlier, the classical method was not feasible because the newborn does not produce enough saliva to be measured easily. Thus, a new method for conditioning the newborn's head-turning response was developed and refined at the Prague Institute (see Fig. 2.1); this, of course, required the design and construction of new equipment, specifically a crib to be used during the experimental sessions:

> The most important part of this crib is a special head cradle, constructed from thermoplastic styrene and lined with soft styrene foam padding, in which the infant's head is placed during an experimental session. The cradle is attached to a horizontal axis and rotates when the infant turns his head. It is necessary to be able to shift this axis in a vertical direction according to the

FIG. 2.1.   An experimental apparatus for studies of conditioned head turning.

size of the infant's head. . . . Properly placed switches turn on light signals that indicate to the experimenter when the head movements exceed ±15° from midline (the limits of the neutral position of the head) or ±45° (the criterion of a positive response turn to the left or to the right). (H. Papoušek, 1967a, pp. 264–265)

These experimental procedures began during the second to fourth day of life, and were scheduled to replace one of the regular morning feedings each day except weekends. Initially, the babies were fed without conditioning so as to allow a period of adjustment to the apparatus and to a new method of feeding. This also permitted the experimenters to record baseline head-turning rates prior to initiating a series of conditioning procedures, as follows.

First Procedure: Establishing a Simple Conditioning Response

The conditioned response (CR) to a bell was first trained by using reinforcement of milk when the infant turned to the left. According to H. Papoušek (1965), this side was chosen because of a prominent tendency of newborns to turn to the right. The milk was presented by a research assistant seated behind the infant, and was administered through a nipple attached to a thermos, thus allowing a precise amount to be measured and controlled. Over the course of 10 trials per session, each reinforcement the infant received contained approximately one tenth of the portion typically consumed during a normal feeding. The intertrial intervals were timed to last approximately 1 minute, but were varied randomly to avoid conditioning to time. According to Papoušek,

Unlike the classical conditioning design, the interval between conditioning stimulus and reinforcement is not constant. Milk is presented to the infant as soon as he turns his head to the left, and the bell stops ringing one or two seconds after the infant starts sucking. This arrangement makes it easier to analyze the latency of the conditioned response. The child learns to turn his head as soon as possible since the quicker his response, the sooner he gets his milk. The gradual shortening of latency is indicative of adjustment to the experimental arrangement. (H. Papoušek, 1967a, p. 266)

In cases where the baby did not respond to the conditional stimulus (CS) within 10 seconds, the assistant would elicit a head turn by using tactile stimulation to the infant's left mouth region. If this still failed to elicit the required response, then the assistant would manually turn the baby's head to the left and insert the nipple in its mouth. At the completion of the reinforcement, the assistant turned the infant's head back to midline and removed the nipple. The criterion established for successful conditioned response was five consecutive correct responses per experimental session.

Second Procedure: Extinction of the Conditioned Response

The next procedure involved presenting the original conditioning stimulus for 10 seconds without reinforcement of the infant's behavior. Again, each session included 10 trials, and the criterion for successful extinction was 5 consecutive trials during which no head-turning response occurred.

Third Procedure: Re-Conditioning

(Repeat, analogous to the first procedure.)

Fourth Procedure: Discrimination Training

For this procedure, a buzzer was introduced so that when the infant turned to the *right* side, reinforcement was administered in the form of milk (as before). The purpose was to detect the infant's ability to discriminate between two different signals, bell and buzzer, and to learn the contingency on which reinforcement will be delivered. As H. Papoušek (1967a) explained, "The infant is now trained to turn his head to the left to the bell and to the right to the buzzer. In every session five signals of each kind are applied in random order. Six consecutive correct responses constitute the criterion for conditioned discrimination" (p. 267).

Fifth Procedure: Double Reversal of Discrimination

Finally, the reinforcement procedure was reversed. In this last protocol, turning in response to the sound of the bell was reinforced from the right, and turning to the buzzer was reinforced from the left. This was then reversed again, back to the original order. The same criterion for discrimination was used as described in the previous procedure.

One concern of the researchers was based on their awareness of the importance of establishing the infant's optimal state of alertness (or "optimal excitability of the Central Nervous System," according to Pavlov) as a prerequisite for effective conditioning. In order to monitor this, Papoušek constructed a pneumatic transmission method referred to as a "kymograph" (H. Papoušek, 1965) to record the infant's breathing and general motor activity during the experimental procedures. A 7-channel polygraph was used to record stimuli presentation, respiration, head turns, and motoric activity; as described earlier, the infant was resting in a "stabilimeter crib," with the limbs partially restrained so as to avoid excessive activity that might disrupt the equipment or procedure. As the baby moved, an elastic pad oscillated and transmitted this to the polygraph record:

> The actogram of the infant's general movements is recorded pneumatically from the elastic mat on which the infant lies in its crib. Respiratory movements are recorded pneumatically too, while head-turning is recorded electrically with the help of two potentiometers attached to the axis of rotation of a special frame that turns with the head. By lifting or lowering the axis of rotation of the head frame, the weight of the head can be balanced so that even a small, premature newborn encounters no difficulty in moving the apparatus or maintaining a neutral position; under normal conditions, however, he does not hold his relatively heavy head in a central position during the first months of life. (H. Papoušek, 1965, p. 104)

One of Papoušek's strengths as a researcher was his remarkable ingenuity and technical skill when the situation required developing equipment "from scratch." Sameroff gave the following account of what he saw at the Institute for the Care of Mother and Child:

> So here you are behind the Iron Curtain and you don't have the availability of the western equipment and advances—so, he'd make his own! He'd blow glass to make pens (for the polygraphs)! You take glass tubes and you kind of pull out the ends so they are very thin and then cut them off, put the ink through them, etc. And he would develop—this was their own model of transducers—where there would be a little air bag attached to a pen and when the kid moves, it changes the pressure in the bag which moves the pen back and forth. And so this is all put together . . . the most you'd have is this piece of paper running around. Then they have things called "kymographs" where they

are on a drum and the paper is around this can kind of thing and all you'd do is turn the can and it traces—it was very primitive stuff. The stuff that was used in the 20s and 30s—and making it by hand essentially. So he was really committed to doing this research! (Sameroff Interview, February 4, 2000)

An additional methodological precaution pertained to scheduling of the infants' daily activities, including the timing of research sessions: "Infants were tested in the late morning, approximately 10 minutes after their regular sleep in the fresh air. The routine schedule of feeding and sleep in the sequence of sleep, feeding, and waking enabled us to examine the subjects in comparable states of hunger and wakefulness" (H. Papoušek, 1967b, p. 255).

THE CHALLENGE TO CLASSICAL CONDITIONING APPROACHES

In designing these conditioning studies, Papoušek decided early on to combine elements of both associative and operant conditioning into one experimental design, thereby modifying classical conditioning approaches (see Fig. 2.2). His decision was based on the feeling that this more closely resembled natural learning situations in which the children typically obtain rewards as a result of their own activity:

> Our methods were chosen so that the newborn could obtain a biologically relevant reward through his own activity. He had to learn to rotate his head to the left at the sound of an electric bell. Only when the head-turn followed the acoustic signal was the infant rewarded with a portion of milk. We thus combined the advantages of both forms of conditioning: the conditioned signal, the bell, enabled us to record latency too as a powerful parameter. The operant aspect of the paradigm motivated the infant to obtain reinforcement through the quickest response possible. Thus latency could be construed as a measure of adaptation. (H. Papoušek, 1977, p. 7)

As Papoušek's research gradually became known, the uniqueness of this approach had an important impact on other infancy researchers at the time. This is perhaps best captured in the following quote by Lewis Lipsitt, a professor at Brown University, who was among the leading American scholars to use similar techniques in his own studies of infant learning:

> I became very familiar with his research both from reading those things that had been translated into English and from discussions with him, and it was on those occasions that I learned about this terrific technique that he had which I always described as putting classical conditioning and operant learning together. He didn't know very much about operant learning, but he . . . had made this innovation whereby he wasn't just using elicited responses which are characteristic of classical conditioning, but he was then reinforcing the re-

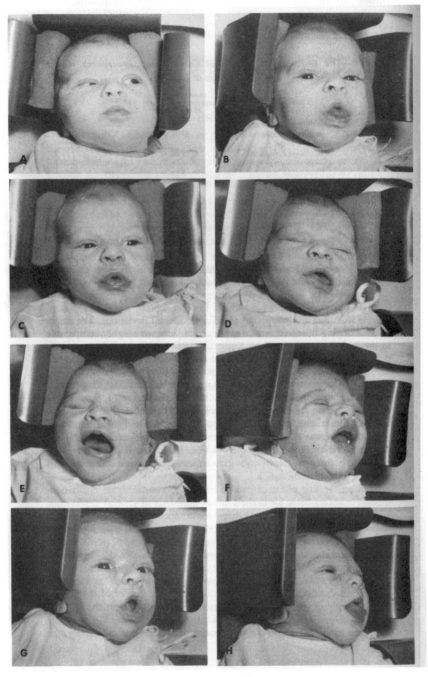

FIG. 2.2. (Continued)

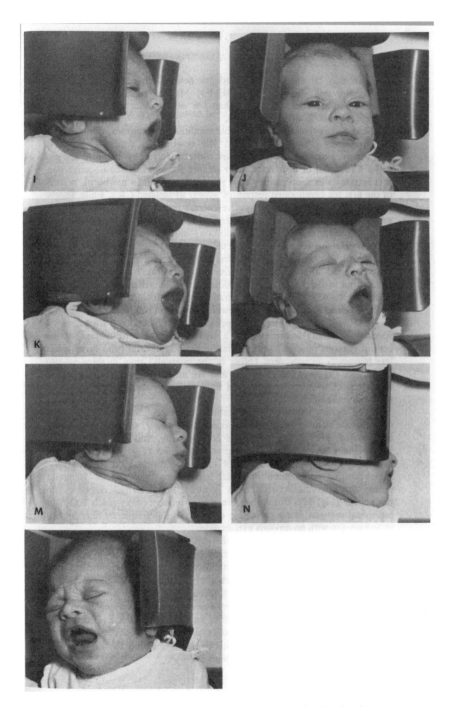

FIG. 2.2.   A photographic history of conditioning and extinction in a neonate. This infant, a boy, was 4 days old at the beginning of conditioning (A)
and about 3 weeks old by the end of the extinction procedure (O).

sponse when it occurred and not reinforcing it when it didn't occur. It had to with this conditioned head-turning paradigm that he had developed in Prague at the Center for Mothers and Infants. And that always seemed to me, and still seems to me, like a very vast contribution to the field, that he had the ingenuity to do that. Because he developed a powerful technique for teaching very young babies, including prematures. He was the guy who came up with the very best infant conditioning work of the era, of that time. . . .

I think it was so ingenious that he came up with this technique. . . . He struck on this technique of varying classical conditioning, which ordinarily involves reinforcing every single trial—and he instead reinforced only contingent upon the appropriate behavior. And that's what characterizes operant conditioning as opposed to classical. In classical there is mandatory administration of the unconditioned stimulus that elicits the response, whereas in operant learning the reinforcer—the reward, as it were—is delivered contingent upon the occurrence of the appropriate response. So, for example, what he did was to touch the baby at the corner of the mouth, which elicits a head-turning response. But it doesn't happen all of the time, that is, the response doesn't occur all of the time. So what Hanuš did was to reinforce it only when it occurred. And, thereby, he pumped up—he "jacked up" the occurrence of this response by delivering a reinforcer contingent upon the occasion of the response. And that's what made his techniques unique. (Lipsitt Interview, May 4, 2000)

The opportunity to observe infants in a consistent environment during their first 6 months meant the research team in Prague could follow patterns of individual children's development and compare age-related differences in learning, state regulation, sleep–wake cycles, and so forth. What they observed may seem self-evident now, but was truly a new view of infancy at the time: By the end of only 1 week, significant differences could be detected in the number of correct versus incorrect responses to the conditioned head-turning procedure (H. Papoušek, 1977). But as the studies progressed with the same infants, even more intriguing patterns emerged: "The course of conditioning in newborns differs in several ways from the course of conditioning in older infants or adults. Just as former studies have indicated, the rate of conditioning, slowest in newborns, undergoes a striking developmental change during the first half year of life" (H. Papoušek, 1967a, p. 268). In the case of newborns, for example, the total course of learning (conditioning to criterion) took more than twice the number of sessions as required by older babies, for whom experimental conditioning procedures did not begin until they were several months old (see Table 2.2, modified from H. Papoušek, 1967a, p. 268). Furthermore, for many of the youngest babies, only the first conditioned response and its extinction were successfully completed. Nevertheless, the evidence led to the conclusion that newborns not only can learn, but they can also detect environmental changes contingent on their own activity, and then adapt to such changes.

TABLE 2.2
Infant Age and Duration of Conditioning Procedures

Age (Days) @ Beginning of Experiment:	N	# Sessions to Criterion
3.42	14	76.02
85.78	14	47.76
142.50	16	30.26

Older infants (3- to 5-month-olds) clearly learned faster than newborns: "The acquisition curves for the older infants were steeper and smoother, from which we conclude that the ability to learn develops very quickly in the first half year of life, and especially in the first three months" (H. Papoušek, 1977, p. 17). In addition, older infants showed more emotional reaction when their responses were met with success, that is, they expressed their pleasure more clearly via both facial and vocal positive reactions.

The newborns were found to be highly motivated learners as well, but their efforts resulted more often in overexertion or an appearance of overstimulation; perhaps to protect themselves from becoming overly aroused, the newborn babies were often observed withdrawing abruptly as if "playing possum." In this state, the infant is quiet and not moving, shows little attention to the environment, the eyes are unfocused or staring, and heart rate and breathing become slow and regular. Essentially, the infant appears to be sleeping, but Papoušek and others have interpreted this as a "biological fuse" that allows self-protection by the immature organism against sensory overload (H. Papoušek, M. Papoušek, & L. S. Koester, 1999). Older infants were better able to cope with the demands of the experimental situation, so that when they needed to withdraw from further stimulation they did so by turning away, protesting, and so forth.

In addition to age-related changes, striking individual variability was also observed. In a major departure from classical conditioning studies according to Pavlov, Papoušek also addressed the question of individual differences, a subject that preoccupied him early on, and remained an important theme even after his later defection from Prague. Considering all of the controls the researchers were able to introduce at the Prague Institute (e.g., regulated sleeping and eating cycles), the wide range of individual differences in speed of learning was somewhat unexpected. According to Papoušek,

So you know, the group showed conditioning. But does each of the babies show conditioning, or only some of them, and why? And you cannot study the cause of conditioning. So for these reasons I sort of combined the elements of both methods—it was not actually a combination, it was a new design, but it was then used as "instrumental conditioning." And we were studying each in-

fant individually and up to achievement of certain criteria. Remember I said
we maintained very strict criteria. So let's say in our design we were sort of telling the baby "when you turn to the left, you'll get milk, but only if you hear a
signal—if the signal doesn't come, it's in vain." So the child learned to respond faster and faster with the left turns, but also in a differentiated way.
Stopped turning to the left if there was not a signal signaling that now the
condition was here for achieving something. Which I thought was more comparable to natural situations. Because, you know, the mother may be preparing a bottle. The child may hear the sounds, may already know them, and may
show anticipatory sucking. But he cannot change anything by sucking. But after all, here and there he can hear similar sounds which do not mean anything because the mother is not preparing the milk for him, she's now preparing something else in the kitchen. The sounds may be similar, but the child
has to actually differentiate, perhaps according to the course of time. So, you
know, if there is a time of regular feeding, then he may find those sounds
more relevant than at other times. So this was seemingly more complex.
(Papoušek Interview, October 22, 1999)

Sameroff described this as another unique contribution of the Prague
studies; more interesting than significant group differences was the idea
that the rates and patterns of learned responses were actually quite variable
from infant to infant. To be sure, the conditioning studies were demonstrating success even with infants, which at that time was significant in and
of itself. But Sameroff found the next step in the process to be even more
intriguing:

Hanuš' unique approach was, instead of saying in . . . 50 trials, does the Control group have more than or less than the Treatment group. He said, now,
let's look at individuals. How each child individually learns. And then we can
tell not that they're better than 50% criterion, but we can trace it day to day to
when they actually learn. So you can look at the process of learning and take it
apart, and that was part of the excitement. So he was conditioning every day
and you could follow the whole process of the kids learning and every kid
coming to criterion at some point, rather than the group curve or something
like that. (Sameroff Interview, February 4, 2000)

Beyond the concern with individual differences, there was also the lingering issue of previous studies that had been less successful at establishing
newborn learning. Based on his own work, Papoušek concluded that the
critical difference was that operant methods (conditioned head turns) were
more effective; those who relied on purely classical methods showed no
learning. H. Papoušek (1977) commented that his colleague Sameroff interpreted this discrepancy by claiming that classical conditioning required
the baby to integrate and associate several perceptual modalities (i.e., the
conditioned and unconditioned stimuli), a task that presumed a certain

level of cognitive development. Papoušek's own interpretation was slightly different:

> Our own interpretation of the discrepancy in results has to do with the early postnatal regulation of motor activity. With operant conditioning, the infant obtains a reward through his own activity, i.e. reinforcement is contingent on his rotating his head in a particular direction. The recognition of contingencies is already evident in newborns. This enables newborns to form expectations about the course and consequences of their movements. The fulfillment of these expectations, through repetition of the movement, regularly elicits pleasure. Such pleasant emotional experiences represent effective mechanisms for inner reward, an important component of intrinsic motivation. . . . In summary, we can conclude that the sooner the newborn organism is enabled to achieve a biologically relevant environmental change contingent on his own activity, the more likely it is that learning will occur. (H. Papoušek, 1977, pp. 15–16)

CONCLUSIONS

Shortly before his death, when asked about the importance of Prague and the Institute for the Care of Mother and Child for his life's work, Hanuš admitted: "I have to say, and to be honest, to say it in relation to Prague, that those years gave me the immediate experience with children on the one side, which I knew just as if they were my own babies, and with their mothers on the other" (Papoušek Interview, October 15, 1999). In other words, for Papoušek, the most important thing about the Institute was that it afforded him the ability to work directly with his research subjects on an everyday basis, and to do so over an extended period of time. Indeed, it seems that it was the ability to pursue theory in combination with practice—in a setting involving medical doctors and psychology researchers with different interests and disciplinary perspectives—that provided Papoušek with the opportunity to develop a scientific view of infancy that corresponded with the practical insights gained by working with his subjects firsthand. The result was an integrated and dynamic view of the infant's mental, behaviorial, and physiological development that formed the basis of his views for the rest of his life. It also provided the basis for continuities in his later views of parent–infant interactions and the Papoušeks' theory of Intuitive Parenting (see chap. 7).

Chapter 3

The Scientist as a Policy Figure: Child-Care Reform and "The First Swallow" of the Prague Spring

Hanuš Papoušek frequently told gentle but ironic anecdotes about the obstacles he faced as a research scientist at the Institute for the Care of Mother and Child—about administrators and bureaucrats who lacked the kind of flexibility researchers needed to conduct innovative experiments and observations, ingenious ways to compensate for the lack of laboratory equipment and financial resources, and so forth. Yet, there was another dimension to Papoušek's professional life other than that of a dedicated researcher: He had a deep and abiding interest in problems of public policy and how to improve the lives of infants and parents in the everyday world. Relatively early in his career, in addition to his research, Papoušek started applying his scientific knowledge to many of the practical problems and concerns that parents and children faced at home, at school, and at the workplace.

Thus, as early as 1959 and still only 37 years old, he accepted an invitation from the Czech Ministry of Health to embark on a study tour of day-care facilities in the Soviet Union. After his return, Papoušek wrote a report recounting his impressions that proved to be the beginning of a long-standing association with the Ministry of Health. Among other things, he served in the influential post of secretary and general coordinator of the Ministry's research studies in the area of infant health and day care. Through this role, he became involved in a day-care reform movement that some Czech observers subsequently called a "first swallow" or early signal of the 1968 Prague Spring (Matějček Interview, October 6, 1999). Perhaps his involvement in this reform effort is what prompted Jerome Bruner to say that Hanuš was "a perpetual Prague Spring waiting to happen" (Bruner Interview, January 30, 2002).

The following is a case study of how a pediatrician and research scientist such as Hanuš Papoušek helped bring about important policy changes in the closed socialist society of Czechoslovakia, during an era of political liberalization in the 1960s. The eventual abandonment of Soviet-style day-care policies was a complex process that involved many different factors and continued for a number of years. First and foremost, it was due to the courage, integrity, and tenacity of dedicated professionals, scientists, intellectuals, and journalists who were both Party and non-Party members. Additionally, it involved the willingness of Ministry officials to remain receptive to scientific data and evidence presented to them. In 1967, the Czech Communist Party finally adopted new day-care policies that gave mothers and fathers the option of staying at home with an infant or young child, while at the same time receiving financial support—but only after another socialist country, Hungary, had taken the lead. A unique convergence of factors led to the Czechoslovak Socialist Republic's (ČSSR) adoption of this new policy at that particular point in time. Throughout this process, Papoušek and his ideas about infancy and the role of parents played a vital role.

THE STALINIST YEARS AND "COLLECTIVE EDUCATION" IN THE 1950S

Upon seizing power in 1948, Klement Gottwald and the Czech Communist Party proclaimed the creation of a "people's democracy" and a special "Czechoslovak road to socialism." By the time a Central Committee was chosen in 1949, however, these slogans were replaced by calls for the establishment of a Soviet-styled "dictatorship of the proletariat." Within one year, private ownership of land and industry was eliminated and a command economy with centralized planning, controls, and pricing was installed. Gottwald himself was bestowed with a Stalinist personality, police terrorism became common, foreign travel was forbidden, and foreign trade was reoriented from West to East. The new Communist system achieved substantial progress in the status and employment of women, even though women still lagged behind in terms of equality with men in other realms. By 1963, the number of women in the labor force more than quadrupled, and more than two thirds of all employed Czechs were women with higher education.

After Stalin's denunciation in 1956, uprisings occurred in Poland and Hungary; the response of the Party leadership in Czechoslovakia, however, was to impose new restrictions and announce the adoption of a new constitution in July 1960. The country's name was changed to the Socialist Republic of Czechoslovakia and the "transition to Communism" was pronounced legal and complete. At about the same time, the first economic studies indicated that the Soviet-modeled economy was starting to stall, and a number of economists argued that whereas the fundamentals of socialism needed to be preserved, the Stalinist program of economic organization should be radically revised if not discarded altogether. Signs of a general standstill and a sense of purposelessness began to appear throughout Czech society (Korbel, 1977). The system itself seemed ripe for change.

Throughout the 1950s, the Communist Party adhered to policies concerning early education and childrearing that were fairly simple. These were based on the assumption that the mistakes of the past had been due to innate human selfishness or egocentrism, and thus required a new approach. This selfishness was perpetuated above all by the family and was caused by the love of parents who wished to do only good for their children, without paying sufficient attention to what would be good for the socialist society at large. It was a vicious cycle in which selfishness and egocentrism were handed down from one generation to the next. The cycle would need to be broken first, in order to create a better kind of person and socialist society. The intervention imposed by the government for this purpose was collective rather than family-based childrearing and education (Matějček Interview, October 6, 1999).

As a first step, in 1950 the Czech government abolished the family-based system of foster care for orphans and replaced it with collective institutions that were created under the Soviet slogan, "Through Collectivity to Collectivity." It no longer made sense for foster children to live in families if the family did not have a future, so young children without parents were assigned to live in government-run "crèches" and children's homes. By the end of the 1950s, and at great expense, a nationwide network of crèches had been put into place for infants and young children under age 3, supervised by the Ministry of Health. Children from ages 3 to 6, on the other hand, were placed in group homes under the control of the Ministry of Education. The assumption was that most children below age 3 would be cared for in crèches (even if they had parents in the home) because the vast majority of mothers, as part of an egalitarian attitude toward men and women, would be at work. Women had a right to pursue their own careers and their own emancipation; if children were in need of care or education before reaching school age, then they could be raised either partially or fully in such institutions. Significantly, "collective education" was introduced in all of the Soviet-dominated countries, but important differences emerged from one country to the next in terms of the actual percentages of children being cared for in the crèche system. In Czechoslovakia, the number of children in crèches was never more than 25% from 1950 through 1968, after which the percentage declined. In the Soviet Union, the highest number reported was 40%, whereas in the Democratic Republic of Germany the highest number reached 85%, a figure attained in the 1980s. In

Romania, the crèche system remained in place under the regime of Nicolae Ceausescu until the late 1980s.

As this system of "collective education" was being put into place in Czechoslovakia, members of the Ministry of Health thought it would be useful to document the advantages of collective education, although certain lower ranking advisors felt that the possible disadvantages ought to be addressed as well. As a result, surveys were commissioned to examine the impact of group care at a number of facilities throughout the country. The most noteworthy of these studies was one carried out by two psychologists, Josef Langmeier, professor of psychology at the Pediatric Medical School of Charles University, and Zdeněk Matějček, a psychologist at one of the government's mental health research institutes in Prague. As part of an effort to inform itself about day care in other countries, the Ministry arranged for Hanuš Papoušek to receive a governmental grant to gather information about group child-care facilities in the Soviet Union. Somewhat surprisingly, no one seemed to know whether Soviet researchers had undertaken any kind of assessment of their own crèches and children's homes, despite the establishment of these institutions since shortly after the 1917 October Revolution.

After collecting and analyzing their data in the ČSSR, Langmeier and Matějček first presented the results of their survey at a conference of the Czech Pediatric Society in Bratislava in 1961. Their presentation created a major stir. Instead of reporting that institutionalized group care had important advantages, as had been expected, they reported having found almost exactly the opposite. Langmeier began their presentation by outlining a general theory of deprivation, and Matějček followed with a summary of longitudinal data showing that at 18, 24, and 36 months, children raised in group care settings showed deficits in mental development, social behavior, ability to adapt, and speech and language development when compared to those raised at home (Matějček Interview, October 6, 1999). At Bratislava, it was primarily medical doctors and professional administrators working in the crèche system who took the most immediate note of Langmeier and Matějček's findings, and who soon afterward began calling for alternatives to group homes for the youngest children. Child-care workers and administrators of institutional homes for children age 3 years old and up, on the other hand, were more reticent in calling for change. One reason for this may have been that group homes for infants and toddlers were still under the control of the Ministry of Health and its non-Communist minister, the Catholic priest Plojhar. The system of homes for older children, on the other hand, was under the jurisdiction of the Ministry of Education, a stronghold of the Communist Party. It has also been suggested that the difference in social status between medical doctors and educators in socialist Czechoslovakia played a role. Medical doctors and pediatricians enjoyed a higher social status than child-care workers and administrators, and hence may have felt more confident in speaking out authoritatively (Korbel, 1977).

Hanuš Papoušek visited the Soviet Union for 3 weeks in May 1959, when he was awarded a governmental grant to visit Leningrad and Moscow. Because it was his first visit there, he spent approximately half of his time meeting with Soviet developmental researchers at leading institutions such as the Pavlov Institute in Leningrad, and the other half visiting day-care sites in and around Moscow. (See chap. 2 for more about his meetings with Soviet developmentalists.) All were collective facilities in which the children were separated by age group in accordance with official regulations and guidelines. All 1-year-olds were grouped with other 1-year-olds, all 2-year-olds with 2-year-olds, all 3-year-olds with 3-year-olds, and so forth. This meant that children changed groups and care providers on a regular basis according to their birthday—an approach that troubled Papoušek a great deal.

While in Moscow, however, Hanuš also had the good fortune of being hosted by a man named Tschermanov, a progressive thinker who was considered the Soviet patriarch of all group child-care facilities. Tschermanov, who had visited Prague and had come to trust Hanuš, knew that Hanuš' Russian was fluent enough not to require a translator, so he invited Papoušek to a special conference that foreigners normally were not allowed to attend. Forty years later, Papoušek still recalled vividly what Tschermanov said:

> "Look, if you're really interested in something special, I'm going to invite you to this conference. But as a foreigner you'll have to promise not to participate in the discussions. We'll do it just between the two of us. This is a special conference with heads of day care facilities from all different regions to talk about why so many facilities outside Moscow are not complying with official policies and regulations." And so I sat there and just had to hold my mouth laughing, because here was a rare opportunity for me to understand something very important about the Soviet Union, which was that someone could admit that he voluntarily or willingly *deviated* from official instructions. But the remarkable thing was that Tschermanov simply replied, "Well, this is Russia, you know. There's a big cultural difference here. If Moscow decides to regulate something, not everybody will follow. Some regions have their own heads, and sometimes they are right." And as a result, I learned that some Soviet facilities had already decided ten years ago to combine the different age groups. Sometimes it was because of lack of personnel or space, so they put all age groups together. And as a result, people like Tschermanov and some other officials in Moscow had already decided as early as 1958 that it was important simply to listen to the experience of people in the field, and to make adjustments in policies that would accommodate them. (Papoušek Interview, October 15, 1999)

Back in Prague, Papoušek prepared a lengthy report of his visit to the Soviet Union, including an account of the conference. In essence, what he reported was that Soviet day care was driven primarily by ideological, political, and organizational considerations that had been put into place largely on the basis of administrative convenience. Notably missing, Papoušek wrote, was a thorough scientific understanding on the part of Soviet researchers about the needs of the young children and parents that the Soviet day-care system was intended to serve. Most Soviet day-care facilities had been created in the 1920s under conditions of great hunger, enormous labor shortages from so many men having died in the war, and large numbers of women who suddenly had to leave home and work in the factories. Forty years later, from a scientific and developmental perspective, it was clear that the effects of these facilities on children were virtually unknown. Among the few studies available were two recent publications by researchers from the Soviet Academy of Arts and Sciences, Tchervonow and Yavlalina, neither of which was available in Czech (Papoušek Interview, July 17, 1998). What Czech Ministry officials needed to know, Papoušek stated, was that both studies compared the effects of family-based versus group care and came to conclusions similar to those reported by Langmeier and Matějček.

After submitting his report, Papoušek was initially apprehensive about the Ministry's response. After all, he had painted a picture of the Soviet model that was not very rosy. What would happen to him if all they really had wanted was a false glorification of his impressions? To his surprise, however, the response proved to be somewhat different than he had feared. Although the Ministry decided it would not be wise to publicize his report, it turned out that a good number of officials were pleased with what he had written:

> You know, the Ministry of Health genuinely appreciated what I told them. "How could you write such a report? Didn't you even worry about someone reading it who might realize that you spoke the truth about the real role of official instructions, ideologies and policies in the Soviet Union?" And the amazing thing was that shortly thereafter, in 1960, the Ministry came back to me and they said, "We want you to apply for a World Health Organization (WHO) stipend, so you can go to Scandinavia and prepare a similar report for us next year." I guess this business with the truthfulness at the Soviet conference must have had an influence on them and on me, so when I received the stipend for Scandinavia, I tried to do the same thing. And I have to say, I tried to do the same thing with everything I said later about day care as well. (Papoušek Interview, October 15, 1998)

What Papoušek learned from this experience was that there were individuals in the Ministry (although not necessarily the majority) who were less interested in politics and ideology, and much more open-minded and receptive to scientific data than he had anticipated. Moreover, he was also told by Ministry officials that they intended to nominate him as the first

Czech to receive this prestigious World Health Organization (WHO) fellowship, which would allow him to study some day-care systems in Western Europe. It was an opportunity Papoušek eagerly accepted. Under the WHO fellowship, he traveled to Sweden and Great Britain in 1961. In Sweden, he became acquainted with the system of family centers, in which mothers took neighbors' children into their homes. He was impressed that these centers were financed by the Swedish government, and admired the flexibility they provided for mothers. Additionally, he learned that Swedish pediatricians were more than just medical doctors. Like those in Czechoslovakia, they were trained to see children not only when they were sick; individual children were examined on a regular basis even if they were healthy, families were consulted, and childrearing and parenting advice was given. He was also very much impressed that, by the early 1960s, Sweden together with Czechoslovakia had one of the lowest infant mortality rates of any country in Europe. In Great Britain, Papoušek was impressed by the many different services offered through the National Health Care System, including a variety of public and private day-care centers and preschools. There were both full- and part-time day and residential nurseries from age 0 to 2 and 2 to 5, run either by the government or by nonprofit and religious organizations (Papoušek Interview, July 17, 1998).

After completing the WHO fellowship, Papoušek started serving the Ministry of Health on a relatively regular basis, while at the same time continuing his research at the Institute for the Care of Mother and Child. He was assigned to increasingly responsible roles, all having to do with day care. In 1963, he was appointed to the influential post of secretary of the Ministry's Governmental Research Project on the Care of Children in Preschool Facilities, a position he held until 1970. By his own account, this enabled him to review all Ministry research studies pertaining to the nation's crèches and early child-care centers. In 1965 and 1966, he was also named the Czech government's delegate to binational day-care conferences with Sweden and Italy, and in 1966 he was named the chief organizer of an important international conference on day care in socialist countries that was to be held in Prague. His appointment to this latter assignment was not coincidental. Papoušek urged the Ministry for several years to hold such a conference, and from the very beginning was actively involved in shaping the agenda and inviting the participants (Papoušek Interview, July 17, 1999).

THE ROLES OF *CHILDREN WITHOUT LOVE, LITERÁRNÍ NOVINY,* AND HELENA KLÍMOVÁ

Not long after the 1961 Bratislava conference, a number of events occurred that previously would have been virtually unimaginable in socialist Czechoslovakia. Even many Czechs were caught by surprise. One event was the

1963 release of a Czech film that gave a very negative impression of the country's group care facilities and yet somehow managed to escape official censorship. Shown in movie houses across the country, it became surprisingly popular and stirred widespread public indignation. How was it possible for the government to allow Czech children to be treated in such a deplorable fashion? The other event, partially triggered by the film's release, was extensive newspaper coverage publicizing the views about day care of some of the country's leading medical doctors, psychologists, and day-care professionals. What began as a discussion about day-care problems at a relatively specialized professional conference in Bratislava, suddenly became something of a public cause challenging some of the central ideological tenets of the entire political and social system.

The idea of making a film about youth homes came from Dr. Damborská, the director of a children's home facility in Luhačovice. The documentary was titled *Children Without Love* and drew extensively on the studies originally presented by Langmeier and Matějček. Without providing commentary or interpretation, it showed the infants and young children in institutions to be much more passive and unhappy than those raised in their families. One reason the filmmakers had been able to avoid the governmental censorship of the arts was because they claimed that their film was a documentary, made without aesthetic aspirations. Moreover, it did not arouse suspicions because many of the people involved were Party members. As Matějček, who served as a consultant to the directors, recalled: "Some were members, some were not. . . . Even the Party people became engaged, and that was good. So it was not an 'anti-Party' movement as such. Sure, some of the 'anti-Party' people were involved, but not officially. The Party members didn't demonstrate any opposition, so in this way the film could get through" (Matějček Interview, October 6, 1999).

Shortly after becoming popular at home, *Children Without Love* also succeeded in attracting considerable international attention. Following its release in Czechoslovakia, someone secretly managed to attach the documentary as a trailer to Miloš Forman's famous film *Der Schwarze Peter* (*Černý Petr*), smuggled it out of the country, and submitted it as an entry for the 1963 Venice Film Festival. At Venice, *Children Without Love* won three first prizes in its category, creating even more of an uproar among hard-liners. Precisely who was responsible for smuggling the film out is still not publicly known.

Equally important as *Children Without Love*, however, was the work of a talented young journalist named Helena Klímová. Klímová worked for the reform-minded biweekly newspaper *Literární Noviny*, probably the most influential Czech publication to promote social, economic, and cultural reform. Indeed, by the mid-1960s, *Literární Noviny* was perceived by many Party officials as the country's "second seat of power." A mother herself, and wife of the promising young writer Ivan Klíma, Klímová wrote articles related to women's issues, health care, and children, and had become aware of the discussions about child care within the professional and scientific communities. Beginning in 1963, she wrote a series of articles about Czech day care that hit Prague "like a bombshell," as she later recalled (Klímová Interview, April 26, 2000).

In one of her articles with the metaphoric title "Like a Meisener Apple, Like a Rose," Klímová (1963a) cited some of the negative views that were circulating within the professional day-care community. Somewhat provocatively, she called Czechoslovakia's orphanages and full day-care centers grossly deficient and in many cases even harmful. Although the facilities were generally very hygienic, well-organized, and medically well-staffed, she wrote, institutionalized care remained a giant social experiment, the benefits of which were unsubstantiated and not at all clear. Citing Michaličková and Švejcar from Prague, and the British psychiatrist John Bowlby, Klímová reported that the emotional development of children was being neglected, and the role of the mother as the source of moral, emotional, and social development was being diminished. Maternal care was essential to the healthy development of the young child; its quality could not be measured by the number of hours per day, but only by the degree of enjoyment from the reciprocal relationship between mother and child. The enjoyment and mutual reciprocation of emotions are possible only if the healthy relationship between the child and mother are continuous and not disturbed, she maintained. Even a mother with poor parenting skills can contribute a great deal to her child (except in the worst cases) by offering a sense of security from which the child can begin to explore the world (Klímová, 1963a).

In addition to writing about the mother, Klímová also focused on professional views pertaining to infants themselves; here she cited results of studies conducted by Dr. Damborská, the director of a crèche in Luhačovice who had also instigated the making of *Children Without Love*. Damborská had undertaken a "live experiment" at her center that was designed to demonstrate different types of attachment and adaptability with three infants who were presented with new toys. The first two infants were children from her center—one was accompanied by an "auntie" or caregiver from her own crèche, the other was left with a stranger. The reactions of the first two infants, although different in degree, indicated insecure attachments and impaired adaptability. The third infant was a child living at home, accompanied by the mother for the experiment. This child freely explored the toys and, with the loving encouragement of the mother, even played with a rather frightening, large teddy bear.

Based on this demonstration, Klímová explained the basic concept of adaptability in terms of its essential role in healthy child development, and proceeded to cite the following statistics from Damborská's research: When compared to children living in families, institutionalized children showed three times as many signs of poor adaptation; fear reactions occurred twice as frequently; and panic was not observed at all in children living with families, but occurred eight times in institutional settings. Damborská's conclusion was that emotional adaptation in the case of institutionalized children from age 24 to 40 weeks was significantly worse than that of children living at home. In the case of institutionalized children, the beginnings of impaired socioemotional development could be observed. Further research also revealed that institutionalized children were delayed in the areas of play, language development, and the rate at which they gained weight.

Klímová's conclusion was that institutionalized children, even in high quality facilities such as the one in Luhačovice, have a poorer start in life. Genetic predisposition was unlikely to have caused such deficits; it was more reasonable to conclude that the environmental differences experienced by institutionalized children compared to those living at home were responsible. Factors thought to explain these differences included the following: monotonous, unstimulating institutional life; lack of continuity of care due to frequent changes in personnel; and children with no sense of being protected and nurtured, hence their natural curiosity was replaced with mistrust and fear.

Finally, Klímová also discussed the condition of "hospitalism," characterizing it as a phenomenon that occurs in children who live in an environment where "care" is understood only in terms of material provisions (e.g., in hospitals, institutions, poor day care, and even negligent families), and where children do not receive sufficient stimulation or emotional support. Hospitalism results in feelings of profound sadness and disappointment, as well as withdrawal from the surrounding world. Children with this condition seek relief in self-stimulating activities such as intensive thumb sucking and repetitive rhythmic movements. By adolescence, they may have developed a syndrome referred to at the time as "anetic." The most effective intervention for children suffering from hospitalism is adoption into a warm and nurturing family.

Klímová (1963a) also described her observations of children in a weeklong residential preschool facility in Prague. She spent a considerable amount of time in this establishment, and offered readers poignant anecdotes of children longing for home and for their parents, whom they saw only on weekends. In addition, she provided a summary of the latest research concerning the impact of full-day, full-week preschool on the social and emotional behavior of children. Recent studies had found that the affective expressions of children in such facilities were superficial and flat. On Saturdays and Mondays they appeared even more listless than on other days of the week. As the week progressed, there was an increase in "nonconstructive" and self-stimulating activities such as playing with the hands, mouth, and nose, as well as mechanical, pendulumlike movements, unnatural grimaces, and facial expressions. When the institutionalized children were asked to draw pictures of their days at home when the family was together, 70% of the children depicted either themselves alone, or a family without a child. To emphasize the point, Klímová's article depicted a child's drawing with two sides to it: One side portrayed a child alone with a dog and a canary, and the other side showed a mother and father with a snowman. Immediately next to this drawing was a picture by another child the same age, but from home-based child care; in this picture, the child was shown in the midst of a family.

Klímová concluded that children without adequate individual attention suffer from a lack of emotionally sensitive care, and fail to develop a secure basis from which to feel confident, protected, and loved. As a logical consequence of inadequate attention to their early developmental needs, these children are likely to develop psychological problems later in life, such as difficulties establishing and maintaining deep emotional relationships. The later characteristics of many of these children were described as a lack of empathy, feelings of belonging, conscience, respect, and other dimensions of emotional and moral life. Her article ended by observing that the recent Czech research studies on the negative impact of residential day care were "works of conscience" by diligent individuals who found the care provided for many Czech children at that time to be distressing at best.

In the same year, Klímová published yet another "bombshell" titled "Children and Day Care: The Professionals Are Talking" in *Literární Noviny* (Klímová, 1963b). First, she interviewed Josef Švejcar, a medical doctor who was the head of the 1st Children's Clinic in Prague. This was followed by another interview, this time with Hanuš Papoušek. In response to Klímová's questions, Švejcar stressed that the most important thing for children is that their physiological needs be satisfied first, and that the primary emotional bond is maintained between the child and the mother. The mother–child relationship was described as the basis for all future relationships between the child and other human beings. On the one hand, because the size of the family had decreased in preceding years, interaction with other children was seen as beneficial for proper social development. Enrollment in day care, however, needed to be adjusted to the needs of the child rather than simply to the working hours of the mothers. Švejcar suggested that the ideal solution would be for a child to attend day care only after the end of the second year, not longer than 6 hours per day, and in a facility with a ratio of at least one caregiver per eight children. He proposed that after 6 hours in day care, a child should be looked after exclusively by the mother.

In her interview with Papoušek, Klímová asked him to compare the advantages of family upbringing to those of collective care. Papoušek replied that both types of upbringing could have positive and negative effects. Therefore, the goal should be to combine the best features of each. Papoušek indicated that the quality of family life in Czechoslovakia was not always satisfactory. On the one hand, relationships within the family were the stepping stones for establishing the child's relationships with the outside world, and the family should provide the child with a stable environment and positive examples of how persons interrelate. On the other hand, family care can also lead children to become egocentric, and the quality of life is not inherently optimal in all families. In addition, some families are not able to provide adequate space for play and exercise, especially those living in large cities.

Collective care can supplement family care, Papoušek maintained, especially in situations of deficiency, and can serve an important social function. It frees up the parents for work, culture, and recreation, and can also be organized as a form of education that provides opportunities for learning and new discoveries by the child. One major drawback of collective care, however, can be greater exposure to infectious diseases. In addition, some parents may think of it as a substitute for the upbringing they themselves otherwise would have to provide, thus releasing them from the obligation of having to deal with the child on a daily basis. This is a big mistake, he argued. Day care can never completely substitute for parental care, especially in the areas of language development and emotional support; it should only be considered as supplemental to the care provided within the family. The child needs to know that it belongs within its own family, and that it can always return to the security found there. In addition, stable contact with her child is important for the mother, because it is through this intimate relationship that the child also elicits the art of mothering.

Weeklong institutional care clearly is undesirable, Papoušek observed, and the trend at the time was beginning to be toward less reliance on this arrangement. As in the Soviet Union, Czech crèche children were doing better in the areas of physical and motor development, but they often lagged behind in language and emotional development. The problems with day care often lie in issues such as the length of stay and the age at which a child should first be enrolled. It is difficult to say exactly when a child should enter day care, but Papoušek offered the following as guidelines for the kind of care parents should choose:

1. The maximum length of care outside the home should be four hours per day. Day care is a strain on young children; they tire quickly.

2. Parents should be allowed to choose an approach that is individualized and flexible. They should be able to wait with enrollment until the need arises, and children should be given sufficient time at home in order to recover from illnesses.

3. Children should be allowed to adjust to day care gradually. Mothers and fathers at first should be allowed to be present, and to stay until the child stops missing them.

4. During the second year of life, children should not stay in day care for more than eight hours per day, sleeping time included, but it would be better if their stay did not exceed six hours.

5. The working hours of mothers should be reduced. Such a reduction would have several advantages: the number of day care places available would double if each child attended only four hours per day; more women could enter the workforce, and work productivity would increase. (The first four hours of an eight-hour shift had been found to be generally more productive than the last four hours.)

6. The presence of mothers in a day care facility could help to decrease the already heavy workload on the staff.

Finally, Papoušek offered the opinion that, all too frequently, day care was evaluated only from medical and hygienic points of view. It was also important to view day care as a social and educational institution, and more attention should be given to the attitudes and moral development of the child. Making reference to his recent trips abroad, Papoušek noted that half-day shifts and the presence of mothers in day-care institutions were well-established practices in several foreign countries. Another positive step might be to follow those Soviet examples outside of Moscow in which preschool classes were age integrated, and Swedish examples of family-based centers that were more flexible and less costly than regular day care. As Papoušek concluded, many child-care issues were in need of careful research, and financial support for such studies should be a government priority.

In addition to Švejcar and Papoušek, Klímová also interviewed economist Jiří Prokopec, a researcher at the State Commission on Population. Prokopec suggested that a reduction in the work hours for mothers was feasible from an economic viewpoint, as was maternal leave for as long as one year. (In response to charges from Party women's groups, he also acknowledged that fewer work hours might limit the career prospects for women.) From the perspective of state finances, however, a reduction in mothers' work hours and wages would lower government expenditures, making it possible to use these savings instead to pay those mothers who cared for the youngest children at home. Providing financial incentives for mothers to remain at home with very small children would produce long-term social value and benefits that needed to be rewarded.

Not surprisingly, Klímová's "bombshells" did not go unanswered. Among the newspapers to launch a sharp attack was the official organ of the Communist Women's Organization. It argued that women who stayed at home were lawbreakers and in violation of the government's family laws. They were "leeches on society," and family child care at home was a "bourgeois" concept. The vehemence of this attack finally led to the publication of a statement by several researchers at the Institute for the Care of Mother and Child. Appearing in *Československá Pediatrie* in spring 1963, the statement read:

> We need to repeat our views toward these problems. . . . We are fully in agreement with the conception of day nurseries as published by the Ministry of Health. Lots of experts have been involved in addressing problems to enhance this concept. This conception is that a combination of collective care (as in nurseries) and family care is important, but permanent institutionalization (as in orphanages) should be kept to a minimum. Problems of child-rearing can be complex. Some of the articles appearing in the press acknowledge this and recognize the difficulty of separating these problems from those of working mothers. Long-term research into childrearing is necessary to bring a serious basis of knowledge to the formulation of childrearing policies. At present it is important to emphasize not just the quantity, but also the quality of these institutions. The decisive link is the highly aware, dedicated day care worker. For long-term institutional stays, the most important factor is the education and training of the nursery and day care workers themselves. (Kubát, H. Papoušek, & Štolová, 1963, p. 468)

Three names appeared at the end of the statement: Kubát, Štolová, and Papoušek. In addition, Hanuš Papoušek wrote two other articles about day-care problems in 1963 and 1964, both published in *Československá Pediatrie*. The articles were titled "A Pediatrician Looks at Some Ideological Problems in the Upbringing of Children," and "Some Problems of Child Care Institutions." In each case, Papoušek was the sole author. Even more so than is reflected in the joint statement, both articles support the need for greater involvement of mothers and families in the care of their children.

In the first article, Papoušek contended that a central problem in the day-care debate was the lack of ideological clarity about the role of the family in general, and about the nature of the relationship between men and women under socialism. Even though the Communist system gave families a great deal of support, it had become apparent that the idea of providing support for *children* within the family was being neglected to an alarming degree. Everyday one saw that parents were making too few efforts to create a happy family life at home, and too little attention was given by parents to ensure that their children were properly educated and reared. Moreover, mothers in the workplace were encountering problems with employers who showed little understanding for the difficulties of having young children at home, and too many parents failed to understand the importance of their own influences on a child. The problems with institutional care were that it sometimes created developmental delays in the psychological functioning of children, and it did not provide sufficient emotional support and social stimulation. The risk was that collective care could cause psychological disruptions that children were not always able to overcome later in life. To be sure, some children have genetic impairments or are subject to negative influences (e.g., parental substance abuse) from pre- and postnatal development, but the negative effects of institutionalized care could not be overlooked.

The second ideological problem, according to Papoušek, was the failure of Czech society to promote the importance of adequate childrearing wherever the opportunity arose—in families, institutions, schools, and other aspects of public life. Young parents, men as well as women, needed to gain a better understanding of their responsibility for childrearing in both collective and family settings, but in most cases the role of collective facilities in the childrearing process was being overemphasized. At the same time, parental childrearing practices sometimes came into conflict with the rules and regulations of group care, especially during the school-age years. According to Papoušek, this brought pressures and influences to bear from various sources that led to moral and psychological confusion, especially during adolescence.

Childrearing needed to be looked on not only as a professional problem, but also as an ideological one. Active participation in childrearing must come from an understanding of its societal importance, and deficits in childrearing should be viewed as a consequence of ideological ignorance. It was not enough to educate parents about what was already known, but about ways to solve new ideological problems as well. The role and function of the family in socialism and Communism, the relationship between childrearing in family and group institutions, and the best way to enhance the abilities of children all were unresolved problems. Although social factors sometimes arise that have a negative impact on the childrearing process, these factors also needed to be understood with regard to their political implications. Pediatricians needed to view themselves as more than medical practitioners who were concerned only with physical problems. If pediatricians understood problems from both the professional and ideological viewpoints, they could do a better job of bringing about the right cures and interventions (H. Papoušek, 1963).

In "Some Problems of Child Care Institutions," Papoušek's primary purpose was to point to the need for more and better kinds of scientific research, and to encourage this much more openly than ever before. "The issue of group day care has been widely discussed, making it clear, from a scientific point of view, that many of the medical and educational problems involved in group care have not been adequately resolved," he began (H. Papoušek, 1964, p. 1117). To be sure, a combination of group and home child care would be ideal, but the problems of the first years of life are important and complex, and research concerning these problems needed to be more thorough and sophisticated than was the case then. The problem of women needing to work and provision of adequate child care was a worldwide phenomenon. Much more research-based understanding was required, both qualitatively and quantitatively, in accordance with rigorous scientific standards and methods. More studies were also needed in regard to the incidence of infections, speech development, and emotional and personality development, especially in cases where collective childrearing was more prevalent than family-based care.

Adopting an official-like tone, Papoušek outlined a research agenda that the Ministry of Health would further through grant awards for the upcoming year:

> In the ČSSR, we need more research concerning the historical, climatic, social and cultural conditions. . . . With more specialists and researchers now looking at these issues, this will help the Ministry of Health develop better policies. Accordingly, in 1964, as part of the state's research plan, grants have been awarded to study problems of collective versus family-based care, ideally focusing on two main questions:
>
> 1) Basic research concerning the ontogenesis of psychological functions and immunity against illnesses: The goal of this research should be to uncover optimal circumstances for preventive and educational care for children 1–3 years of age, and to provide suggestions for how to evaluate this kind of care, both from a medical and educational point of view.
>
> 2) Research into the current problems connected with collective institutions for 1–3 year olds, concerning both medical and educational care: Studies should be initiated that look at nutrition; how to improve immunity; strengthening of physical competencies; guidelines for the enrichment of speech development, emotional development, and social interactions; the appropriate proportion of family vs. collective childrearing; and the conditions under which institutional care becomes unavoidably necessary. (H. Papoušek, 1963, p. 1117; translation by Katarína Guttmannová)

To write so openly about the ideological dimensions of the Czech government's day-care policies was a bold and courageous act. In so doing, Papoušek was dealing with a sensitive situation in much the same way as he had done once before. In 1953, the problem had been the push by pro-Soviet hard-liners to adopt Pavlovian theory as the model for all Czech science. In that case, Papoušek dealt with the problem as constructively as possible by writing that, from a physiological and medical standpoint, Pavlov's findings and methods were of interest for their applicability primarily with regard to problems of disease. From a scientific viewpoint, however, much more work needed to be done. In 1963, in addressing the thorny issue of day care, he sought to be as constructive as possible by maintaining that although both collective day care and family-based child care could have advantages and disadvantages, mothers and families needed to be much more involved in day care than policies allowed.

THE 1966 INTERNATIONAL CONFERENCE
ON SOCIALIST DAY CARE

As the movement for greater liberalization grew, the barriers to international cultural, educational, and scientific contacts between Czechoslovakia and foreign countries began to diminish, and the number of foreign visitors invited to attend cultural and scientific conferences grew dramatically. Beginning in 1961, numerous international congresses in the fields of medicine and the natural sciences were held in Prague. Perhaps the most famous international meeting in the cultural field was held in 1963, when Edvard Goldstücker, a recently freed political prisoner, organized a conference on Franz Kafka. (Although acclaimed throughout the world, Kafka had been on the Czech government's list as a "decadent, bourgeois writer.") Travel by foreigners to Czechoslovakia rose impressively between 1961 and 1966, as did Czech travel abroad, and peaked in 1968.

In the field of early child care, Papoušek also became very active in attending and organizing international conferences in Prague. In 1965, he was instrumental in helping to organize a Czech–Swedish binational conference at which he served as governmental delegate. Perhaps even more important was the major international day-care conference referred to earlier, involving all socialist countries in October 1966, for which he served as the key planner and organizer. Cosponsored by the Ministry of Health, the Institute for the Care of Mother and Child, and Charles University, this conference proved to be crucial in finally persuading the Czech Communist Party to adopt an official change in their day-care policies. As it turned out, however, it was up to the Hungarians to pave the way.

In planning the conference, Papoušek gave considerable thought to how the agenda should be organized, deciding that all presentations would address both the pros and cons of three different options: group day care; home-based care with maternal leave; and family centers such as in Sweden (Klímová, 1966). But Papoušek also decided to keep one element in the program a secret. He later said:

> Okay, so the government gave me full support for everything I needed for the conference. But what I didn't tell them was that at one point in the program there would be an analysis of each alternative by economic specialists from the Czech Planning Committee, in other words the top people responsible

for making the government's decisions. If they said, "This alternative is economically all right," then the government in fact would say it was fine. But if they said, "This is economically not all right," then the government wouldn't take it very seriously at all. (Papoušek Interview, July 17, 1998)

According to newspaper accounts, the entire conference was remarkably "open and scientifically objective" (Klímová, 1966, p. 7), but suddenly there was a moment that took many by surprise. According to Papoušek, it came during discussions of the economic implications of the second alternative, family-based care with payment for mothers who stay at home. Was it possible that it would not cost the government any more money if the mother could decide for herself whether or not to send the child to day care? At first the analysis seemed implausible. After all, the expenses for keeping the center open would still be there, and child-care workers were all paid by the state. To build more day-care centers would require a tremendous financial investment by the government. But with the mother having the option of staying at home (even with a government stipend), the result could be reduced costs in terms of new facilities and day-care staff. In fact, as the Czech economists assured the conference participants, under the stay-at-home option, it would be possible to argue that the government would be better off financially. In any event, it would not be possible to say it would cost the government more.

The Hungarians and the Poles were among the delegates who responded most positively to this reasoning, in addition to the Czechs. The Soviets were taken by surprise because, although they had previously considered the stay-at-home option as a possible alternative, they had not gone to the trouble of calculating its advantages in economic terms. By the end of the conference, however, several of the Soviet delegates appeared at least interested in knowing more; they approached Papoušek saying, "We need that information. It could be of great interest to us" (Papoušek Interview, July 17, 1998). The response on the part of the East German delegate, on the other hand, was immediately hostile. As Papoušek recalled vividly 30 years afterward, a woman by the name of Frau Schmidt-Kolmar was outraged:

She got all red in the face and almost went through the ceiling. "You want to push women back into the kitchen," she yelled. "That's not acceptable. It's ideological nonsense and dangerous. And I'm not surprised, because we're in Prague and we know all about the funny ideas going around here." . . . And so we all just stood around and looked at each other thinking, "Aha, so that's what we have here!" (Papoušek Interview, July 17, 1998)

The East German reaction was distinctly negative, but Papoušek was surprised to learn that the Czech government was unwilling to take any action, despite the calculations of the Czech economists and the interest of many in the Ministry of Health in the stay-at-home alternative. The primary reason for their reluctance seemed to be the East German delegate's reaction. "The Czechs were really scared," as Papoušek later reported. Frau Schmidt-Kolmar was not only in charge of the East German government's day-care policies, but her husband was a member of the East German Party's Central Committee! As a result, Papoušek was disappointed not only in his own government's response, but concerned about himself as well. "I was really worried about what would happen to me. . . . But at least there were no *immediate* signs that they would arrest me or fire me from the Institute" (Papoušek Interview, July 17, 1998).

As fate would have it, the delegate from Hungary, Emmi Pickler, was an influential woman who played a key role in that country's Ministry of Health. Pickler was a trained psychologist, responsible for the entire government's day-care policies, and in good standing with the Party. As Papoušek remembered:

> Emmi came to me and asked whether I could give her copies of the alternatives. So I secretly gave her all the economic calculations and she returned to Hungary with them. And that's how it happened that while Czechoslovakia was afraid of introducing any kind of reforms whatsoever, Hungary introduced them only three months later, in January, 1967. . . . You would have to know Emmi to understand how she made it all happen. . . . She was another Yvonne Brackbill! . . . She died later, and her daughter became responsible for Hungary's day care affairs. . . . And after Hungary introduced the reforms, the Czech government said, "Well, Jesus Christ, maybe we shouldn't have been so scared." And two years later, in 1968, they introduced the same reforms as the Hungarian government. They took the money saved from introducing stay-at-home care and invested it in the improvement of the already-existing day care facilities. And they introduced home care and all kinds of other things for the young children. It was much better to build new centers at the preceding levels than having more and more sick kids. (Papoušek Interview, July 17, 1998)

And thus it came that, in 1968, as Czechoslovakia's political liberalization reached full force, the Czech government also abandoned its long-standing policies of collective education and allowed mothers the option, with pay, of caring for infants and young children at home. Even after the Soviet crackdown in August 1968, this new, more flexible policy was not changed, and it remained in place for the duration of the Communist era.

In the late 1990s, Zdenek Matějček, Helena Klímová, and Hanuš Papoušek each looked back and reflected on the pre-1968 day-care debate. Were ČSSR politicians and policymakers responsive to suggestions for social policy changes if the recommendations were based on solid psychological research? "Yes," Matějček replied, but only after a long pause. "In this respect only, though. I can't say it was so in other policy areas. But in this particular case it was truly research driven, and that was because Hanuš was part of it" (Matějček Interview, October 6, 1999). Even after the Soviet crackdown in 1968, were recriminations taken against Matějček for what Langmeier, he and others had said or done? "As for myself, I wasn't a 'Party man' or so," he recalled. "But no, I was always allowed to go abroad if the foreigners would pay. And I was allowed to continue my work" (Matějček Interview, October 6, 1998).

Helena Klímová, on the other hand, had a different response. Following publication of her articles about the 1966 conference, she was fired from her job. After struggling for a time, she decided to change careers and eventually became a psychotherapist. Looking back, she said, "You know, I would say that what we launched was a human rights campaign. Today I would call it a 'human rights for infants' campaign. It started in 1963 and was the first beginning of any kind of human rights movement in this country. . . . It's just that at the time it was not called the rights of infants and children. Or human rights of any sort! It was simply called, let's say, 'the needs' of infants. It was disguised in psychological language. . . . I would say it was the first attempt to defend any kind of human rights, anybody's human rights" (Klímová Interview, April 26, 2000).

As for Hanuš Papoušek, he remained worried about himself and the safety of his family for the rest of his years in Czechoslovakia. Although allowed to continue traveling abroad, he eventually left Czechoslovakia on a permanent basis in 1970 (see chap. 6). Why was the Czech government so worried after the 1966 conference? Was it because the East German woman had spoken out so strongly, or was something else going on?

You know, there was a time when East Germany played an important role in the Eastern bloc. As a matter of fact, it was well known that Brezhnev responded mainly to pressure from the East German government when he decided to occupy Czechoslovakia in 1968. . . . I would never have thought about such things again. That whole day care business was a kind of adventure which did not belong to my scientific activities. It was just something I did on the side, you know, with the left hand over there, in addition to my research. (Papoušek Interview, July 17, 1998)

But surely there was something, despite his dedication to science, about the continuing theme of science and politics in his life? "Yes, that's for sure," came Papoušek's reply. "And actually, politics is an explanation for many of my later decisions in life" (Papoušek Interview, July 17, 1998).

Whether the advocates for day-care reform used some of Hanuš' scientific ideas without his consent remains unclear, but his involvement in the public debates left an indelible impression on him. Ever the optimist, he believed that as long as politicians and policymakers maintain an open mind and do not become fearful, scientific knowledge can prevail over ideological and political argumentation. A more democratic attitude toward science, he believed, would result in more humane and egalitarian policies and an improvement in the conditions of human life. Despite fears for his own well-being and that of his family, this was a hope that remained with him the rest of his life.

Chapter 4

Early Recognition Abroad

By 1960, Hanuš Papoušek had established himself as one of the major scientists at the Institute for the Care of Mother and Child and his reputation within Czechoslovakia was growing. Brief trips had taken him to visit research institutes and day-care centers in the Soviet Union, Great Britain, and Scandinavia, but his contacts with Western researchers were still almost nonexistent. Outside Czechoslovakia his name and work remained virtually unknown. Beginning in 1961, however, this changed rapidly. Scientists from Western Europe and the United States began visiting his laboratory in Prague and extending invitations to attend important international scientific conferences and meetings, putting him in contact with influential networks of scholars and researchers in the Federal Republic of Germany, France, Switzerland, England, and especially the United States. Despite ongoing ideological tensions and political differences, American and Western European countries began showing greater interest in scientific exchange and dialogue with researchers from Eastern European countries and the Soviet Union. Significantly, at about this same time, Czech authorities also began demonstrating a much more open and tolerant attitude toward allowing Czech scientists, intellectuals, and cultural figures to make visits and to establish exchange contacts with professionals in Western Europe and the United States. Clearly, important shifts on both sides were underway.

By all accounts, the first American to visit the Institute for the Care of Mother and Child was Frank Palmer, who made his initial trip to Prague in summer 1961. Palmer, with a doctorate in psychology, worked as a staff member for the Social Science Research Council (SSRC) in New York, and returned for a second visit in summer 1962. On his second visit, Palmer was accompanied by William Kessen, professor of psychology at Yale University, and recently appointed chairperson of SSRC's Committee on Intellective Processes Research. These early visits proved to be an important turning point in Papoušek's life, resulting in the first invitations to attend a number of scientific meetings in Western Europe and the United States.

What was it that prompted Palmer's visits to the Institute for the Care of Mother and Child in the first place? From the Czech perspective, why would someone representing a research organization from a capitalist superpower suddenly be interested in finding out more about the infancy research being conducted in a small, Eastern European, socialist country? More specifically, why would this person want to talk with a pediatrician/researcher such as Hanuš Papoušek? When asked why their first meeting had taken place, Papoušek later said:

> You know, I think it was almost sheer luck. One day when I was working in my lab there was this American guy who was on his way back from Moscow. And his experience in Moscow was that they introduced him to the directors of the institutes, but he never saw a laboratory and never was allowed to talk with the younger researchers. Then he came to Prague and with just one call to the Ministry of Health he was on his way to the Institute, the laboratory was open to him, and I took the day off to tell him about our research and show him our equipment. He explained to me how important it was for him and his friends to have direct contact with researchers and have open discussions about research problems. . . . At first no one was with him, but his best friend was Bill Kessen, and he was looking for contacts for Kessen. And then a year later, in 1962, he came back with Kessen. (Papoušek Interview, October 15, 1999)

But was it really that simple? Were factors other than "sheer luck" at work? Were Palmer's interests purely of a research nature or did he have political or ideological motivations as well? On another occasion when he was asked about Palmer's initial visit, Papoušek gave a somewhat different answer: "You know, there were always people who knew more than I did. When this first visitor came from the United States, I was very naïve." Then, in the quiet voice and gentle humor that accompanied him all of his life, he observed:

> It turned out he was an employee of the CIA. Because after he left, I was called to the Police to report how I ever got the idea of having contact with him. And I told them, "Well, the Ministry of Health sent him to me and asked me to do them a favor and [host] an American delegation. Don't blame *me* for contacting him. Go to the Ministry of Health and ask them. How should I know if someone is CIA or not?" You know, if a scientist came, I couldn't simply ask, "Excuse me, are you in the CIA?" (*Laughter*). But you know, when the Police said that, I was not surprised. (Papoušek Interview, October 19, 1999)

Was Palmer really an agent of the American government's Central Intelligence Agency? If so, from the point of view of the history of developmental psychology and infant studies, would this have been particularly important? Papoušek realized, and as some of his closest friends agreed, he was sometimes able to engage in a certain degree of paranoia or what today might be called "conspiracy theory." Despite his lifelong insistence on scientific rigor in the realm of infancy research, the realm of politics could be quite a different story. Was this also the case with regard to his first meeting with Palmer? More on this topic later. For present purposes, suffice it to say that from the very beginning, Papoušek felt kindly disposed toward Palmer, and the two remained good friends until Palmer's death in the late 1970s. Apart from Papoušek's individual recollections, the general "Zeitgeist" of the Cold War and other background information concerning Palmer's visit must also be considered.

As far as Czechoslovakia was concerned, the beginning of the 1960s marked a fundamental shift in attitudes and policies toward the Soviet-modeled policies and programs of the Communist government, even though the Prague Spring did not occur until 1968. Beginning with the first signs of economic decline in the late 1950s, significant numbers of Czech scientists, intellectuals, artists, and musicians became increasingly critical of their own government's hard-line policies, basing their dissatisfaction largely on the fact that the promised economic, social, and political reforms were not producing the results for which so much of the population had hoped. As a result, many members of Hanuš Papoušek's postwar generation became interested in alternative models and policies. Like their forefathers, they looked with more open minds to social, political, and cultural developments in France, Germany, England, and for the first time also the United States. Moreover, despite the Novotny government's strong ties to the foreign and military policies of the Soviet Union, increasing numbers of government administrators began to display a much more tolerant attitude toward Czechs seeking permission to familiarize themselves with and travel to the West. As historians of post–World War II Czechoslovakia have pointed out, a trend toward increasing contacts with Western Europe and the United States began in 1960–1961, culminating 7 years later in the Prague Spring of 1968 (Korbel, 1977).

A review of annual reports published by Institute for the Care of Mother and Child from the early 1950s through the 1970s reveals that this general trend is also reflected in the scholarly activities of the Institute. Throughout the 1950s, these reports showed that Institute members had virtually no contacts with researchers from other countries, with the exception of occasional visits to the Soviet Union, German Democratic Republic, or other Eastern bloc countries. Moreover, all Institute reports from this era were published in Czech only. Beginning in 1962, however, a number of significant changes took place. First, the authors of the Institute's annual activities report, comprised of its director and five of its most senior scientists, suddenly took note of the fact that "a great number of scientific workers from abroad, from Belgium, Brazil, Bulgaria, Columbia, Cuba, Denmark, Finland, France, GDR, FRG, Great Britain, Holland, Hungary, Indonesia, Japan, Poland, Senegal, Sweden, USA and USSR, came for long or short stays to the Institute for studying visits" (Institute for Care of Mother and Child, 1967, p. 5). Moreover, also starting in 1962, the report's authors noted that fully 40% of the Institute's scientific papers now were being published in foreign journals, and that institution-to-institution ties had been established with international organizations such as the World Health Organization, the International Biological Union in London, the International Planned Parenthood Association in Copenhagen, and the Population Council in New York. Third, and perhaps most importantly, for the first time in its history the Institute suddenly started publishing its reports not only in Czech, but also in English. Clearly, a conscious effort toward pursuing a less Soviet-bound and more open attitude toward Western contacts was underway. Sadly, however, publication of the Institute's annual activities report was discontinued after 1968.

On the American side, early Western contacts with Hanuš Papoušek and the Institute for the Care of Mother and Child must be seen in the sociopolitical context of the Soviet–American rivalry during the late 1950s and the immediate impact of the Sputnik era. Shocked by this first Soviet space launch, the Eisenhower administration had responded to widespread fears in the United States about reports of Soviet scientific and technological superiority. Among other things, this event led to the appropriation of unprecedented amounts of federal money in the United States for improved scientific education and research, including the field of psychology, as demonstrated by the work of key scientific organizations such as the American Psychological Association and the Social Science Research Council. In both organizations, much greater emphasis suddenly began to be placed on reexamining the dominant trends in their own academic fields, and on seeking opportunities to gain a better understanding of scientific trends from colleagues and counterparts in Europe and the Soviet Union. It is in this context that one must view such actions as the May 1960 decision by the American Psychological Association to send a first-ever delegation of senior American psychologists on a study trip to the Soviet Union. More relevant to the life and ideas of Hanuš Papoušek was the decision by SSRC to send Frank Palmer to the Institute for the Care of Mother and Child. (Unbeknownst to the senior scientists involved, the APA board of directors had accepted a $15,000 grant to support this effort from an organization calling itself the "Society for the Investigation of Human Ecology." Only later, in 1977, was it discovered that the Central Intelligence Agency had secretly funded the grant, hoping to learn more about Soviet behavioral research; Street, 1994, p. 258.)

In June 1959, leaders at SSRC decided to undertake a significant effort in the areas of infant learning and early childhood development. After a number of exploratory conferences and meetings, its board of directors formed a new committee called the Committee on Intellective Processes Research. Shortly thereafter, the board created a second committee, the Committee on Comparative and Developmental Behavior, whose task was the exploration of new directions in early human and nonhuman developmental research. Through these two committees, which complemented the work of existing committees on simulation of cognitive processes, SSRC became one of the major players in furthering scholarly explorations into the earliest cognitive processes in human development, and in the "cognitive revolution" in U.S. psychology generally.

The persons initially appointed to the Committee on Intellective Processes Research were leading figures in early child development and developmental psychology at the time: Roger Brown of the Massachusetts Institute of Technology; Jerome Kagan of the Fels Institute; William Kessen of Yale University; Paul Mussen of the University of California–Berkeley; Harold Stevenson of the University of Minnesota; and Lloyd Morrisett, Jr., of the Social Science Research Council. A. Kimble Romney of Stanford University was appointed to the group one year later. The members comprising the second group, the Committee on Comparative and Developmental Behavior, were equally renowned scholars: Harry Harlow of the University of Wisconsin; Eckhard Hess of the University of Chicago; Harriet Rheingold of the University of North Carolina; Robert Sears of Yale University; and again Harold Stevenson of the University of Minnesota. Generously funded by grants from the Carnegie Foundation of New York, General Electric Foundation, and National Science Foundation, these committees organized a 4-year sequence of conferences and seminars that began in fall 1959 and culminated in 1964 with a training and research institute for 30 to 40 highly qualified graduate students from across the country (Social Science Research Council, SSRC, Archives, Box 168, Folders 168, 962, 963, Rockefeller Foundation Archives, Pocantico Hills, NY). In all, Papoušek received invitations and funding to participate in four of these conferences, providing some of the most formative experiences of his early intellectual and professional life. Indeed, from this time onward much of his biography was related to one or another of the people he encountered at these events. Many came to visit him in his laboratory at the Institute for the Care of Mother and Child and remained important friends long after his defection to the West.

As documented in SSRC reports from May and September 1959, the Committee on Intellective Processes took as its starting point the observation that many Americans had become troubled by the inadequate teaching of reading, arithmetic, and elementary science in their schools. Whether or not it was an observation directly attributable to post-Sputnik fears is difficult to say, but it was a concern widely shared among the American public. The Committee accordingly defined its purpose to be the promotion of research and understanding concerning processes of intellective development in the first years of life. Stating that the word "cognition" had come back into American psychology as a name for the rather complex information processing that took place between stimulus and response, its members felt that the somewhat archaic expression "intellective processes" would be an appropriate term for describing the focus of its work. The reference to intelligence was chosen as a reminder of the notion that information processing is a skill that can be well or poorly developed. The Committee went on to assert that the development of intellective processes, as a research topic, had long been subordinated in American child psychology to the study of evaluative and motivational processes, and the expression "socialization" of the child seemed for many to make exclusive reference to the process of value internalization. The later writings of Jean Piaget, it continued, were still relatively unknown in the United States, but they provided important examples for the study of intellective development with respect to topics such as number, logic, and geometry. In addition to Piaget's work, the field of linguistics was singled out for its potential to articulate basic descriptions of a set of norms clearly intellective in nature but also involved in socialization. Few Americans as of yet were familiar with Piaget, linguistics, information theory, or computer simulation, the Committee concluded. Clearly, much more needed to be done (SSRC Archives, Box 168). In other reports, the Committee noted that

> interest in the development of intellective processes is common to several areas of social science and that research and well-founded theory on this subject would provide both a foundation for educational practice and have important implications for the psychology of personality and learning. In recent years there had been little research on this subject in the United States. Child psychology was focused on physical growth and on social and emotional development. Intelligence testing had its justification in prediction and selection more than in contribution to theory. Studies of higher mental processes principally explored the intellect of the convenient college sophomore. Piaget had written extensively on various phases of cognitive development, but primarily from the naturalistic point of view. While Piaget's writings had been favorably received, American psychologists had done little to develop and extend Piaget's ideas, to relate his work to their own, or to form alternative conceptions. The high level of activity in several areas of psychology, together with new ideas coming from studies of the thought process in adults, made it appear that the time had come to bring together persons interested

in the development of intellective processes. (SSRC Archives, Box 168, Folder 962, Rockefeller Foundation, Pocantico Hills, NY)

The Committee's activities consisted of conferences on various aspects of children's thinking, and the subsequent publication of conference results. Conferences typically included not more than 25 participants and emphasized extensive discussion and creation of personal ties, with the resulting publications disseminated in the United States and abroad.

The first SSRC meeting attended by Hanuš Papoušek was organized in summer 1962 in Oslo, Norway. It was planned as a sequel to a prior conference that William Kessen had organized in Dedham, Massachusetts, in spring 1960, the purpose of which had been to give Americans a better understanding of the developmental theories of Jean Piaget and his colleagues in Geneva. How did Piaget's theories about the development of intelligence, cognition, and behavior, as well as his method of inquiry, differ from those of American psychology, in particular the latest work on computer simulation of human thinking conducted by Herbert Simon? Was there anything to be learned from Piaget? Among the presenters at the Dedham conference were: Bärbel Inhelder, Piaget's main coworker; William Kessen of Yale University; Harold Stevenson; Daniel Berlyne, the University of Toronto; and Herbert Simon, a future Nobel Prize winner from the Carnegie Institute of Technology. Shortly after the Dedham conference, the Committee decided it would be useful to find out more about European child development research beyond that of Piaget and his colleagues. For this purpose, several Committee members, while traveling in Europe in summer 1961, made contacts with and invited 10 to 15 leading Western European researchers to the Norway conference. Frank Palmer, the Committee's staff member, was assigned to visit the Soviet Union and Eastern Europe, including the Institute for the Care of Mother and Child where he and Hanuš Papoušek first became acquainted.

The Oslo conference was held in Voksenasen, a student hotel outside the city, from June 26 to August 1, 1962. In addition to Papoušek, the Europeans invited were Bärbel Inhelder (Switzerland); Heinz Prechtl (Netherlands); A. R. Jonckheere, Eric Lunzer, Neil O'Connor, and M. D. Vernon (all from England); Kjell Rooheim (Norway); Per Saugstad (nationality not indicated); Smesland (first name and nationality not indicated); A. V. Zaporozhetz (Russia); and Zofia Babska and Alina Szminska (Poland). From the SSRC committee, Paul Mussen was selected as program chair for the conference, and additional American participants included Jerome Kagan, William Kessen, and Frank Palmer. (This list was derived from notes and committee meeting minutes in the SSRC Archives.)

For the first 3 days, the Europeans presented their research results and theoretical ideas in 2-hour sessions. The fourth and fifth days were spent on a trip to Bergen and Stavanger, with no scheduled presentations but the informal professional discussions and reports by American committee members about their own research. Copies of the key presentations and a summary of the discussions were published in a Society for Research in Child Development *Monograph* titled *European Research in Cognitive Development*, edited by Mussen (1965). Papoušek presented a paper reviewing some of the different kinds of data and physical functions that were being measured at the Institute for the Care of Mother and Child and discussed the early experimental studies in which infants demonstrated the ability to learn at a much earlier age than had previously been thought. His presentation attracted major attention.

Returning to the United States after the Oslo conference, Kessen submitted a report to the other members of the Committee stating that Palmer and he had visited the Institute for the Care of Mother and Child in Prague:

> It was a productive visit in its own right, but I call attention to it here as a model for what can be done after a conference. The notion of concentrated study in a single laboratory is, in my opinion, a sound one. The two-hour visit accomplished some purposes, but for the knowledge we need of techniques and preconceptions in foreign laboratories and clinics, only the extended visit will do. I recommend that the Council consider the possibility of supporting graduate students and postdoctoral psychologists in travel of this kind to foreign countries, particularly in Eastern Europe. (SSRC Archives, Box 168, Folder 962, Rockefeller Foundation Archives, Pocantico Hills, NY)

Kessen clearly was impressed with what he saw in Prague, but he was less impressed with the methodological rigor of other European researchers. The following were among his general points:

1. A gulf exists between European and American styles of research. The Norwegians, for instance, are more operational and anti-"metaphysical" than the Americans. Many other Europeans do not have the commitment to experimentation and careful design that American psychologists make their ideal. The Americans are seen by the Europeans as doing brilliant research on trivial problems and the Europeans are seen by the Americans as doing sloppy research on interesting ones.

2. Despite the genuine amity among conference participants, there still is a great deal of distrust of the Americans by the East Europeans. They tend to see us as Greeks with gifts. They have no conception of the independence of the Council and its work from the federal government, and all our attempts to explain this seemed unsuccessful. It will be a long time before the suspicions and reservations of the Easterners are greatly reduced.

3. There is a striking diversity of aims, techniques, and attitudes among research workers in the field of children's thinking. There is no single theory, no standard method, no canonical list of problems. For this reason increased communication channels and support for research are valuable. (SSRC Archives, Box 169, Folder 962, Rockefeller Foundation Archives, Pocantico Hills, NY)

Despite his misgivings about European research, Kessen nevertheless recommended that SSRC help establish a separate European committee to carry on with further work, or to enlarge the existing New York-based committee to include Europeans. In fact, one of the decisions reached by the Oslo attendees had been to create an independent European Committee on Behavioural Science Research in Early Development, with three persons chosen as members: Bärbel Inhelder, Hanuš Papoušek, and Heinz Prechtl, with Prechtl as chairperson. Selection to this committee proved to be the first of many times that Papoušek either volunteered, or was chosen for a leadership position in an international research organization.

After Kessen's report was submitted, the Committee again sent Frank Palmer to Europe, where he convened a meeting with Inhelder, Papoušek, and Prechtl in Geneva in February 1963. The purpose of the meeting was to establish better communications among the participants at the Oslo conference and to begin circulating research articles and papers for comments and scientific feedback. Prechtl described the intellectual concerns of this new, independent European committee as covering the "behavior of the newborn, conditioning in early infancy, motor development, language development, cognitive and thought processes, etc." (SSRC Archives, Box 346, Folder 2046, Rockefeller Foundation Archives, Pocantico Hills, NY).

Palmer was optimistic that the Social Science Research Council would be able to provide limited funds to help the Europeans in their efforts to form an offshoot of one of the Council's standing committees. After returning to New York from Geneva, however, he was unsuccessful at finding additional money and the European group did not meet a second time. Nevertheless, several of the Europeans (eventually joined by a number of Americans) began circulating unpublished research papers to its members and referred to their informal scholarly circle by names such as the "International Club on Infancy Correspondence" or "CRI" (Conference for Research on Infancy; Clifton Interview, March 23, 2000; titles vary according to the source). According to archival SSRC documents, the group also had much more far-reaching plans, all oriented toward the goal of stimulating further research on infancy, such as "to organize small study groups . . . ; to assist in organizing training courses for younger scholars to acquaint them with new methods; to explore the possibility of establishing a current research information exchange and to maintain communication with SSRC . . . ; to facilitate visits by investigators to research centers other than their own" (SSRC Archives, Box 346, Folder 2046, Rockefeller Foundation Archives, Pocantico Hills, NY). Little did this small group know that their informal "correspondence club" would rapidly attract additional members and begin organizing regular research conferences, often at the campus or home of one of its members. This small group eventually grew into the large professional organization now known as the International Society on Infant Studies (ISIS).

After the Oslo conference, Papoušek received his first invitation to visit the United States in June 1963. The invitation came from the Social Science Research Council, this time from the Committee on Comparative and Developmental Behavior. The major purpose of his trip was to attend a conference in Madison, Wisconsin, on the topic "Learned and Non-learned Behavior in Immature Organisms." A number of the conference participants, such as Lewis Lipsitt, Harriet Rheingold, and Harold Stevenson, became Hanuš' lifelong friends and respected professional colleagues.

In addition, Palmer took Papoušek on a whirlwind coast-to-coast tour that included giving lectures and research colloquia at six major universities and research institutes, all within a 3-week time period. The trip was organized by Palmer, who met Hanuš on his arrival in New York and personally accompanied him to every site. Driving by car the entire time, Palmer took Papoušek for presentations at New York University, the National Institute of Mental Health, Yale University, University of Wisconsin, UCLA, Stanford University, and University of California–Berkeley. (One might ask whether it was Palmer or Papoušek who drove. Hanuš' reputation as a driver was widely known among his friends, who found themselves wondering just how many speeding tickets he may have accumulated along the way! When it came to research, Papoušek was a model of caution and meticulous attention to detail; when it came to driving, however, he tended to throw caution to the wind.)

Papoušek's own recollections of this trip are very revealing. First and foremost, he was struck by the great interest people expressed in his work wherever he went:

> The interest for infancy research was something so new, that many psychologists just didn't know yet how you can do research with babies. They had no idea how to organize it—how to do it! They had only the first experience with neonatal research, using the first few days with mothers staying in the hospital, and doing research with newborn babies. So the interest was tremendous, all major universities wanted me to come and report what we were doing in Prague. Of course, there were reports by Bill Kessen on what he had seen at the Institute in Prague, and by Frank Palmer from SSRC, so there was a kind of prior knowledge before I even realized there was something like that. But the interest was tremendous and sort of compelled me to go from East Coast to West Coast and you know, stop at different places and give papers. . . .

As for Palmer, Papoušek said:

Whenever I came to the States, this guy (Palmer) was responsible for my behavior. That means he had to supervise everything. So it was not surprising
that he drove me all the way across the country. . . . He arranged all the visits,
all the lectures, and we became very good friends (laughter), although I knew
who he was. Frank was very open, and he appreciated so much open information on the Soviet system. I don't know if he profited from it professionally—I
didn't care. But he was explaining so much to me. And that was so vital to me
for the further visits, that I simply paid him back with information from my
side. And because I had been to the Soviet Union, he was very much interested. And so you know, we kept exchanging information, teasing each other.
I called him a Capitalist, "a bloody Capitalist," and he called me a "bloody
Communist." There were certain points in our discussions when I just could-
n't buy everything from him, you know, which was common for me in the
United States, and vice versa as well, of course. (Laughter). . . . It was very difficult for him to understand how we Czechs, sort of quietly and without much
resistance, could have accepted the change to Communism in 1948. So I said
to him, "what do you think about what the Americans did at the Crimean
Conference at Yalta? They decided we should belong to the East, then signaled us that we shouldn't expect any help! And then the Russians came and
. . . they knew how to win the elections. And once the Russians were there,
there was no way back. So you can either protest and end up in prison, or have
ugly remarks in your files about your behavior around that time. And that's
about the only thing we could have achieved. . . . So one decides, okay, there
is no way to help us from the American side; we have to help ourselves. And so
we tried to find our way. . . ." My talking with Frank about this facilitated everything, because Frank knew enough about this. (Papoušek Interview, October 19, 1999)

Did Hanuš Papoušek have a paranoid streak in him? Was Frank Palmer a
CIA agent? Perhaps in the final analysis, these are not the important questions. Their friendship was an important episode in Papoušek's life, Palmer
helped him enormously during his early visits to the United States, and the
two remained good friends until Palmer's death in the late 1970s. (At least
one other person told the authors in an interview that after his retirement,
Palmer acknowledged that he had worked for the U.S. intelligence services,
although it was not entirely clear whether it was before, during, or after his
time with SSRC.)

Hanuš Papoušek made his second trip to the United States in June 1965,
again at the invitation of the SSRC. By this time, however, Frank Palmer had
left the SSRC and taken a faculty position at City University of New York, so
the person serving as Hanuš' host was William Kessen. Like Palmer, Kessen
drove him from one location to the next, although there is no information
indicating that Kessen was employed by the CIA. This time, Hanuš' itiner-

ary consisted of research presentations at the University of Minnesota and participation in an SSRC conference on "Early Behavior: Comparative and Developmental Approaches" in Stillwater, Minnesota.

Hanuš had to arrive late at the conference because of difficulties getting a visa. This time, however, the problem came from the American officials. Stillwater, Minnesota, was near the site of American military rocket silos, and therefore a restricted, "top secret" area. Apparently, Harold Stevenson in his role as convener of the conference had been questioned extensively about Papoušek and the reason for his visit; the only solution was for Stevenson to promise to carefully monitor Papoušek's location at all times during his stay in Minnesota, and to ensure that the guest from Czechoslovakia left immediately after the meetings were over (Papoušek Interview, July 16, 1998). When Papoušek did finally make his appearance, Stevenson interrupted the proceedings to welcome him and to explain the irony of the situation to the other participants: "Gentlemen, we finally have Hanuš here, and I have to explain what has happened because you are probably not aware of the difficulties he has faced to get here. Stillwater, MN is a prohibited zone for citizens of the Socialist world. So those of you who think that there are only prohibited zones in the Soviet Union where *Americans* are not allowed to travel, might be interested to know that there are also similar restrictions right here in our own country" (Papoušek Interview, July 16, 1998). Papoušek later commented that he had been greatly impressed by Stevenson's handling of this situation, and that of course he himself would never have dared to make such an announcement back in his own country!

Hanuš returned soon after for another lecture at the University of Wisconsin, and to give colloquia at Brown and Syracuse Universities. In addition, between these trips to the United States, Papoušek participated in two other international meetings cosponsored by the SSRC; both included biologists, psychologists, and ethologists, and were held at Burg Wartenstein, Austria, in conjunction with the Wenner Gren Foundation. One was a symposium on behavioral consequences of genetic differences in man, held September 17–25, 1964. The other, which took place July 19–25, 1966, was devoted to interrelationships between biological and cultural adaptation.

PAPOUŠEK'S FIRST EXTENDED STAY IN THE UNITED STATES: DENVER, COLORADO

Papoušek took a third, much longer trip to the United States, lasting from Christmas 1965 to summer 1966. During this time, he served as a visiting faculty member at the University of Denver. Although he again took the occasion to lecture at numerous universities and research institutes, he was able to spend most of his time in one place and devote much more effort to familiarizing himself with various American schools of psychological, biological, and developmental thought. Most importantly, he had access to a research lab where he was able to construct his own equipment and conduct his own research. It was during this time, with the help of American graduate student Paula Bernstein, that he conducted experiments in which he further refined his conditioning methods for studying infant learning.

The person responsible for inviting Hanuš to the University of Denver was Yvonne Brackbill, chair of the department of psychology at the time. Brackbill herself was a pioneering figure in the infancy field, having been one of the first Americans to travel to the Soviet Union, and having compiled an extensive bibliography of Soviet research in the field. She and Hanuš had gotten to know each other when Brackbill made a stopover in Prague on one of her trips to the Soviet Union, at which time she had extended an invitation to him to spend an entire semester in Denver. A grant from the National Institute of Mental Health made it possible for Brackbill to invite a visiting scholar such as Papoušek, and to fully support his stay in Denver.

By all accounts, his time in Denver was very enjoyable and rewarding, for Hanuš as well as for the faculty and students at the University of Denver. Most everyone in psychology at the University of Denver was doing classical conditioning studies at the time, but every Tuesday, Brackbill organized poker parties for the researchers and students in her lab. According to Hiram Fitzgerald, one of Brackbill's graduate students, it was during the poker sessions that everyone in fact learned about infant development:

> It was a no-holds-barred opportunity to learn. . . . The poker parties were well attended and exciting, because we knew that Hanuš was working on adapting classical conditioning to operant conditioning, and he was building bridges between psychology and biology. . . . Yvonne was the one who taught us science and the ethics of doing science, but it was Daniel Freedman and Hanuš Papoušek who gave us theoretical grounding in the field. . . . It was Norman Mahr at the University of Colorado Medical School, also in Denver, who coined the term "developmental psychobiology." But it was from my readings and discussions with Hanuš that I learned about the linkages between biology and psychology. Even about the notion that there was such a thing as intuitive behaviors, and all the ways in which this was related to that in the human newborn. (Fitzgerald Interview, November 14, 2002)

While affiliated with the psychology department at the University of Denver, Papoušek also was given access to a research lab at the University of Colorado Medical School. There he was able to use infants 1 to 3 months old as subjects for continuing his head-turning experiments from Prague. He did not bring his original head-turning equipment, but he was allowed to build new equipment in Denver and, with the able assistance of Paula Bernstein, modified his classical conditioning methods. In Prague, he had found that newborn babies were able to learn, a finding that he and his colleagues interpreted as a human-specific capacity. However, it was not long after that he had become aware of research indicating that the same capacities could be demonstrated in newborn rats. Realizing that the capacity to learn may not be the distinguishing feature between humans and animals, Papoušek proceeded to ask himself whether or not there is something else other than the ability to learn so early that made the human species unique. Finding himself drawn to explorations of the specific capacities that made humans different, he revised the methods he had used previously for conditioning newborns: A visual reward was presented from the midline that the baby could activate by turning the head to the left. It was a simple turning-on movement that the infants needed to learn, and they mastered it readily. The subjects learned to turn first to the left and then immediately back to watch for the reward. Papoušek described what he and Bernstein found as follows:

When we had this methodological access, we were then able to go in the direction of cognitive processes. It was as if we were introducing small concepts. Changing the strategy. And we . . . simply changed the strategy and observed the consequences. And we saw that if the baby all of a sudden found out that his capacity didn't work any more, it might have been looking, perhaps even chaotically, and then he started experimenting from the very beginning, looking for what might be behind it. And then we introduced other strategies like, for instance, turning twice to the left, and then only every second time. And the astonishing thing was not only that 4-month old babies are doing it, but that they can do it rather quickly, usually within one session. But within one session out of two consequent movements, they put it together in one gesture which was like (demonstrates . . .) and then wait. So now it wasn't experimenting any more, but it was, so to say, knowing "I have to do it twice." And they adjusted the speed of the response in a way that violated all our expectations because a *double* response lasted less than half a second. Did you know that human adults need a *minimum* of half a second of cognitive "irritation" to become aware of the stimulation? And so again we were at a loss. What were we doing with the babies? They were showing us capacities that went seemingly beyond the capacities of conscious behavior. And yet in 4-month-olds, what kind of consciousness can one expect? They were able to discover rather complex rules: 3 times to one side, 4 times to one side. Two—once to the left, once to the right; twice to the left, twice to the right. We didn't really succeed in going that far, though. It was obviously already too difficult for them because it was asymmetrical—let's say twice to the left, three times to the right. But if one did not know the rules but could only observe the babies and try to find out the strategies based on objective information—this was something tremendously difficult for an adult to try to find out. And that's what it all meant. We would sit down together, observe the experiment, and ask each other to say when we thought to ourselves, "I know the rule." This was tremendously difficult. Well, we started this in Prague, and I elaborated the method with Paula Bernstein in Denver, where we tested it. . . . Then I returned to Prague and continued the studies, well, kind of played further with this. (Papoušek Interview, October 19, 1999)

As on his first two trips to the United States, Papoušek traveled extensively from Denver to give guest presentations at numerous other institutions and conferences, including the University of Colorado Medical School; the first Symposium of the International Correspondence on Infancy Research at Harvard University; the Child Study Center, University of Minnesota; New York University; National Institute of Mental Health; University of Kansas; UCLA; and Presbyterian College, St. Petersburg, Florida. Significantly, while visiting the National Institute of Mental Health, Papoušek also received an invitation to become a member of one of its advisory boards. This invitation also involved a small honorarium paid in U.S. dollars over the next few years. When he first arrived in Bethesda, Maryland, a member of the NIMH administrative staff realized that, officially, it would not be possible for Hanuš to be an advisory board member because he was a citizen of an Eastern European country. "But then the guy simply said, 'Oh well, okay, we'll let you serve anyway,' " Papoušek later remembered. "That was really funny, because I realized that the same sort of thing also happened in Czechoslovakia. Sometimes people just look the other way" (Papoušek Interview, October 19, 1999).

One unexpected acquaintance Hanuš made in Denver was with the psychoanalyst René Spitz. Having trained with Freud in Vienna, Spitz later emigrated to the United States and became best known for his empirical studies of psychological disorders in infants. René Spitz effectively used his observations to publicize the devastating effects of socioemotional deprivation in institutionalized infants. The term *hospitalism* is attributed to him, referring to the grieving process he documented in youngsters waiting to be adopted from foundling homes. Papoušek later stated that Spitz may have been one of the first to speculate about *intuitive* aspects of parenting, although he had done no systematic research in this area.

Although Papoušek and Spitz often disagreed in their interpretations of infant behavior, the two men shared a number of perspectives such as the value of filmed observations, and the importance of early parent–infant communication (see Emde, 1994, for further elaboration regarding Spitz's contributions to the field). Papoušek and Spitz (Hungarian by birth) also shared a Central European background and a love of the mountains of Slovakia where Spitz reportedly continued to go for "recuperation" (Papoušek Interview, July 16, 1998). Their intellectual disagreements were taken with good humor, perhaps reflecting their similar cultural backgrounds. In fact, Hanuš recalled Spitz as saying, "Remember, Papoušek is from Prague. And if a person from Prague walks across Wenceslas Square and a balcony falls on his head, he only gets flat feet because his head is so hard" (Papoušek Interview, July 16, 1998).

The experience in Denver was apparently Papoušek's first opportunity to discuss and be confronted by a psychoanalytic perspective regarding infancy, and the concepts he explored with Spitz were surely a challenge to his own training and viewpoints. Thus, Denver, already the "capital of psychoanalysis" in the United States (Papoušek Interview, July 16, 1998), provided Hanuš the venue for refining his Prague conditioning methods as well as for considering alternative interpretations and beginning to speculate about the role of parents in infant development. Ironically, the orphanage where Papoušek was able to observe infants during his stay was called the "Infants of Prague Nursery." Most of the systematic infancy research, however, took place in an empty grocery store across the street from the psychology department at the university, along with Hiram Fitzgerald, Paula Bernstein, and others.

One of the lasting friendships that developed during this early stay in Denver was with a young intern in a psychiatric clinic, Robert Emde. Paula Bernstein later was to become his research assistant, and Emde himself became intrigued by the work being done by both Brackbill and Spitz with young infants. After being introduced to Papoušek, Emde's fascination with the potential clinical applications of the exciting research being done in Prague and Denver only increased. Like Papoušek, however, his interests extended beyond the laboratory and the hospitals or orphanages, to the realm of public policies to support the optimal socioemotional development of infants and children. To this day, and after decades of funding by the National Institutes of Health, Emde is an internationally renowned advocate for this cause, and one of the founding fathers of the relatively new Early Head Start programs in the United States. Emde also continues to attribute some of this commitment to the influence of Hanuš Papoušek when the two of them began their friendship in Denver. In April 2000, Emde was invited to deliver the first Hanuš Papoušek Memorial Lecture in Vienna, Austria, at a conference of the German-speaking affiliates of the World Association of Infant Mental Health. Though saddened by the circumstances of Hanuš' rapidly declining health, Robert Emde also saw this as a unique opportunity to honor his friend and pay tribute to his many accomplishments that Emde so admired.

By the end of his stay in Denver, Papoušek was well acquainted with a number of different fields in American science, and personally familiar with many American and Western European researchers in the emerging infancy studies field. Moreover, he was impressed by the far greater opportunities and resources for conducting research that were available in the

United States in comparison to his native Czechoslovakia and other Eastern European countries. In terms of Papoušek's own research, his stay in the United States had allowed him to further develop his own unique approach to conditioning, to become familiar with cognitive research, to explore the role of unlearned or intuitive behaviors, and even to draw comparisons between human and nonhuman infants. He was now fully acquainted with state-of-the-art science in both East and West.

Chapter 5

From Prague to Harvard:
The Transition From East to West

For Hanuš Papoušek, the late 1960s and early 1970s were a time filled with high hopes, bitter disappointments, and great uncertainty. The political thaw that had begun in the early 1960s and culminated in what became known as the Prague Spring of 1968, raised widespread hopes that Alexander Dubcek's call for "socialism with a human face" would bring greater freedom and democracy to all Czechoslovakians. Papoušek and most of his generation were young enough to remember the years of the First Czech Republic and of the Edvard Beneš regime after World War II. Thus, the Soviet-led invasion in August 1968 was every bit as painful as the Nazi occupation in 1938 and the first Communist takeover in 1948.

For Papoušek personally, the decade of political thaw had allowed him to build a flourishing research career at the Institute for the Care of Mother and Child, develop increasing scientific contacts abroad, and to attend conferences and give lectures throughout Western Europe and the United States. At home, he was appointed to several important governmental scientific advisory boards and committees, was able to speak out in favor of reforming the Czech government's child-care system, and to become known for his humane, commonsense advice to parents via public radio broadcasts. In addition, as a leading member of the Czechoslovakian Academy of Sciences, he was becoming increasingly vocal in holding the Academy's Party leadership responsible for what he and others perceived as a serious deterioration in the country's scholarly and intellectual standards.

The political thaw that eventually became known as the "Prague Spring" can be said to have begun on January 5, 1968, when the Central Committee of the Czechoslovak Communist Party, bending to increasing economic and political dislocations across the country, voted formally to end the 14-year reign of Antonin Novotny as head of the Party. Novotny's ouster was greeted with widespread public acclaim, but also sent the fate of Czechoslovakia spinning out of control (see Littell's introduction to *The Czech Black Book*, 1969, for further elaboration). The man chosen to replace Novotny as First Secretary of the Party was a Communist from Slovakia named Alexander Dubcek, who by all appearances was not a reformer or a hard-liner bent on counterrevolution. Once in power, however, Dubcek responded to a popular outcry for more democracy and material comfort and proceeded to advocate a brand of Communism that was not only very humane and open, but also profoundly Czech in nature.

The press, finally free from censorship, poured forth a torrent of criticism. Government and Party decisions were opened to public scrutiny, and victims of the Stalinist purges of the 1950s were "rehabilitated." At the 20th anniversary of the coup that in 1948 had put the Communists in power, Dubcek, standing on a platform shared by none other than Soviet Party leader Leonid Brezhnev, declared that "everything must be really and thoroughly changed" (Littell, 1969, p. vi). The formal document announcing change, the Czech Party's Action Program of April 1968, spoke of embarking Czechoslovakia on a "unique experiment in democratic Communism. . . . The Communist Party does not fulfill its leading role by ruling over society but relies on the voluntary support of the people. . . . A clash of opinions is necessary in the search for the best solution" (Littell, 1969, pp. v–vi). The public debates that erupted throughout the country—in the media, within Party units, among intellectuals, teachers, students, and workers—proved intolerable for Brezhnev and the Soviet Party leaders in Moscow. Previous challenges—such as in Yugoslavia in 1948, the German Democratic Republic in 1953, or Hungary in 1956—had been rebellions against Stalinism and the excesses of tyrannical power. The Czech reformers, although Marxists, were posing the first serious challenge to the Leninist principle of centralized decision making, the monopoly status of the Communist Party, and the dogmatism with which political power was being exercised.

From Moscow's perspective, this was heresy. On August 17–18, 1968, the Soviet Politburo (reportedly by a vote of 7 to 4) voted for the use of force, with Alexsei Kosygin, Mikhail Suslov, Nicolai Podgorny, and Gennadi Voronov taking sides with Dubcek and the reformists (Littell, 1969). On Tuesday, August 20, at 10 p.m., soldiers from East Germany, Poland, Hungary, and Bulgaria crossed the Czech border from four different sides. Soviet storm troopers, arriving under the guise of darkness, stormed and occupied the airport, television and radio stations, and Czech Party headquarters in Prague. At 1 a.m., Wednesday, August 21, the Presidium of the Czech Communist Party, meeting in a special session under the chairmanship of Dubcek, issued the following proclamation:

The Presidium calls upon all citizens of the Republic of Czechoslovakia to keep the peace and not resist the advancing armies, because the defense of our state borders is now impossible. For this reason, our army, the Security Forces, and the People's Militia were not given the order to defend the country. The Presidium considers this action to be contrary to the fundamental principles of relations between socialist states and a denial of the basic norms of international law. (Littell, 1969, pp. 10–11)

At 7 a.m., the Presidium of the Czechoslovak Academy of Sciences convened in an extraordinary session and approved the following proclamation:

"The Czechoslovak Academy of Sciences stands unanimously behind the Dubcek leadership of the Party. . . . We condemn the occupation of Czechoslovakia by the armies of the Warsaw Pact. The occupation is an action contrary to alliance commitments and represents a flagrant transgression of the principles of international law and state sovereignty, which, in its consequences, damages the cause of socialism in the eyes of all the nations of the world. . . . The Presidium of the Czechoslovak Academy of Sciences has succeeded in establishing contact with a large portion of the members of the Academy and with a majority of Academy institutions. They all express their agreement with this declaration, as well as their support for further actions by the Academy Presidium. . . ."

The Academy Presidium has also sent the following telegram to the Embassy of the Soviet Union in Prague:

"Dear Comrades: Since we are unable to establish contact with Soviet scientists, we ask you to transmit to the leadership of the Academy of Sciences of the Soviet Union our protest against the forcible and illegal occupation of Czechoslovakia. . . ."

The Presidium of the Academy has also issued the following appeal, drafted in several languages, to all scientists of the world:

"At this time when our country is being illegally occupied by the occupation armies, we turn to you with an urgent appeal to help our just cause with all means at your disposal." (Littell, 1969, pp. 28–29)

At 7:45 a.m., hundreds of Prague citizens surrounded the Jan Hus monument in the Old Town Square, and a Czech flag was hoisted on top of the statue. An artist, Vlasta Chramostov, went up to a Soviet captain and asked him, "Why did you come? After all, you are our friends. Friends do not come visiting with arms. We want peace, freedom, sovereignty and friendship." From one side of the Square came the constant calls, "Dubcek, Dubcek, Dubcek." In another corner, citizens were singing the national anthem. The Soviet captain finally answered, "Everything will be all right." There were tears in many eyes. The Soviet soldiers and commanders, following orders from their political leaders, knew what the tears of the Czechs meant (Prace, 1968, as cited in Littell, 1969, p. 34).

On Wenceslas Square, smoke from burning houses was rising in the air, while the antenna from a Soviet tank hit the trolley wires, enough to provoke gunfire that for many years would mark the historical façade of the museum (*Rude Pravo,* August 22, 1968, as cited in Littell, 1969, pp. 49–50). In many ways reminiscent of the Nazi invasion in 1938, this latest failure by Czechoslovakia to achieve a more permanent form of democracy confronted Papoušek, like many of his countrymen, with a series of difficult questions. Had the Czech peoples' aspirations for greater freedom and "socialism with a human face" been misplaced? Was this latest reform effort in many ways not reminiscent of the ethical humanism of Thomas Masaryk, whose efforts to bring justice and democracy to Czechoslovakia had also succumbed to foreign attack? Moreover, for Papoušek personally, what would this new political crackdown mean for his commitment to pursue his scientific work and free exchange of scholarly ideas, unencumbered by ideological considerations or political constraints? In the face of political repression, what kinds of compromises, if any, would he be willing to make?

For a short time, many Czechs had the impression that conditions under the post-Dubcek regime had not really changed very much. By early 1970, however, internal political recriminations and further restrictions on foreign travel were being imposed, leading to Papoušek's decision to leave Czechoslovakia if at all possible, and to start a new, if uncertain, life in the West. As on previous occasions, however, he made the best of a difficult situation and, despite many frustrations, ultimately succeeded in his desire to continue making important scientific contributions, and in starting a new and rewarding personal life.

PERSONAL, POLITICAL, AND PROFESSIONAL DECISIONS CONVERGE

From June through August 1968, during the height of the Prague Spring, Papoušek was teaching at Harvard University in Cambridge, Massachusetts. Thinking that events at home were moving in the right political direction, he had decided to accept a summer teaching position from the department of psychology at Harvard University, realizing that he had greatly benefited from his 1966 stay at the University of Denver and that further time in the United States would give greater familiarity with American psychological and infancy research. At Harvard, he taught a course in developmental psychobiology, a relatively new subject, and accepted an appointment as honorary research associate from Jerome Bruner at the Center for Cognitive Studies, where he was able to exchange the latest ideas with leading scholars from psychology, pediatrics, education, and a variety of other fields.

Toward the end of his stay at Harvard, Papoušek was offered a 2-year contract to continue teaching in the psychology department beginning in the fall term. He was pleased to receive the offer and, as fate would have it, signed the contract on August 20—the morning before the shocking news of the Czech invasion. Appalled by this latest aggression against his country, he was faced with an unexpected dilemma. Would it be better to leave Cambridge immediately and to be with his family in Prague? Or, would it be safer—at least for the time being—to stay in Cambridge and fulfill the terms of his contract?

Papoušek later recounted his thoughts. If he did not return immediately to Prague, then would his family be safe? Would the invasion and expected crackdown result in repercussions affecting their welfare if he were not there? If he were to stay in the United States, then what bearing would this have on his long-standing plans of completing his second doctoral dissertation or *Habilitation*? If he stayed, what would happen to all of the data he had gathered in Prague? Would he ever be able to gain access to it again? Not knowing the long-term consequences of the invasion, Papoušek came to the conclusion that it would be best for him to interrupt his stay in the United States temporarily, and to ask Harvard to postpone resumption of his teaching contract until a later time. Accordingly, he contacted the Czech Ministry of Internal Affairs and received official approval to go back to Prague, while the administration at Harvard assured him he could resume his teaching contract in January 1970. With these approvals from both sides, Papoušek purchased a plane ticket and returned to Prague in late August.

In fact, when he called his Prague friends and family from Cambridge to inquire about the political situation a few days after the invasion, he was told that people were still able to leave the country with relatively little interference. Moreover, stories were circulating of the Czech security guards at the borders making their own decisions about whether or not a person could leave, irrespective of "official" permission. When he arrived in Prague, Papoušek was relieved to find his family unharmed; he resumed his previous position at the Institute for the Care of Mother and Child, and initially was not aware of major changes having taken place. After a few months, however, it became evident that even at the Institute for the Care of Mother and Child, the era of political openness and hope for the ČSSR was coming to an end, and the political pressures placed on him personally were beginning to mount.

At the Institute, where he was still the leader of the Party unit, he had played an active role prior to the Prague Spring in helping to oust a hardline Party member named Vojta, who was the director of the Institute. However, Vojta, who had close family ties in the Party's Central Committee, did not leave the Institute after his removal, but was reassigned to a new position with different responsibilities. In addition, Hanuš had worked with scientists from other institutes to organize a new scientific society whose goals were to be more independent of the centrally controlled Czech Academy of Sciences. Also, as head of the Institute's Party cadre, Papoušek had consistently advocated placing greater emphasis on the importance of science as opposed to ideology as the basis for guiding the Institute's research and, unbeknownst even to some of his closest coworkers, had taken a tolerant attitude toward some who held non-Communist and non-socialist views. There was much fear and apprehension that Vojta and the other hardliners still had enough influence within the Party to seek revenge.

In fact, one of the first steps taken after the Warsaw Pact clampdown was to ask all Institute researchers to sign an oath of loyalty to the new regime. Papoušek was fully aware of the likely consequences of failure to sign: Either he would be sent to practice medicine in some small, remote village, or he would have to emigrate illegally to another country as many researchers at other institutes were doing. Nevertheless, Papoušek refused to sign. As it turned out, most members of the Communist organization at the Institute for the Care of Mother and Child also refused to condone the Soviet invasion and openly expressed their opposition, leading Party higher-ups to eventually dissolve the Institute's entire Party cell.

As events unfolded, it also became clear that the renewed repression was taking a heavy toll on Hanuš and his relationship with his family. In particular, despite the Soviet invasion, his wife Draha was not prepared to leave the country, either legally or illegally. A warm mother and supportive housewife, she did not share her husband's professional interests or his proficiency in foreign languages. It became impossible to separate personal from professional considerations in such an important and probably irreversible decision as leaving the country. As a result, Draha and Hanuš agreed to divorce in May 1969. In later years, Hanuš described his efforts to help their three teenage children in Prague understand and cope with the situation, and to give them the option of whether or not to join him. It turned out that Dagmar, the oldest child, was already in the West. So although Dagmar was able to spend a short amount of time with Hanuš, he was not able to see his other children again until 1975.

Despite these problems, or perhaps as a way of coping with them, in fall 1969 Papoušek turned to the task of writing his second dissertation, or *Habilitation*, as it is known in German universities. His topic was the development of learning capacities in the first 9 months of human life. The dissertation was completed in December 1969, when he was awarded the prestigious Doctor of Sciences degree in developmental psychology by the department of pediatrics at Charles University.

For all the political restrictions being imposed, however, Papoušek still was allowed permission to travel to international conferences until late

1969. In June 1969, for instance, he had little difficulty obtaining reentry permission from the Ministry of Internal Affairs to lead a seminar in Munich at the Max Planck Institute in the child psychiatry department, led by Gertrud Bleek. This was a unit for which he had already given a seminar once before, in May 1967; several researchers there had begun a collaborative research project with the Institute for the Care of Mother and Child that entailed periodic travel between Prague and Munich between 1967 and 1969. Moreover, in July 1969, Papoušek was allowed to attend the 19th International Congress of Psychology in London, where he co-chaired a symposium on learning processes in human infants.

By late summer 1969, however, he and his colleagues were caught by surprise when the Czech Academy of Sciences and the Ministry of Foreign Affairs suddenly declared it necessary to reduce scientific contacts with two specific countries—West Germany and the United States. The rationale was that these two countries had tried politically to "misuse" the situation following the Soviet takeover. In reality, these happened to be the only two countries still offering monetary support for Eastern European scholars to participate in conferences abroad; now this opportunity was abruptly terminated. Their own government was not offering funds for international professional travel, so this further restriction drew the Iron Curtain even more tightly around the Czech borders.

Accordingly, when Papoušek applied for permission to present a paper at a convention of the American Academy for the Advancement of Science to be held in Boston on December 24–27, the Ministry of Internal Affairs turned him down. For Papoušek, it was the last straw. Having finished his *Habilitation,* he decided to seek whatever means possible to leave Czechoslovakia. The remaining question was whether to choose an illegal or legal route. He had the offer from Harvard to begin teaching there in January 1970, but what good would this do without permission from the Ministry of Internal Affairs?

He was no longer employed by the Institute for the Care of Mother and Child because he was waiting for word from the Ministry of Internal Affairs. Hanuš later described his dilemma: "Here I was saying good-bye to all my friends, because I was hoping that one day I would get my visa so I could disappear as fast as possible. If I met an acquaintance on Monday, I had to act as if I was expecting to be gone, forever, on Tuesday" (Papoušek Interview, July 15, 1998). What made it doubly difficult for anyone to understand why he was still in Prague was the fact that the Institute could no longer pay him a salary. He explained, "It's no fun in a Socialist country if all of a sudden you stay there and have no salary. There's nothing you can do! There was no flexibility. I couldn't do anything. I was just helpless! It was *hell,* I have to tell you. . . . With my parents for instance, every time they had to say good-bye, it was under the assumption that it would last for who knows how long—the rest of one's life or something? It was really a living hell" (Papoušek Interview, July 15, 1998).

AN UNEXPECTED LOOPHOLE

In July 1970, while an international medical conference was being held in Prague, Papoušek found a loophole in the Czech authorities' foreign travel restrictions. It came about by sheer coincidence and allowed him to flee to the Federal Republic of Germany on July 6, 1970. The remarkable feature of this provision was that members of state scientific committees[1] were allowed to travel abroad on "urgent business," for no more than 3 days, with permission from the Ministry of Foreign Affairs—without requiring the usual prior permission from the Ministry of Internal Affairs. Moreover, Papoušek's escape was aided by several German researchers at the Max Planck Institute for Psychiatry in Munich.

As it happened, a child neurological congress was held in Prague, with prominent participants from numerous Western countries in attendance. Among these was Joest Martinius, a scientist from Munich who was part of the same group of child neurologists from the Max Planck Institute with whom Hanuš was already working and who periodically visited the Institute for the Care of Mother and Child. Through conversations with the Czech colleagues attending the congress, Martinius was well aware of the severe limitations that had been put on scientific contacts, and knew that the possibilities of attending other foreign medical conferences for someone like Hanuš were now almost nonexistent.

While he was waiting to hear about his visa and permission to return to Harvard, Papoušek learned, quite by accident, of the special provision that made foreign travel possible for members of the "scientific committee." This unexpected news gave Hanuš the loophole he needed, and the decision was finally made. After his initial reaction of disbelief ("Jesus Christ, you're sure that is still possible?"), he immediately went to see Martinius, who was in Prague at the time, informing him that "if you can somehow arrange that I can come to Munich for some urgent reasons, just for 1 or 2 days, then I could get out of the country" (Papoušek Interview, July 16, 1998). (Martinius made regular trips to Prague for their research, and was accustomed to carrying mail back and forth in an effort to facilitate East–West communication for Hanuš. He was well aware of the risks for both men, but his commitment to his Czech friend prompted Martinius to take on this latest assignment; Martinius Interview, July 2002.)

---

[1]Papoušek was secretary of the Governmental Research Committee on the Care for Children in Preschool Facilities.

Martinius returned to Munich and immediately took up the matter with Detlev Ploog, director of the Max Planck Institute for Psychiatry. A careful pretext was then devised whereby Papoušek was sent an "urgent and official" invitation requesting his assistance with the completion of a final report for their joint project on newborns. Apparently, the dramatic wording had the desired effect of appearing to be in need of immediate attention, and the Ministry granted approval for Hanuš to go to Munich in July 1970 "for 3 days of consultation." In reality, those fictitious 3 days were the beginning of a new life for him.

A BRIEF STOPOVER IN MUNICH

Following an anxiety-filled train ride from Prague, Hanuš was greeted at the main railway station in Munich by friends from the Max Planck Institute (i.e., Gertrud Bleek, Joest Martinius, and Mechthild Schulte), as well as his longtime friend Heinz Prechtl, who was also in Munich at the time. Although all were close friends, Hanuš was especially pleased to see Mechthild, a researcher at the Max Planck Institute with whom he became acquainted during his earlier visit in 1969. During those seminars, Hanuš and Mechthild discovered that they shared many interests, not only psychological and medical research, but also classical music and mountain hiking. Within a short time, Mechthild became a significant part of Hanuš' new life in the West.

The only personal documents he was able to smuggle over the border were rolled up tightly and hidden in a thin ceramic wine bottle, which was then presented to Mechthild as a "gift." Later, retrieving Hanuš' papers from the narrow mouth of the bottle—without breaking it—proved perhaps more difficult than carrying it across the border. Today, this ceramic bottle can still be found in the Papoušek home, a fully intact and poignant reminder of the family's history.

Upon arrival in Munich, Papoušek went almost immediately to the American Embassy to explain his situation, requesting a visa for the United States. Initially, it appeared that this would not be possible because he had left all of his official papers in Prague; eventually, and after much persuasion on his part, the U.S. officials agreed to use their special diplomatic services to get Hanuš' files from Prague at the earliest opportunity. This was not done without certain suspicions, however, as indicated by the response of one member of the diplomatic corps: "We have no materials on you, nothing; you could be *anybody* in our eyes—you could be a spy, even if you are also a highly-qualified specialist being offered a position at an outstanding American university . . ." (Papoušek Interview, July 15, 1998). (This was not the first time suspicions about his personal documents had been raised, nor was it to be the last. Earlier, while still in Prague, Hanuš received the rather mysterious notification that someone was traveling through Switzerland en route to the United States under the assumed name and passport of "Hanuš Papoušek"! Indeed, it turned out that his Czech passport was missing, although it later reappeared just as mysteriously.) While waiting for the visa, sponsors at the Max Planck Institute insisted that Papoušek should "disappear" or essentially go into hiding in Lauterbach, a small Bavarian village, so that no one could easily find him in Germany. Eventually, Hanuš was able to obtain the visa he needed, went to the United States after several weeks in Germany, and arrived in time to assume his position at Harvard.

The official response of outrage from the Czech Ministry of Internal Affairs was swift, as Hanuš recalled:

> I had finally decided to leave the country, sort of illegally. . . . They immediately closed that hole when I stayed in Germany. I was the only one who happened to become aware of it and then used it. . . . From Munich I then informed the Czech government that I was by chance in Munich, and I was told by the American side that Harvard had been waiting for me since the first of January. If I did not come immediately they would forget the whole contract. So I said, "I hope that I am acting on your intentions if I now go to the United States without returning to Prague, in order to facilitate that intent within time." The answer from the Ministry was *furious*! (Papoušek Interview, July 15, 1998)

Despite this infuriated response, Papoušek did not sever all of his ties with the Czech governmental officials. While remaining abroad without official permission, he refused to seek asylum as a "political refugee" in the Federal Republic of Germany or the United States, and continued to retain his Czech passport for a number of years to come. In this sense, Papoušek was quite literally caught between East and West, while seeking to build a bridge between both.

IMPLICATIONS FOR THE FAMILY AND COWORKERS IN PRAGUE

From the Czech side, threats of repercussions followed, both for Hanuš and his family. They were not specific, and it was clear that he was punishable by Czech law for illegal emigration. Papoušek's daughter, Dagmar, was already in Munich at the time working as an *au pair* girl, and preparing to complete examinations in German language proficiency. Hanuš discussed with her the option of staying with him in Germany, but eventually she decided to return to Prague and complete her schooling there. Political repercussions ensued in Prague, however, which prohibited Dagmar from studying at the university; as well, Hanuš' daughter-in-law was fired from a job in one of the Ministries (where she helped to organize international travels). These consequences initially thwarted Dagmar's dreams of studying medicine. However, she was allowed to train at a laboratory school, obtained excellent grades there, and was professionally prepared for high-level laboratory jobs at universities and outstanding medical facilities. Today she is employed as a medical assistant in the Pediatric Cardiac Unit of Motol, a large university hospital in Prague, where her husband, Vladimir Komárek, is a pediatric neurologist.

Hanuš Jr., the older son, had completed his degree in electrical engineering and already had a secure job, so his career was not as directly affected by his father's departure. The third child in Prague, Jirka, was still in school at the time but decided to study at a special international school for hotel management rather than pursue a university degree. In 1975, the Czech government gradually began to ease travel restrictions for children whose parents lived abroad. Hanuš' children were able to leave Czechoslovakia on a limited basis, not more than once a year, and his aging parents could make occasional trips to Munich and serve as liaisons between the Prague children and their father.

Perhaps most important is the perspective of the Prague children as revealed in a retrospective statement provided by daughter Dagmar (personal communication, February 25, 2000):

> We had a happy childhood, though we were not exactly well off. Dad worked a lot and didn't have a lot of time to spend with us. However, the little time that he had left, he used to the fullest to our advantage. We went on trips, mountain hiking, he taught us how to swim and ski, he taught us the names of various birds, flowers and trees, we'd go camping. He would teach us how to behave in nature and to love it. He taught us to love music and showed us the way to appreciate art, to be humble and modest.
>
> At the time that Dad left, we were only able to write to each other, a few calls now and then. It wasn't easy but one couldn't really do anything about it at that time. I think it was hardest for mom and my younger brother. We only met up with Dad again in 1975 and were limited to one visit a year. I'm very grateful that he brought us up the way he did. All the good things I learned from him I tried to pass on to my children. We all have great respect for him, are proud of him, and love him very much.

Papoušek's sudden departure also affected colleagues at the Institute for the Care of Mother and Child, who felt the loss of a valued colleague, leader, and mentor. Further contact and exchange of ideas were severely restricted by the Czech government. As Hanuš reported, "They were prohibited from quoting my publications and it went so far that scientific references were censored. I don't know if you can imagine it, that for a scientific reference you are compelled to omit one author! You know, this is simply, for us, unbelievable, but that was one of the consequences" (Papoušek Interview, July 15, 1998).

Back in Prague, there was evidence that Papoušek's former coworkers decided intentionally to keep their own scientific productivity at a minimum, in order to signal to the outside world that things were not in order when internationally renowned scholars decided it was necessary to leave the country. According to Hanuš, "There was kind of a protest, a silent protest against the Russian occupation—which I did not realize for some time. So after a couple of years I started asking them (via correspondence), 'Where are your publications? How come the production is so low?' The answer they gave surprised me, because they told me 'Do you *want* us to publish, and to show that everything is in order in Czechoslovakia?' " (Papoušek Interview, July 15, 1998).

Beyond the walls of the Institute for the Care of Mother and Child, ordinary citizens before Papoušek's departure had grown accustomed to hearing the voice of pediatrician Dr. Hanuš Papoušek on their local radio stations. His regular broadcasts of parenting and childrearing advice had been recorded in advance and continued to be aired for several months after his departure. Many loyal listeners simply could not believe that, despite his presence on the radio, the "Dr. Spock" of Czechoslovakia had fled the country illegally.

UNDERSTANDING THE EFFECTS
OF THE "IRON CURTAIN"

From today's perspective, it is often difficult to fully comprehend the harsh realities of the Cold War and the effects of this historical era on the exchange of ideas and scientific progress among scholars on either side of the Iron Curtain. One of Papoušek's oldest and closest European friends was Heinz Prechtl, who was then on the faculty at the University of Groningen. As mentioned earlier, Prechtl happened to be in Munich to meet Hanuš at the train station at the time of his defection, and was in the party of friends and colleagues waiting for the emotional reunion. Although the visit was officially supposed to be just a few days, they all knew the real reasons: "Because he was facing problems, of course. Because he was very much on the Dubcek side. He would have run into difficulties, probably in jail. I think he had to leave. It was a life-saving decision. And he could not conform in any way with the new direction of the Communist Party" (Prechtl Interview, April 28, 2000).

Papoušek's son-in-law described the situation in the former Czechoslovakia as one that many Americans find hard to understand:

We were here as in a prison. . . . The border was closed . . . and because I was not a member of the Communist Party, . . . for 18 years I was not allowed to go abroad. And at the same time it was not allowed, or it was dangerous for people who emigrated such as Hanuš to come back, because it was at risk of being captured and put into prison. So . . . it was very difficult for us to communicate with people abroad. It was really like in, like a prison. The Iron Curtain was really very tight.

Hanuš was very active in the '60s in research, . . . and he realized I think in 1969, that there was no future in the Czech Republic for people who would like to be *very* active in science. And so I think that was the reason to leave. . . . So if you are a scientist, you need contacts, you need to travel to other countries to see another lab, to discuss the problems. You need papers—there was no Internet in the '60s! Now it is no problem—I can click on *MedLine* and will obtain in some minutes a lot of information, what happened in the last two weeks, I can ask outside contacts about new papers, and so on. And so there were no journals, and no information. And information, *information* is extremely important for everybody and especially for scientists. . . . After the Russian occupation, only people who cooperated with secret police and with the regime were allowed to travel. And so can you imagine, if it is not possible for you to travel outside of Montana, not to another state, and to spend 20 years only in Montana? It's terrible. (Komárek Interview, November 8, 1999)

Thus, the barriers to scientific exchange were insurmountable, but the threat to his own personal freedom was perhaps even more of a concern both for Papoušek and for his family in Prague. As Komárek reported, once a person has experienced freedom and democracy, it is very difficult to return to a totalitarian system.

Of course, when Hanuš traveled abroad earlier, his family members were rarely allowed to accompany him. This increasing exposure to Western ideas, people, and lifestyles may have indirectly contributed to the decline of his first marriage, because his wife was unable to share in these important experiences. According to Arnold Sameroff, who lived in Prague and worked closely with Hanuš during the 1960s, "part of the deal with taking trips abroad, is you never took your family. You wouldn't take your wife for instance, but you'd always have to leave, I don't want to say 'hostages' but *essentially*—it figures. It was true. If they took their families with them, they'd never come back. So that also enhanced the separation between Hanuš and his family. . . . When he *did* take trips, they were not allowed to come along. So the more he wanted to get involved in the international community, the more it separated him from the family" (Interview, February 4, 2000).

Hanuš' second wife, Mechthild, corroborated these views, when she responded to the question, "What do you perceive as the most politically difficult aspects of his life in Czechoslovakia, and the most compelling political reasons for his leaving?":

His impression was that, from that time on, after the Russian invasion, he would not be allowed any more to do the kind of research which he wanted to do. And the freedoms which they had gotten in the past years, to travel and to have the international contacts, would be much more restricted again—nobody knew for how long. I think this was the main reason. Of course also the disappointment, because his hope was that the Prague Spring movement, this humane form of Socialism, and democratic form of Socialism, would be able to develop and provide a third way between the big "blocks." But it turned out that this wouldn't be the case. This was a big disappointment for Hanuš. It was not easy for him, because the family was there and he had to leave the family behind without knowing whether he would see them again; this was not easy. (M. Papoušek Interview, October 22, 1999)

RETURNING TO HARVARD UNIVERSITY

After finally obtaining the appropriate visa for travel to the United States, Papoušek again took up residence in Cambridge, Massachusetts, in time for the fall 1970 semester. Jerome Bruner had been the key person at Harvard who requested permission from the Czech government for Papoušek to work in the United States. Apparently, this became a source of amusement later, when Bruner liked to remind Hanuš that this was the first case he knew of in which Harvard University was required to seek permission from another country's government to employ a citizen from that country. In addition, the Czech government responded by making the visa conditional: Papoušek would be required to continue at Harvard the research in which he had been engaged at the Prague Institute. As Papoušek once recalled, Bruner's firm but diplomatic reply was "we are not used to dictating to our scientists what to do and what not to do. . . . We will assure Hanuš Papoušek that he can do whatever he likes once he's here, that we support scientific activities in general, and that we don't impose any conditions" (Papoušek Interview, July 16, 1999).

Coming from his position as director of an entire unit in a prestigious and unique research institute, the transition to being just one of many renowned scholars at Harvard may have been somewhat difficult for Papoušek. Suddenly he was expected to teach, oversee a research laboratory, and adapt to expectations of the American academic workplace. Clearly, Hanuš was appreciative and realized how invaluable this opportunity was, but he later commented (with his usual good-humored chuckle), "I was exploited!"

Papoušek assumed a variety of responsibilities at Harvard: teaching developmental psychobiology (still a very new field at the time), offering seminars in social psychology to Jerome Kagan's students, teaching a laboratory course at the request of the Dean Richard Herrnstein, working as a senior researcher at the Center for Cognitive Studies under the direction of Jerome Bruner, designing new investigations to advance knowledge about

infant development, and eventually collaborating on research with Peter
Wolff at the Boston Children's Hospital. George Miller and Jerome Bruner
had founded the center in 1960, with substantial funding by the Carnegie
Corporation. Bruner (1983) described this new venture: "I suppose everybody has a somewhat different notion of what the 'center' of psychology is.
We had our idea. We thought it was concern for the distinctly human forms
of gaining, storing, transforming and using knowledge of all sorts—what
makes humans human. Call them cognitive processes. They were certainly
being neglected—particularly at Harvard" (p. 122). This vision was well
suited to the ideas Papoušek had been developing at the Prague Institute,
even though his research there was generally referred to as "conditioning
studies." Far from limiting his thinking to a strict behaviorist model, he was
increasingly fascinated by the infants' displays of affect, evidence of cognitive processes, and physiological reactions to the learning tasks.

The Harvard opportunities were clearly exciting for someone coming
from Eastern Europe in the early 1970s, but the combined teaching and research load made it difficult for Papoušek to prepare manuscripts for publication, especially in a language other than his mother tongue. Nevertheless, the Center for Cognitive Studies and the Children's Hospital provided
intellectual stimulation, abundant resources for the pursuit of scientific investigations, and an impressive array of scholars and students on the cusp of
new discoveries about the human infant. His colleagues included Marc
Bornstein, Tom Bower, T. Berry Brazelton, Kurt Fischer, Patricia Green-
field, Marshall Haith, Colwyn Trevarthen, and Ed Tronick.

Perhaps most important and influential in his life, however, was the arrival in Cambridge of Mechthild Schulte, who came to Harvard on a one-
year postdoctoral fellowship to study psychiatry at Harvard Medical School.
In 1972, Hanuš and Mechthild decided to get married in the United States.
Marc Bornstein, one of Papoušek's closest American friends, explained
what it was that drew Hanuš to the United States: "There was something
about what he saw, what could be done here, that maybe in Eastern Europe
he couldn't have done. He probably said to himself, 'I have to try. It's a
better place to try to do what I have to do.' So he left Czechoslovakia, and
now the question is 'Why?' And there were two positive things. They were
Mechthild and *Freedom.* Those are two pretty powerful things" (Bornstein Interview, March 10, 2000).

PAPOUŠEK'S RESEARCH AT HARVARD: ADDING
MOTHERS TO THE PICTURE

Several of Papoušek's studies are of particular interest from this time at
Harvard: one of "self-recognition smiles," one of "social referencing," and
another that he referred to as "experimentally induced mother–infant de-

tachment." Often the ideas emerged initially during Bruner's Wednesday morning "Donut Seminars," which brought together the diverse group of interested scholars in the center to discuss research, theories, and methodology.

One topic, for example, centered around the observation that 4-month-old infants already displayed "self-recognition smiles" upon seeing their mirror image. Was this truly self-recognition, or was the baby merely responding to seeing another baby (or to the "babyish" appearance that is known to elicit a variety of social responses in most humans)? Or, as Papoušek queried, might the infants be trying to communicate with someone who appears to be moving with absolute contingency in relation to the infant's own movements? Another possibility was that the direct eye-to-eye contact possible with a mirror image played a role in eliciting these smiles.

The challenge was to design an experimental or observational method that could control for various possible confounds and lead to firmer conclusions about the phenomenon being studied. Papoušek's creative mind, his technological expertise, and his insightful observational skills all contributed to the solutions to such problems. In one instance, the idea of substituting a television image for the mirror image offered an ingenious way of isolating certain factors. (When this was first suggested to Bruner, Papoušek was amazed when the following morning there were two video recorders on his desk, and a technician from the center waiting to provide instructions and assistance.) This may well have been a turning point for Papoušek, having had little prior exposure to television at all (Papoušek Interview, July 16, 1998)!

The result was a study in which the infant was facing two video monitors, one providing apparent eye-to-eye contact via simultaneous playback of the infant's own image, and the other playing an image of the same infant but recorded from an angle that precluded eye contact. These two images were both contingent on the infant's own behaviors, but allowed the eye gaze component to be isolated. In a subsequent session, the second image (in addition to face-to-face) was a playback of the previously recorded session, and was thus no longer contingent. (Apparently results of his study were never published. However, "Mirror Image and Self-Recognition in Young Human Infants: A New Method of Experimental Analysis" appeared in *Developmental Psychobiology* [H. Papoušek & M. Papoušek, 1974], and was based on similar methodological explorations developed during his stay at Harvard.)

A second study undertaken at Harvard was a pioneering effort to examine the phenomenon now known as "social referencing": the infant's tendency to observe and then follow, or imitate, parental models about emotional responses to an ambiguous or potentially threatening event. Certainly this was taking Papoušek even further into the realm of cognitive processes. But, the data were lost and results remain unpublished, although

Hanuš described the procedures and results as follows: The infant (age 4 months) was exposed to a neutral object, in this case a toy dog covered with grey cloth and lowered from the ceiling in front of the child. A battery control mechanism allowed the experimenter to activate the dog's barking and movement so as to attract the attention of the infant. One group of parents was instructed to first exhibit a *fearful* response to the toy, whereas the other group was asked to demonstrate a *joyful* or pleasurable response—similar to work being done by Joseph Campos around the same time. Later, the order of responses was reversed, and infant behaviors were again observed. The first finding was that infants looked at the mother's face when the strange object appeared, and then actually imitated her facial expression.

The next results were surprising and somewhat unsettling for a pediatrician always watching for potential clinical implications of child development research. Those parents who modeled a *positive* response to the toy during the first exposure found it very easy to reverse this effect by subsequently demonstrating a fearful or *negative* response to the barking dog. However, for those infants who were first exposed to an *anxious* or fearful response by the parent, the modeling effect was not so easily extinguished or reversed; that is, these babies found it difficult to assume a more positive approach to the barking toy dog (even when that was being modeled) after first seeing the parent's fearful reaction. It is not difficult to imagine that such patterns might help explain the later development of phobias or anxieties.

Finally, and also during his stay at Harvard, Papoušek attempted to answer a challenge posed by Bruner regarding the possibility that 3-month-old infants already had become satiated with their mother's interactions—a controversial finding that had been reported somewhat earlier by Jaroslav Koch, a colleague in Prague. Infants first learned how to pull a bar to open a curtain revealing a clown puppet with a drum and drumsticks. A second curtain also opened nearby, revealing the mother greeting the baby and saying, "Hello, here I am!" for 5 seconds, at which time the curtain closed again and the mother disappeared. Using this procedure, Koch demonstrated that the infants quickly discerned what the two alternatives were, and began showing preference for the toy clown over their own mother. A disturbing finding, if this initial interpretation was correct!

The fact that the infants began to respond somewhat negatively toward the mother, as if rejecting her overtures, was controversial and difficult to explain if one relied only on the surface interpretation. Not satisfied with this explanation, Papoušek decided to explore the phenomenon further while at Harvard. Could it be that the mother's behavior was actually violating some expectation that the infant had already learned, some "rule" of early interactions between parents and their infants? Or, as Bruner asked at the time, was it possible that 3-month-olds already had *concepts*, or *schemas*, of their mother's behavior?

Intrigued, Papoušek designed another study, this time using 4-month-olds so that if the "satiation hypothesis" were correct, then there would be an even greater likelihood of finding it at this later age. More interesting than this hypothesis alone, however, was the question of whether or not infants at that age already have concepts and expectations about interactions with their mothers. By violating an infant's concept, one might then be able to observe negative behaviors that would confirm the suspicion that babies have already learned a great deal about predictable social exchanges within a few short months. But what maternal behavior might one manipulate to test this out?

Papoušek and others in his group noticed that whenever a mother was in the lab and had to leave the infant briefly, she not only sought permission from the researchers but also from the infant. That is, she would always address the baby in a certain reassuring way, and then explain repeatedly that she would be leaving for a short while and would return quickly. Reunions following these brief separations showed no difficulties in reestablishing pleasant interactions between the two. In other words, even with very young infants, mothers seemed to have developed "rituals" for leave-taking, thus providing the research team with a logical behavior to modify for their purposes. However, Papoušek was nearing the end of his 3-month stay at Harvard (1968), and there was not much time left for initiating and refining a new experiment. With Jerome Bruner's support, efficiency, and encouragement, 40 infants were promptly recruited and the study proceeded in full gear.

The plan was to use intermittent periods of darkness (i.e., the lights suddenly went off for 3 seconds during a normal interaction), at which time the mother would disappear behind a curtain. The timing of these interludes was unknown to the mother, so she was unable to prepare the baby as usual for her absence. No rituals of departure were permitted, as she was to simply move behind the curtain and wait for her signal to return. The effects were similar to the findings of "maternal over-satiation" reported earlier by Papoušek's colleague in Prague. When the mothers first reappeared, infants typically responded by staring briefly, then greeting her cheerfully. With two or three repetitions, however, infants began turning away from the mother, actively rejecting her efforts to renew contact by fussing, crying, or turning away.

In fact, the results were so dramatic that mothers actually became distressed and asked what the experimenters had done to the infant while she was out of sight! Most claimed to have never experienced such a reaction from their child before, and reported that feeling rejected by their own child was unpleasant, painful, and intolerable. In some cases, it was even difficult to convince the mothers that nothing had been done to the babies during this simple manipulation, and because infrared film was being used it could not be played back to the mothers immediately in order to reassure them.

In addition, Harvard was in the midst of litigation involving the ethics of embryological research in another department, so Papoušek was quite hesitant to publish his results right away, fearing that concerns about the treatment of human subjects might be raised. When the results did appear in print (H. Papoušek & M. Papoušek, 1975), the following subjective reaction was included: "These experiences surprised the mothers as well as the observers, and we noted with some relief that the children's relationship with their mothers recovered quickly after the experiments ended!" (p. 259).

The decision to leave the United States for Germany after 2 years coincided with several significant events. During this time, Hanuš Papoušek and Mechthild Schulte (a German citizen) were married in Boston. In 1972, Jerome Bruner was leaving Harvard for Oxford University. And by then, Hanuš had met Detlev Ploog and the two had discussed possible research opportunities at the Max Planck Institute for Psychiatry in Munich. There were again forces pulling the Papoušeks in various directions, however, and the dilemma of whether or not to remain in the United States and become citizens was made more difficult by job offers at both American and Canadian universities. Their next path as a couple was unfortunately made clear with the sudden death of Mechthild's father, a renowned scholar and chair of the adult psychiatry department at the University of Tübingen, Germany. It was important to be closer to her family at such a time, so the Papoušeks moved to Germany in 1972.

The experience at Harvard had served an important function, especially for Hanuš, because it provided a needed intellectual and personal transition from his earlier situation in Prague to becoming a citizen of the "West" and establishing a second family. In terms of his research, it also led him more in the direction of using new technology to document fine details of the adaptive behaviors of parents and infants.

As Bruner (1983) commented, "The question is not where or when the mind begins. Mind in some operative form is there from the start, wherever 'there' may be. The question, rather, is about the conditions that produce human minds that are richer, stronger, more confident" (p. 152). Papoušek showed in his Prague studies that infants "from the start" possessed many more capabilities than many scientists had assumed. He had also become aware of the optimal conditions needed in order for researchers to demonstrate these capabilities, such as attending to the infant's state of arousal, readiness to interact, and so forth. Now it was time to examine how human parents might be supporting the infant's development in ways that indeed enriched and strengthened the child's emerging mental capacities, even when these strategies did not appear to be at a conscious level for the parent.

Chapter 6

The Early Years in Munich

Toward the end of his 2-year contract at Harvard, Hanuš Papoušek was 50 years old, still carried a Czech passport, and was living in the United States without a permanent visa. Professionally and personally, he was a man without a country. Although he enjoyed the intellectual vibrance of Harvard and Cambridge, he felt uncomfortable with the dominant social and political norms of both East and West, especially at the height of the Vietnam War. In Prague, he had put great hopes in a humane form of socialism as an alternative to both sides, and international exchange of scientific and intellectual ideas as a means for bridging some of the ideological differences between East and West. What would the future hold for him? Recognized as a brilliant scientist with ground-breaking ideas about the capabilities of infants, Hanuš also knew that his prospects for permanent employment at Harvard were uncertain.

Theoretically speaking, one option was to return to Czechoslovakia; as a practical matter, however, this too was questionable as long as the hard-line government of Gustav Husak remained in power. A second option was to take a position at a university or research institute in the United States or Canada, where he knew firsthand that the conditions and financial support for conducting high quality research were as good as anywhere in the world. Indeed, a number of offers had already come his way. In the end, however, a third option, driven primarily by family considerations, prevailed.

Following the death of her father, Mechthild felt drawn to return to Germany. At about the same time, Hanuš received a job offer from the prestigious Max Planck Institute for Psychiatry in Munich. A short train ride to

113

the Czech border, Munich was where he and Mechthild had first met and was within easy reach of his family in Prague in case the divisions between East and West were to subside. In the summer 1972, Hanuš decided to accept the offer from the Max Planck Institute and move to Munich. He and Mechthild would start new research careers there, raise a new family, and continue to work and make frequent trips abroad until his death in May 2000.

The move back to Germany was an easy adjustment for Mechthild, but it was much more difficult for Hanuš. First and foremost, it meant having to write in yet another foreign language. Although he had a facility for languages, in Prague he had written almost exclusively in Czech, and in the United States he needed help from friends to publish articles in English. In Munich, Mechthild helped him write research publications in German for the first several years. In addition, the move to Munich meant having to adjust to a culture and society with which Hanuš never truly felt at ease. In part, this undoubtedly was the result of unresolved attitudes that he, like many Czechs of his generation, felt toward Germany after the brutal Nazi invasion and occupation of the Czech lands in 1938. Even though he was well received within the Max Planck Institute itself, there was a certain ambivalence about the extent to which he was genuinely satisfied in his new homeland. Was it an instance of an emigrant having to change countries one too many times?

More than anyone else, Detlev Ploog, director of the Max Planck Institute for Psychiatry, was responsible for bringing Papoušek to Munich. Ironically, this was the same person who had signed the "urgent request" that enabled Papoušek to escape from Czechoslovakia in 1970. Appointed director of the Munich institute in 1970, Ploog was a prominent psychiatrist and primatologist who was every bit as committed as Hanuš to the pursuit of science as a process for seeking greater truth. As head of West Germany's premier psychiatric research facility, Ploog had trained in England and in the United States under the neurophysiologist Paul MacLean at the National Institutes of Health. He was determined to restore the international reputation of postwar German psychology and psychiatry after the appalling compromises it had made as a result of Nazi politics and ideology. Ploog was careful to conduct an extensive international search and, after meeting Papoušek, felt he had made the right decision in not only hiring Hanuš, but in bringing Mechthild back as well:

> Both of us worked on a very close basis with scientific colleagues in the United States, and for me, as well as for Hanuš, the United States was almost like a second home. . . . There was this great stroke of luck that I was invited to give a talk at Harvard while Jerry Bruner was still there. It was at Bruner's place that I got to know Hanuš, and we talked for a long time. And at that point Papoušek was not married, but . . . I already knew Mechthild from Tübingen

and Munich and all that. Mechthild had worked in our Child Psychiatry Unit, and Mechthild and Hanuš had gotten to know each other in this unit (when he came from Prague and gave occasional seminars). And so it wasn't just a sense of promoting the well-being of science, but of promoting the well-being of a marriage as well. I must say, that union produced some of the most splendid scientific results I have ever witnessed. (Ploog Interview, October 15, 1999)

Ploog's vision for the Institute was grounded in an ethological approach to the study of human behavior, and he was convinced that it was important for scientists in his field to ask themselves what it is that ultimately separates human beings from other forms of life. He explained, "I firmly believed that what makes the human species different from other species in the animal kingdom is the ability to speak. Although all mammals have some way of vocalizing and communicating with each other, the human species is unique by virtue of its speech. . . . One has to go to the roots of behavior in humans, and the roots of human behavior lie within the child, specifically the infant" (Ploog Interview, October 15, 1999). Strongly influenced by MacLean's work on the role of the brain in relation to emotions, social contact, and communication, he returned to West Germany convinced that, in order to treat human pathologies and psychoses, it was essential to gain a better understanding of the physiological structures and innate capacities with which each person is born (Ploog Interview, October 15, 1999). In addition, he was persuaded of the need to combine research and clinical approaches, especially in relation to the study of early human communication. As Peter Wolff commented, "You must know what Ploog brought to that place. What he was trying to do was to marry clinical science and basic science" (Wolff Interview, December 21, 1999).

As part of the Institute's focus on language disorders and speech therapy, Ploog established a laboratory under the direction of Sigrid Hopf for the ethological study of communication in nonhuman primates, the first such facility in Germany. From its inception, Ploog and Hopf focused both on brain and behavior rather than viewing the two separately, investigating how brain functions influence behavior, communication, and interactions. As a logical extension, Ploog also created a unit in child psychiatry in order to examine the roots of parent–child communication as possibly related to later pathologies. The head of this new unit was Gertrud Bleek, although she made it entirely clear from the start that she was interested only in doing clinical work, not research. Bleek and her team concentrated almost exclusively on treating children with language disorders, autism, and various forms of childhood psychoses.

To complement the work of the primate lab and Bleek's clinical unit, Ploog saw Papoušek as someone who could head a new research unit with a focus on the interdisciplinary study of physiology, behavior, and communication in human newborns or neonates. According to Ploog, "What I had done was to look around in the world to see where there were people who could combine all this" (Ploog Interview, October 15, 1999). He was certain that Papoušek's background in pediatrics, biology, neurology, and infant conditioning would provide the ideal intellectual foundation for this assignment. Ploog also felt that because Hanuš was well versed in American psychological research, he would be well received by West German psychologists, among whom American-style behaviorism was still a dominant paradigm. At the same time, because Papoušek had just spent the last 2 years at the Center for Cognitive Studies, Ploog also saw that he had somehow "enlarged his scope. . . . His horizons were broadened as a result of spending time with Bruner, although Jerry also learned from him. They had a good cooperative relationship. . . . And on top of all this, I had my own notions about vocalizations" (Ploog Interview, October 15, 1999). After lengthy conversations, Ploog decided that Hanuš should head a new department called the Unit for *Developmental Psychobiology*: "I was overjoyed when Hanuš decided to come" (Ploog Interview, October 15, 1999).

Unfortunately, Ploog soon had to temper his enthusiasm with the realization that not all of his plans for Hanuš could be realized. When Papoušek arrived in Munich, Ploog had to give him the disappointing news that a number of sudden policy changes had taken place within the general administration of the Max Planck Society, and the creation of a whole new unit was now out of the question, or at least to the extent that either of them had envisioned it. Although both men were deeply disappointed, there was little either could do. It proved to be a situation perhaps all too familiar in the relationship between prominent research administrator and prominent research scientist who share a common vision of the importance of their work. Although the administrator tries hard to do everything possible to please the researchers, the researchers feel they are not receiving the resources and support needed to get the job done. This was also true of Ploog and Papoušek, and as so often is the case, forces larger than either of them were at work.

HISTORICAL BACKGROUND: THE MAX PLANCK SOCIETY

In the 1950s, during a period of massive reconstruction following the war, the Max Planck Institutes had grown by leaps and bounds, with West German science in critical need of rejuvenation. The Max Planck Society, named after the German Nobel Prize physicist, was created in February 1948 as the successor organization to the Kaiser Wilhelm Society for the promotion of science. Provisions for its funding were grounded in the "National Act for the Funding of Scientific Research Facilities" (also known as

the "Königstein Act") of March 24, 1949. This act assured that financial support for science would be provided by the individual German states, and co-
funding by the federal government in Bonn followed soon thereafter. The
Constitution of the Max Planck Society emphasizes autonomy and academic freedom in terms of research priorities at each Institute, so that despite financial connections with the government, the scientific integrity and
independence of individual Institutes was to be respected.

Whereas the 1950s witnessed a concentrated effort on the part of the
German government to reestablish West Germany's role in the international scientific world, the 1960s saw a surge of growth and expansion during which the number of Max Planck Institutes in a variety of disciplines
grew to an unprecedented 52, more than double the number in its founding year. One of the goals during the 1960s was to promote new areas that
could not easily be supported by other funds. In the 1970s, however, the
Max Planck Society faced the reality of no longer being able to afford un-
limited expansion. Although most existing Institutes were allowed to remain at their current level of funding and size, additional funding was to be
invested in the creation of new research Institutes in other disciplines.
Throughout the system, the only possibility for establishing new programs
was through the elimination or shutting down of Institutes at other loca-
tions. Between 1972 and 1984, 20 Max Planck Institutes (or programs)
closed their doors.

It speaks for Ploog's high standing in West German science that, despite
these retrenchments, he nevertheless managed to prevent Papoušek's new
position from being completely cut. This was probably due largely to the clinical applications of the Institute's research, which played a central role in
Ploog's own scientific goals. As a result, he made it possible for Papoušek's
contract to be honored and his position to be secured, although Hanuš was
only given one small office, no laboratory, and for the next 16 years to come,
no staff to assist in carrying out his research (Papoušek Interview, July 16,
1998). Given this less than ideal situation, it is easy to understand why
Papoušek at times remained somewhat skeptical of the degree to which the
Max Planck Institute as a whole was completely supportive of his work.

Finding himself without the facilities, equipment, or staff for which he
had hoped, Papoušek once again managed to come up with creative solutions to what at first appeared to be a difficult situation. Hanuš decided to
find a new way of gathering data that did not require extensive research assistance or equipment. Adapting observational techniques and new technologies first used at Bruner's center in Cambridge, he bought a portable
movie camera and went into the homes of German parents and infants, recording their interactions in an effort to observe parents and infant learning in an "ethological setting." This was a task that took up most of his time
during his first 2 years in Munich. Hanuš later described these events:

You take the life contingencies as they are available. I didn't return to the States or anything like that. I just thought well, we'll do what we can do. And I bought a film camera, and went to families and spent as much time as possible in families observing mother–infant interactions, or family interactions, in German families. It appeared relatively easy to find interested families, and I collected a lot of very interesting material, which then helped me to develop projects afterwards, when I got a set of rooms. (Papoušek Interview, July 16, 1998)

I actually didn't assume that I would organize something like I did in Prague here in Munich. I was . . . interested in some kind of cooperation with those who were studying the development of communication in non-human primates. . . . And then to care for both ends of the early dialogue: that means, the development of the infant's vocalizations, that's what Mechthild did in detail; and the other thing was the parental behavior. . . . Mechthild then concentrated on the vocal expressions in mothers, and the infant-directed speech in mothers, and I cared for the other aspects of parental behavior and tried to compare mothers and fathers. Like for instance . . . eye-to-eye distance, and all those strategies which facilitate visual contact and which are human-specific. So we did it in triads: fathers interacting with the babies, and then comparing mothers and fathers. (Papoušek Interview, October 22, 1999)

In other words, what initially started out for him as another struggle within unexpected, extenuating circumstances, in the end resulted in the creation of a whole new research agenda for examining the behaviors of infants and their parents.

THE FOCUS OF PAPOUŠEK'S NEW RESEARCH

In taking a new direction, the focus of Papoušek's work began to shift from conditioning and learning studies in neonates to infant learning in his/her naturalistic environment with an emphasis on the role of parental behaviors. This new focus was not a total departure from the kind of work he had done before, although some American psychologists viewed his later studies as being altogether disconnected from his more experimental work in Prague. Quite the contrary, Hanuš' work allowed him to look more closely at many subtle but revealing details he learned from his research experiences in Prague. Whereas Mechthild began to focus mostly on infant vocalization, it became increasingly clear from his observations of German parents and infants that mothers could only partially report about their attitudes and about the practical interventions incorporated with their infants on a daily basis. Papoušek, picking up on some of Ploog's ideas about the importance of innate human behaviors, began to see that many important aspects of maternal behavior seemed hidden even to the mothers

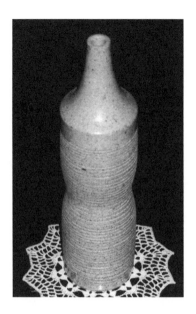

Wine flask filled with personal documents, smuggled into Germany as a "gift" when Hanuš defected from Czechoslovakia.

Kraepelin Str. entrance, Max-Planck Institute for Psychiatry, Munich.

Dr. Detlev Ploog, Director, Max-Planck Institute for Psychiatry, Munich.

Papoušek with video laboratory, Max-Planck Institute for Psychiatry.

The Munich family enjoying the mountains: Tanja, Silvia, Mechthild, and Hanuš, 1986.

Papoušek collaborating with researcher Lynne Koester at Gallaudet University, Washington, DC.

1995

Society for Research in Child Development

Award for Distinguished Scientific Contributions
to Child Development

Presented to

Hanus Papousek

For his pioneering research on developmental changes in infant learning,

For his vision and creativity in exploring the early development of
communication and intuitive parenting,

For his commitment to innovating developmental methods that
cross disciplines, species, and cultures,

For his lifelong dedication to discovering knowledge that can lead to
interventions for improving the lives of children and their families,

For his unusual character and courage in carrying out research of
importance in the midst of challenge and adversity.

Society for Research in Child Development Award for Distinguished Scientific Contributions, 1995.

Arnold Gesell Preis awarded to Hanuš and Mechthild Papoušek.

Participants at Ringberg conference on nonverbal vocal communication, July 1988 (Germany): L to R: Uwe Jürgens; unidentified; Klaus Scherer; Peter Marler; Mechthild Papoušek; Charles Rahn; Kimberly Bard; Barry Lester; Detlev Ploog; Anne Fernald; Roberta Turner; Kimbrough Oller; Rebecca Eilers; Michael Owren; Hanuš Papoušek.

Hanuš and Mechthild Papoušek vacationing in their beloved Alps.

Occupied with one of his favorite hobbies—Papoušek as photographer.

Hanuš and infant daughter Tanja.

Silvia, Hanuš, and Tanja Papoušek.

themselves, and certainly to the scientific observers still struggling to develop adequate methods and equipment for examining these interactions "under a microscope."

Although Hanuš had been sensitized to this issue as a result of observing and working with each mother–infant dyad over a period of nearly 6 months at the Institute in Prague, he was not fully prepared for the prevalence of these nonconscious parenting behaviors when he began filming naturalistic family interactions. In Munich, he became acutely aware of this phenomenon, and began to notice that there was a system involved that had yet to be described in the scientific literature about parents or infants. It was a finding that intrigued him. Pursuing this inquiry further, Papoušek soon realized that many parental behaviors with infants offer highly effective supports for the development of early communication, even before the child is ready to engage in actual language use. Equally fascinating was the fact that most of these parental interventions occur too rapidly to fall under conscious control by the parent. It did not take long before the concept of "Intuitive Parenting" was born. Thus, it is possible to say that it was the initial lack of staff and equipment at the Max Planck Institute that inadvertently resulted in the opportunity to gather new data in the natural setting of families at home with their young children. From these preliminary explorations came the theory that Hanuš and Mechthild were to substantiate, document, and develop fully over the following two decades of research together. Chapter 7 offers a number of specific examples illustrating some of the insights that led to their elaborated theoretical perspective.

Hanuš went about finding new ways to make observations. At the same time, Ploog's original dreams of creating a full research unit did not fade. Several years after Hanuš came on board, ambitious plans were made for a new building that would have included an ideal space for parent–child observational research. The necessary equipment, offices, and a research team would all have been part of the "package," as well as a large sheltered playground, which could have easily been modified for demonstrations and seminars (Papoušek Interview, July 16, 1998). Unknown administrative factors and time considerations once again intervened, however, so that only some of these goals were realized. Nevertheless, Hanuš finally received some grants to hire several young German researchers to carry out studies in his unit, although not with the supporting staff for which he had also hoped. In addition, as his unit became more established, young foreign students and postdoctoral students began arriving on a somewhat regular basis to work under his tutelage.

When asked to reflect on why it never became possible for him to hire a full contingent of researchers, and whether this might have led many in his position to seek other employment opportunities, Hanuš responded philosophically:

Well, this is probably something which changes with time; but when you have something, you may find it too little—particularly when the [subject] matter of interest is so complex that you could experiment in several directions at one time, and again and again and again. And then when you once have to close it and leave it [as was the case when he retired], then you actually realize that it is very difficult to find another opportunity for doing your research. (Papoušek Interview, October 22, 1999)

One cannot help but think that his philosophical attitude may well have been the result of insights and realizations arrived at after the fact, and his reaction was more one of frustration at the time it occurred. Although it was never directly suggested to him, it should come as no surprise that Papoušek sometimes harbored suspicions that because he was an immigrant from a socialist country (and former member of the Communist Party), he could never hope for generous financial support and a "far-reaching career" at a German research institute (Papoušek Interview, July 16, 1998). Coupled with this was the feeling among some German colleagues that Hanuš tended to mistrust others, and he feared that someone might steal or misuse his data (although this latter phenomenon, of course, is not unknown in the United States either). This tendency, interestingly enough, was not reported by his earlier Prague colleagues. Was this perhaps because of his having to learn to live in a more open and free society after having lived most of his life amidst secrecy, suspicion, and political repression before coming to the West? Or was this due to the frequent mistrust and difficulties he encountered with the German authorities? On the one hand, he radiated so much optimism and trust in his research, and so much love for his subjects. Yet, on the other hand, there was a certain modesty and introversion that undoubtedly had to do with difficult life circumstances as well as personality (Ploog Interview, October 15, 1999).

The larger picture of Hanuš' years at the Max Planck Institute is one of an extremely innovative and industrious researcher whose work gradually attracted ever more attention. What also pleased the Institute's leadership was that, during times of tight budget, Hanuš' managed to attract extramural funding to support his scholarly work, and was often successful in obtaining funds from major donors such as the Deutsche Forschungsgemeinschaft, the Alexander von Humboldt Foundation, the Volkswagen Foundation, and the Stifterverband für die Deutsche Wissenschaft. These grants supported Mechthild's research as well as that of various visiting international scholars, and thus provided important additional resources for Papoušek's Developmental Psychobiology Unit. All this was done despite a notable lack of technical and clerical personnel, or students who could be trained to carry out behavioral coding, data entry, data analysis, and so forth. In part, the lack of trained students was due to the system of higher education in Germany; in Munich, for instance, little was being done at this time in areas of experimental developmental psychology, even at the Maximilian University with which Hanuš was affiliated. Opportunities to mentor promising young students from the university and to have them assist in his laboratory were relatively rare.

A SECOND RESEARCH CENTER IN BONN

In 1975, Papoušek received an unexpected invitation that initially held promise for overcoming some of the lack of support that he felt from the Institute in Munich. This came in the form of a major new developmental psychobiology research project that was to begin in Bonn, Germany. Although he initially refused on the grounds that he could not possibly fit this into his schedule, he was eventually convinced that this was a unique opportunity worth exploring. The new project in the capital city was to be quite prestigious, bringing together funds and scholarly interests from the various scientific foundations throughout Germany (e.g., Stifterverband, Deutsche Forschungsgemeinschaft, Volkswagen, and others). There was clearly the potential for this to be a very high-level research program focused on the development of children, with facilities including a preschool for employees' children and offices for representatives of the participating foundations (Papoušek Interview, July 16, 1998).

Part of the appeal of this offer was that Mechthild would be able to collaborate and receive a salary from the new research funds, and a secretary would also be provided (Papoušek Interview, July 16, 1998). This would enable them to continue living in Munich, with Hanuš commuting between the two cities on a biweekly basis. Mechthild and he had already collaborated on research while they were at Harvard, and her interests were being drawn increasingly in the direction of exploring parent–infant interactions in greater detail—particularly after the birth of their daughters in 1975 and 1977, which provided ample opportunities for observing infant development in the natural environment of their own home. With advanced training in psychiatry, Mechthild was well-prepared to contribute to careful observations of human behavior, and by then she had much experience translating and editing Hanuš' writings in this area.

For 5 years, Papoušek directed the research project in Bonn as well as his research unit at the Max Planck Institute for Psychiatry in Munich. One of the primary advantages seemed to be the opportunity to receive grant money from a number of different foundations to further support his efforts. The purpose of the Bonn research, however, was to investigate the development of older children, primarily from age 3 years, as these were the ages available on site in the nursery school for children of employees. Papoušek revealed, *"It was very interesting because I was allowed to establish a re-*

ally first-class laboratory with remote television facilities for documenting anything, everything at any time. I was able to sit, you know, in a sort of dispatching room and just push buttons and document what was going on here or there or in individual classes or at the playground" (Papoušek Interview, July 16, 1998).
Papoušek recognized this as an outstanding opportunity, but it was relatively short-lived. After only 5 years, the project had to be terminated because the child care facility in Bonn was closed, although he was fortunate to be able to move a major part of the equipment to his laboratory in Munich. This enabled him to expand and upgrade his research facility there, which was particularly important given the rapid advances in film and video techniques for documenting observations (Papoušek Interview, July 16, 1998). Equally advantageous was the fact that the German Research Foundation continued their support of Mechthild's work, enabling her to analyze preverbal vocal communication and to become more extensively involved in developing the theory of Intuitive Parenting with her husband. Nevertheless, for Hanuš, the closing of the Bonn center was perhaps more a relief than a disappointment, because he was being drawn more into an administrative role and left with less time for his actual research (the role he preferred).

EARLY GERMAN COLLEAGUES: ANGELA SCHOETZAU AND GUNHILD KESTERMANN

Although money for full-time research assistants and coders was scarce, in the mid-1970s Hanuš was able to hire a limited number of highly competent German researchers who contributed significantly to the work of his unit. One of these researchers was Angela Schoetzau, a pediatrician by training; another was Gunhild Kestermann, a graduate student who wrote her doctoral dissertation under Hanuš' guidance. Both women carried out innovative studies that provided empirical evidence to support the Papoušeks' emerging theory of Intuitive Parenting.
With support from the Deutsche Forschungsgemeinschaft, Schoetzau was able to observe visual distance regulation and facial expressions by mothers during face-to-face interactions with their newborns, as well as the effects of these behaviors on infants' visual attention. The robust findings indicated that mothers tend to keep a face-to-face distance of approximately 22.5 cm on average when interacting with their infants, and maternal facial expressions become exaggerated during these early social exchanges. As the Papoušeks (1997) noted, parents who are in close proximity to a sleeping infant typically observe from a distance of approximately 40–50 cm, or double that used when the infant opens its eyes. Because mothers are apparently unaware of modifying their behaviors in the presence of an alert infant, it was concluded that these are *intuitive* adjustments that are

well-tuned to the visual capacities of the human newborn (Schoetzau & H. Papoušek, 1977).

Somewhat later, Gunhild Kestermann designed and carried out a study at Papoušek's laboratory as partial fulfillment of her requirements for the doctoral degree (Kestermann, 1982). The goal of her dissertation research was to examine "paralinguistic patterns" of infant behavior that may serve as prelinguistic messages to the caregivers regarding infant state and readiness to interact. Kestermann prepared drawings of infants in which only the shape and position of the hands were varied in each picture (see Fig. 6.1). Subjects in her study were 7- to 8-year-old girls, childless women, pregnant women, and parents of 6-week-old infants. The experimental task required the respondent to indicate for each picture which of the following responses they would be most likely to choose: offer the baby a milk bottle, offer a toy, turn off the light to allow the infant to sleep, or "undecided."

In all of the participant groups, the infant's raised, half-opened hands elicited the offering of a toy; hands at the mouth were responded to by offering a bottle; and gradually decreasing muscle tone (lowering hands and arms) was greeted with turning off the lights as if in preparation for sleep. In follow-up interviews, however, the participants often indicated they had little awareness of any underlying reasons for their responses, and in fact they assumed that the critical detail to which they were responding must have been in the infant's *facial* expressions. In reality, the facial expressions did not vary from one picture stimulus to the next. It was also of interest that the amount of prior experience a respondent had with infants did play a role in this study. That is, women who already had infants responded more accurately than did girls or women without children, and experienced or involved fathers did as well as mothers.

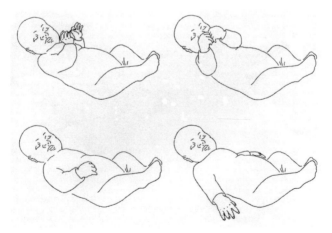

FIG. 6.1.   Stimuli used in Gunhild Kestermann's study of Intuitive Parenting.

COWORKERS, VOLUNTEERS, AND GUESTS
FROM ABROAD

Once he had established himself in Munich, Papoušek continued his penchant for networking and nurturing international contacts, which resulted in a steady stream of visitors to his laboratory and in longer term collaborations by a number of scholars both from within Germany and from other countries. As had been the case in Prague, international visitors began to appear frequently. Most stayed for relatively short visits, although a number stayed for longer periods of time. Not all of them can be listed here, but among them were four Americans: Marc Bornstein, Anne Fernald, Peter Mangione, and Lynne Koester.

Hanuš and Mechthild enjoyed the opportunity to meet and become friends with Marc Bornstein and his wife Helen during the summer 1971, while both couples were in Cambridge, Massachusetts. Bornstein, a student of William Kessen's at Yale, was spending the year conducting infancy research in Boston. This was the beginning of a lifelong friendship and a close personal relationship between the two families, later including the children on both sides. In addition to research and theoretical collaborations, the families traveled together in Europe on occasion, camping and hiking in the mountains and exposing their children to the natural wonders of the Alpine terrain. Hiking was a lifelong passion for Hanuš, whether in the Tatra Mountains of Czechoslovakia, the Alps of Bavaria, Austria, and Switzerland, or the Rocky Mountains of the American West.

Hanuš may have served as a valued and respected mentor for the younger Bornstein, but clearly the relationship was reciprocal: The Papoušeks also sought and valued Bornstein's advice, assistance, and support as he rose to become one of the most productive American scholars in the field of infancy research. Following the completion of his graduate studies in developmental psychology at Yale, Bornstein was awarded a postdoctoral stipend from the Max Planck Society, allowing him to move to Munich and collaborate with the Papoušeks. Their publications together ranged from discussions of the vocal environment of young infants, to the infant's responses to melodies in parental speech, and to further elaborations of didactic interactions between parents and infants.

Hanuš Papoušek's 1979 chapter, "From Adaptive Responses to Social Cognition: The Learning View of Development," was his first to appear in one of Bornstein's numerous edited volumes, in this case a book coedited with William Kessen. As indicated by the title, this chapter provided Papoušek's reflections on infant development based not only on his earlier learning studies, but also on his later more expansive approach encompassing cognition and caregiver–infant interactions that had begun during his time at Harvard. In 1985, a chapter coauthored with Bornstein on "the naturalistic vocal environment of young infants" appeared in a book edited by Tiffany Field and Nathan Fox, in which the Papoušeks for the first time discussed a fascination with infant-directed speech that was to become a more predominant theme in their research in the years to follow (H. Papoušek, M. Papoušek, & Bornstein, 1985). Another article coauthored with Bornstein expanded on a similar theme, this time detailing "infant responses to prototypical melodic contours in parental speech" (M. Papoušek, Bornstein, Nuzzo, H. Papoušek, & Symmes, 1990).

During a sabbatical at the National Institutes of Health in Bethesda, Maryland (1985–1986), the Papoušeks worked in the Laboratory of Comparative Ethology under the direction of primatologist Steve Suomi. This happened to coincide with the planned expansion of Suomi's unit in the direction of human development studies, and he was pleased to hear Papoušek's recommendation of Marc Bornstein for one of the new positions. In the late 1980s, Bornstein became the head of Child and Family Research at the National Institute of Child Health and Human Development in Bethesda, Maryland, with developmental psychologist Michael Lamb assuming a comparable position as head of the Section on Social and Emotional Development. Meanwhile, Hanuš and Mechthild collaborated with Suomi and with another NIH colleague, Charles Rahn, to prepare a chapter addressing possible connections between infants' preverbal communication and later attachment (Papoušek, Papoušek, Suomi, & Rahn, 1991).

The collaboration between Bornstein and the Papoušeks continued as each moved into different phases of their careers, including Hanuš' eventual retirement. In 1992, Papoušek and Bornstein coauthored a chapter applying the concepts of intuitive parenting to infants' verbal development; this appeared in the book entitled *Nonverbal Vocal Communication: Comparative and Developmental Perspectives*, which the Papoušeks themselves coedited with Uwe Jürgens. Further chapters by the Papoušeks expanded considerably on their intuitive parenting framework and appeared in Bornstein's *Handbook of Parenting* (1995).

It generally is not well known in the field of infancy studies that Anne Fernald, now a professor of developmental psychology at Stanford University and internationally recognized for her research on infant-directed speech, got her start in the field as a volunteer in Papoušek's Munich laboratory during the mid-1970s. Prior to graduate school, she and her family had relocated to Germany where her husband, a biologist, was working with Konrad Lorenz at another Max Planck Institute outside of Munich. They went with the intention of staying for a year, but the Fernald family ended up staying a full 8 years (Fernald Interview, May 11, 2000).

According to Anne, it was a wonderful coincidence that Papoušek was near enough to become her first mentor when she became interested in pursuing further studies in the field of human development. Previously, her introduction to the discipline had been primarily based on her own recent experience of having children (in Germany) and reflecting on that process from a very personal, family perspective:

> In another culture you have a heightened awareness of all kinds of knowledge that you just take for granted in your own culture. . . . I heard myself speaking in this strange way in Germany, and watched myself resorting to certain forms of folk knowledge. I thought I knew nothing about how to be a parent, and yet I came equipped with all sorts of assumptions . . . really theories of human development that the culture just imbues you with, quite unawares. . . . I was thinking about these things just in the process of being alive in the world and particularly in that wonderful context. I decided I'd like to explore psychology, whatever that was. I mean I really did not know. When I was at Swarthmore years before, it was rats and mazes and that didn't seem very appealing. (Fernald Interview, May 11, 2000)

Anne took the initiative to seek out Papoušek in Munich hoping to learn more about his research and about the field in general. By simply volunteering to assist him with manuscripts, editing, filing, or transporting equipment for his observations, she was able to become an active participant in the parent–infant research being carried out at the Max Planck Institute for Psychiatry. Naturally, for an inquisitive mind, this also quickly entailed a great deal of reading and one-on-one discussions with Hanuš about infancy research, methodology, and theoretical underpinnings. As Hanuš himself described the situation, "and so she came and just wanted to volunteer. And then she became interested, and you know she's a very active, initiative [sic] woman, and so it was predictable that she wouldn't just look over our shoulders for a long time, but that she would soon be eager to start something!" (Papoušek Interview, October 22, 1999).

By initially accompanying Hanuš on research visits to the Münchener Frauenklinik (Munich Women's Hospital), Fernald was able to observe firsthand the characteristics of mother–infant speech that she was beginning to find so intriguing. In this case, many mothers were "Guest Workers" from other countries, speaking languages such as Turkish, Serbo-Croatian, and Greek. Fernald noticed that when a mother would talk to her baby, perhaps trying to elicit the infant's attention, "They just started to sing in this wonderful way . . . and again, having it be in a language where meaning was just completely inaccessible to me. . . . I heard these wonderful 'calls' " (Fernald Interview, May 11, 2000).

Soon after, Fernald began her first efforts to investigate systematically the acoustical properties of maternal speech: She took along her own portable tape recorder and recorded the mothers' communications to their infants in the hospital. With the help of her husband, plus an oscilloscope from his own laboratory, a Polaroid camera to record waveforms, and graph paper for plotting them, Fernald was on her way to a fascinating study that led to an impressive career and many contributions to our understanding of infant-directed speech. And it was only after this experience that she decided on graduate studies in developmental psychology, which she undertook upon returning to the United States (Fernald Interview, May 11, 2000). Fernald became a well-established professor of developmental psychology at Stanford University.

Her first publication was based on data collected in Munich, analyzed with the assistance of a phonetician (Thomas Simon) at the Maximilian University (Fernald & Simon, 1984). Papoušek described this study as having three components or manipulations: mother engaging in dialogue with another adult, mother talking to a newborn baby, and mother responding to the following instructions:

> We have a special situation here: imagine your baby could go home, but you could not because of some obstetrical complications. Now your baby is back at home with the father, and the father comes and he says, "I don't know what to do with the baby—he seems to be frustrated and is missing you. Could you please talk into the [tape recorder] microphone as if the baby was here, so I can play it back to the baby? Perhaps it will make the baby happier." (Papoušek Interview, October 22, 1999)

Differences among the three situations were dramatic, showing a distinct disparity between adult–infant and adult–adult dialogues, and effects of the presence of the infant. Phoneticians began taking these ideas more seriously, and Fernald was encouraged to publish her findings (Papoušek Interview, October 22, 1999). According to Mechthild Papoušek, Fernald's work continues to be among the most important in the area of infant-directed speech and affective communication in the vocal mode. At the time when Fernald joined Papoušek's lab, Mechthild had begun working there as well and became interested in vocal communication, with a focus on infant vocalizations (Papoušek Interview, October 22, 1999). Although their research interests overlapped considerably, Fernald was soon to return to the United States, where she began her graduate studies in developmental psychology. The research she had undertaken in Munich was published in *Developmental Psychology*, and for a period of time both she and Mechthild Papoušek examined various aspects of infant-directed speech from laboratories on separate continents. Eventually, their research paths crossed again, when Fernald initiated a cross-cultural study that the Papoušeks were able to facilitate in Munich (Fernald, Taeschner, Dunn, M. Papoušek, DeBoysson-Bardis, & Fukui, 1989). In describing her time in Munich, Fernald referred to an era of intellectual excitement about infancy research, and an "entrepreneurial zeal" evident particularly among American scientists (Fernald Interview, May 11, 2000).

Peter Mangione, a graduate student working with Michael Chandler at the University of Rochester, New York, had taken a course there from Papoušek's good friend Arnold Sameroff. As a result of this connection, Mangione was able to work first with Papoušek at the Science Research Center in Bonn, just before Hanuš discontinued his involvement there. In the early 1980s, Mangione moved to the Max Planck Institute for Psychiatry in Munich where he helped develop an elaborate "round-robin" technique for observing differences in behaviors of mothers with their own infants as well as with unknown infants of the same age. For each observation session, three unfamiliar mother–infant dyads (e.g., Family A, B, and C, all with 3-month-old infants) were scheduled together. After videotaping Mother A with Baby A, Mangione and the research team would then videotape Mother A with Baby B and with Baby C; next, Mother B would be observed with her own Baby B and then with Baby A and Baby C, and so on. The goal was to examine which maternal behaviors seem to be stable regardless of behavioral attributes and signals from the infant, and which ones appear to be more easily modified in response to each infant's individual characteristics. Unfortunately, health and family concerns forced Mangione to return to the United States earlier than expected, so that data from this intriguing study were never fully analyzed or reported. (See H. Papoušek & M. Papoušek, 1987, for further methodological details.)

Of the other American visitors, the one to spend the longest period of time working with Hanuš in Munich was Lynne Koester, co-author of this book. Lynne first began working with Hanuš and Mechthild in 1983, when she began a postdoctoral fellowship supported by the Alexander von Humboldt Foundation in Bonn. After an extension of this fellowship, Hanuš arranged for Lynne to continue working in his laboratory with funding by the Max Planck Society until 1987. After her return to the United States, she and the Papoušeks remained in close contact and collaborated on several research projects until Hanuš' death in 2000.

Lynne began teaching child development in the late 1970s at the University of North Carolina–Greensboro, where students were increasingly eager to learn more about infancy—an exciting new area of developmental studies at the time. No one else in that institution's department of child development and family relations was prepared for or interested in offering courses with a focus specifically on infancy research. As was true of many in the profession at that time, Lynne's own doctoral training had little to do with children under age 6; the logical recourse was to apprentice with a "master" in this field. Hanuš agreed to provide the methodological and theoretical training she needed.

Lynne's first year at the Max Planck Institute was primarily taken up with reading everything she could find about the relatively new theory of Intuitive Parenting, as well as expanding her knowledge of infancy research in general. She was also gradually able to become involved with a new aspect of Hanuš' research: microanalytic coding. This brought in the first computer for the Papoušek laboratory, which was shared by the entire research group. The team consisted primarily of students from the Maximilian University (e.g., Monika Haekel, who published studies of father–infant interactions with the Papoušeks), an occasional American student (e.g., Betty Harris, who coauthored publications with the Papoušeks on novelty and play in infancy; M. Papoušek, H. Papoušek, & Harris, 1987), as well as assistants for Mechthild's research. Because there were never more than 2–3 rooms available for the research assistants to share, it was fortunate that many of these students were only at the Institute on a part-time basis.

In terms of collaborative research, Lynne's early work with the Papoušeks involved microanalyses of rhythmic patterns of maternal–infant interactions, examining these across various sensory modalities (i.e., tactile, visual, kinesthetic, etc.). As her stay in Munich continued, Lynne, Hanuš, and Mechthild also coauthored publications on topics such as the role and dynamics of emotional expressiveness in parent–infant communication, and implications of a psychobiological approach to infancy on concepts inherent in the Intuitive Parenting framework. Moreover, in 1985–1986, when the Papoušek family spent the year in the United States at the National Institutes of Health (NIH), Lynne was left to oversee the running of Hanuš' laboratory. At the invitation of Steve Suomi, Hanuš and Mechthild were both able to participate in research at the NIH's Laboratory of Comparative Ethology, where they gathered data on parenting and vocalization patterns of Chinese and American mother–infant dyads. The results of studies at the NIH were published in the journals *Psycholinguistics* and *Infant Behavior and Development* in 1991. While the Papoušeks were away, Lynne worked on her own research and hosted a number of international visitors eager to see Hanuš' lab.

Lynne also had the opportunity to make several trips to Czechoslovakia and become acquainted with a few of Hanuš' former colleagues in Prague. These visits occurred during the mid-1980s when divisions between Eastern and Western European countries were still very evident, and Papoušek himself had not been able to travel back to his homeland since his departure in 1970. Whenever Lynne visited Prague, Hanuš loaded her down with reprints, current manuscripts, and personal gifts for her to take to his former colleagues. Although Lynne knew she was at a certain risk in bringing these materials, they helped to heighten the warmth and enthusiasm with which she was received. These trips offered her invaluable insights into Hanuš' life in Czechoslovakia before his escape to the West.

During the first trip in 1984, signs of "glasnost" and "perestroika" were difficult to discern in Czechoslovakia, where tight governmental controls affected both personal and professional lives on a daily basis. One result was that trips were more complicated to arrange than one might normally expect. First, in order to simply visit the Institute for the Care of Mother and Child, it was necessary to obtain prior written approval from the Ministry of Health. In correspondence requesting to meet with the Institute's researchers, any affiliation with Hanuš had to be disguised by avoiding reference to him or mention of their work together in Munich. Moreover, after arriving in Prague, Lynne found that most of Papoušek's former associates preferred not to talk in their offices because many of the workplaces were "bugged." Despite these inconveniences, however, each of these individuals went to great lengths to welcome visitors from abroad, and made it clear how much admiration and affection they still had for Hanuš Papoušek.

In 1984, but also during subsequent visits in 1985 and 1986, Lynne came to a better understanding of what happens when an authoritarian government stifles the free flow of scientific information. After his defection, Czech officials had taken steps to make sure that Hanuš' name was deleted or blackened out from all publications. It was evident, however, that as much as these individuals seemed incredibly "hungry" for updates about his personal life and most recent research, they were also amazingly knowledgeable, often in minute detail, about those few publications by Papoušek that they had surreptitiously been able to read. Indeed, the government's suppression of Papoušek's publications worked in the opposite way that it was intended; they were read even more closely than might otherwise have been the case. Although official restrictions were still in place, all of Papoušek's former friends and colleagues were extremely eager to hear accounts and gain access to his more recent research findings, and to keep abreast of general research developments in the West.

When the Koesters returned to the United States in 1988, Lynne's training in microanalytic coding of mother–infant behaviors led to a research position at Gallaudet University. There she joined a team headed by Kathryn Meadow-Orlans, investigating the early socioemotional, cognitive, and communicative development of deaf and hearing infants. The collaboration with Hanuš and Mechthild continued at Gallaudet University, the world's only liberal arts university for deaf students, where Lynne had the unique opportunity to examine Intuitive Parenting behaviors in relation to a population of infants and parents that had not been studied from this perspective before. At Gallaudet, Lynne used the Intuitive Parenting approach to explain some of the ways in which parents seem to compensate for a child's hearing loss by expanding the usual repertoire of interactive behaviors. Further funding from the Alexander von Humboldt Foundation facilitated these efforts by providing travel money and payment for graduate student assistants to occasionally spend time working with Hanuš in Munich, and for Hanuš to visit the United States. This resulted in a number of publications, including one applying Intuitive Parenting to interactions with deaf infants (e.g., Koester, 1992, 1994; Koester, H. Papoušek, & Smith-Gray, 2000; and Meadow-Orlans, Spencer, & Koester, 2004), which reflect these later years of sharing data and ideas.

During her years of collaboration with Hanuš, Lynne came to appreciate the qualities that many of Hanuš' colleagues, both before and after his departure from Prague, found so inspirational in him. One of her lasting and memorable impressions of him was based on an experience from the year Hanuš and Mechthild were in Washington, DC, when the Koesters' younger son was hospitalized in Salzburg, Austria, with meningitis. In need of advice and reassurance from a pediatrician they knew and trusted, the family received telephone inquiries from Hanuš about the youngster's illness. Several days later, they received a 60-minute audiotape with the calmness, authority, and reassuring tone that must have endeared Hanuš to parents for years. In a calm, gentle manner, Hanuš carefully explained the antecedents and potential consequences of meningitis with much more depth and clarity than had been provided by their son's attending physicians. Hanuš not only covered the medical issues related to meningitis, but he also had the foresight to discuss the implications of returning a child to kindergarten soon after such an illness. He advised that overstimulation was to be avoided if at all possible and helped the parents to anticipate and plan for the weeks following their son's hospitalization. Again, none of the attending medical professionals had indicated any concern about such matters once the immediate medical crisis was over. This single incident often reminded Lynne that Hanuš was an extraordinarily gifted pediatrician, who possessed both an enormous depth of medical knowledge, as well as true psychological sensitivity and a genuine sense of human compassion.

Other international visitors came to the Papoušek lab in Munich, usually on a short-term basis: Dov and Malca Aleksandrowicz, Judith Auerbach, and Rivka Nowick, all from Israel; Kim Bard, Anthony DeCasper, Carol Erting, Barry McLaughlin, Barbara Rogoff, Steve Suomi, and Peter Wolff from the United States; Heinz Prechtl from the Netherlands; and many others. In addition, Charles Rahn spent time working with the Papoušeks both in Munich and at NIH. It was not unusual to hear visitors express their surprise at the modesty of Papoušek's research facility. The Max Planck Institutes are known around the world as sites of rigorous, high quality research; certainly Papoušek's productivity in terms of publications in English, and the amount of data being generated in his lab led one to expect a somewhat more elaborate arrangement than was actually the case.

PAPOUŠEK AND GERMAN DEVELOPMENTAL PSYCHOLOGY

After moving to Munich, Papoušek's work gained slow but increasing recognition within the small scientific community of German developmental psychologists. Hellgard Rauh, now at the University of Potsdam, was among the earliest scholars to acknowledge Papoušek's work and actively facilitate this process.

Rauh was surprised to find out that Papoušek was no longer in the United States. She took it upon herself to contact Papoušek in the mid-1970s and to encourage him to have more contact with other German psychologists and to help train infancy researchers and build up the field of development psychology at German universities. It was on this occasion that Papoušek confided in her that he did not feel particularly well accepted in German scientific circles, citing the lingering historical skepticism of the German people toward the Czechs. Rauh's response to this at the time was incredulous: "That *can't* be true. It may be true with the pediatricians, but for us psychologists, developmental psychologists, you are an important person. And I would like you to be personally known to young scholars and to publish in our journals. Don't feel alienated only because pediatricians won't accept you. For us psychologists you are an important person!" (Rauh Interview, April 15, 2000). To be sure, later there was growing interest, acceptance, and admiration among pediatricians and other professionals working with infants and parents.

Perhaps Papoušek's hesitancy was also a result of comparing the modesty of his situation and lack of time in Munich with the opportunities he had left behind both in Prague and at Harvard. In addition, there were still repercussions following his defection from the neighboring ČSSR, where his name had been removed from all publications. And, as Rauh noted, it could also be that he felt particularly alienated from the pediatric community in Germany, whose members tended to disregard those doing psychological research as "nonscientific" and altogether too subjective (Rauh Interview, April 15, 2000). It is worth noting that Papoušek had simply not grown up with a pediatric or psychological peer group in Germany, and that he was quite a bit older than the new cohort of developmental psychologists there.

In the mid-1970s, Rauh was part of a group of German developmentalists who recognized the need for a more organized network or structure for the discipline within their country; joining her in initiating this effort were Klaus and Karin Grossmann, Heidi Keller, Leo Montada, and others. One of the goals was to interest more students and young behavioral scientists in joining the field, by exposing them to exciting new ideas and research already being done in Germany at the time. Hellgard Rauh was a primary initiator of a series of special German summer school conferences in developmental psychology, begun in the late 1970s with the support of the Volkswagen Foundation. At the first of these conferences, held in Trier, Rauh accepted the task of organizing a subgroup on early child development. She later recalled having to work hard to convince Papoušek to participate, but feeling pleased that one of the outcomes was a book entitled *Learning in the First Year of Life*, which included a chapter coauthored by Hanuš and Mechthild (Rauh Interview, April 15, 2000). Beyond the German network, international participants in that first German conference on early development included such notables as Jerome Kagan, Michael Lewis, and Ina Uzgiris. Obviously, this was a group with well-established reputations similar to Papoušek's own, and represented an exciting opportunity for the German developmentalists to become more closely connected with scholars both from within their own country and from abroad.

Another conference, held in Berlin in January 1986, also was revealing of Hanuš' relationship with Germany and West German psychology. This was a conference organized by Rauh and H.-C. Steinhausen in conjunction with an international training session for the administration of Brazelton's Neonatal Behavioral Assessment Scale. Although it again took some convincing to recruit Papoušek's participation, part of the appeal was likely the presence of other pediatricians and scholars from a variety of different countries; among the participants were Tom Bower, T. Berry Brazelton, Carol Erting, Rudolf Shaffer, Ed Tronick, and others. Rauh recalled that after Hanuš had overcome his initial hesitation to attend, a poignant incident occurred when members of the conference group went to see the Berlin Wall:

> He [Hanuš] was *extremely* reluctant to come close to the Wall. In front of the Reichstag there was a lawn and there were some sculptures, so I stayed with him there, some 100–150 meters away from the Wall. He said it was the first time since he had left (the Eastern Bloc) that he was so close, and there was some anxiety and aggression coming up in him, and he didn't *dare* to come closer. So we walked by all of these sculptures and he talked about his experiences back in Prague. (Rauh Interview, April 15, 2000)

Toward the end of his career, in the mid-1980s, Papoušek would in fact be honored with the prestigious Dr. Heinrich Hoffmann Medal from the German Society of Child and Adolescent Psychiatry, in recognition of his outstanding contributions to science. However, Papoušek himself never felt fully connected with or integrated into the German developmental psychology community. Rauh and others continued their efforts nonetheless, and felt that toward the end he was actually quite appreciative of their show of support. The theory of Intuitive Parenting began to be found more frequently in German developmental textbooks, where Papoušek was represented as an important figure in furthering the knowledge of early development, preverbal communication, language acquisition, musical development, early play, and parenting (Rauh Interview, April 15, 2000). In Germany, unlike in the United States, the Papoušeks became associated primarily with the theoretical framework and research they developed in Munich. This is easily understood in light of less overall interest and emphasis on experimental approaches to early development in Germany at the time—a situation that has recently begun to change. Hellgard Rauh described this phenomenon well:

In America, experimental research on a natural scientific basis has the highest value and comes closest to the behaviorist idea, or paradigm. And his early research is in many respects highly behavioristic with an ethological touch. But basically behavioristic, or it can be put in that paradigm and works there quite well. . . . So I think that is closest to their idea of proper research. Whereas the interactional research is kind of soft research, much more difficult to register and to analyze in a way that is beyond criticism. I suppose that his techniques that he used here in these interactional paradigms will be recognized only after some time on the scientific basis. In terms of applied research, it has been of immense importance and impact, and probably opened the door for those who had no direct contact with infant research. (Rauh Interview, April 15, 2000)

In the long run, Papoušek earned the respect of German professionals in a variety of disciplines: pediatrics, child psychiatry, psychology, special education, and developmental rehabilitation. Nevertheless, he often felt isolated there due to the scarcity of other infancy researchers.

The transition from Prague and Harvard to Munich was prolonged and sometimes difficult for Papoušek, but also brought with it the joys of renewed family life and the satisfaction of living in circumstances that allowed him much greater freedom and possibilities for scholarly exchanges. Although not always happy with the Institute's support, intellectually and scientifically, his interests expanded as well. The next chapter provides an overview and more detail about the emergence of the new conceptual framework which the Papoušeks developed together: Intuitive Parenting.

Chapter 7

Including the Parent in the Dyad: Developing a Theory of Intuitive Parenting

During his years at the Max Planck Institute, the focus of Hanuš Papoušek's attention turned to research on processes of parent–infant interaction and the development of a theory of Intuitive Parenting, building on his previous emphasis on infant behaviors and mental processes. Developed in close collaboration with his wife Mechthild, the documentation and elaboration of this theory became a lasting accomplishment of Papoušek's scientific career. This chapter explores the major concepts of their Intuitive Parenting theory, its main assumptions and components, and some of the empirical studies carried out to support these ideas. Chapter 8 explores the various ways in which these concepts led to practical applications in more recent years.

In Bornstein's *Handbook of Parenting, Volume 2* (1995), the Papoušeks provided the following overview of the Intuitive Caregiving/Parenting concept:

> The parent (and the caregiver in general) is biologically predisposed as the more experienced partner to lead the infant toward a fundamental socio-cultural integration and, for this purpose, toward the acquisition of a proper cultural communication. The dialogic character of this lead is evident in respect to intrinsic motivations in infants, on the one hand, and to their developmental constraints in behavioral regulation, on the other. The dosage and complexity of didactic interventions are adjusted, according to feedback cues in infant behaviors. Efforts for eliciting and maintaining infant communication are obvious. . . . Intuitive caregiving aims not only at hygienic, autonomic, and emotional needs of infants, but also at the needs to be together with someone, to share experience, to acquire adequate means of communication, and to create novel symbols. (p. 132)

As this overview indicates, the Papoušeks gradually came to view the notion of Intuitive Caregiving/Parenting as a useful integrative concept for understanding many of the processes that underlie interactions between parents and infants. The central idea is that parents and infants have biologically "predisposed" behavioral tendencies that play a part in the communicative process involving both partners of the parent–infant dyad, with the parent as the senior or more experienced leader. Caregiving behaviors serve important communicative, motivational, and emotional functions in support of the early development of an immature infant, and may have been selected over time to optimize developmental outcomes for the human species in general.

ROOTS OF A THEORY: SOURCES AND INFLUENCES

The idea that there are such things as Intuitive Parenting behaviors, and that these are in need of scientific study, had a number of sources and influences. Some sources can be traced to knowledge and insights that Papoušek gained at the Institute for the Care of Mother and Child in Prague while working as a pediatrician and researcher in a lying-in hospital. Others can be found in his experiences while conducting observational studies in a more experimental setting at the Center for Cognitive Studies at Harvard. Equally important, however, was a new focus of attention in the emerging field of infancy studies on the reciprocal nature of communicative processes involving both parents and infants. Each of these factors, together with the development of new observational methods and insights gained in the course of carrying out their Munich investigations, played a role in the development of the Papoušeks' concepts.

Early Experiences and General Insights

Early indications that it might be useful for Papoušek to begin looking at the role of parents go back at least to the 1960s. Although the primary focus of his Prague research was on the infants themselves and their learning capacities, certain practical considerations sometimes arose that prompted him to seek advice from the infant's parents during the course of conducting an observation. In one such case, he was confronted with the problem of how to interrupt an infant's sucking pattern without causing immediate distress that would necessitate the termination of a conditioning session. Papoušek spoke to the mothers to find out if this was ever a problem for them, or if they were simply able to interrupt a nursing baby without negative repercussions. Interestingly, the mothers were only partially able to report back to him about their own behaviors and interventions with their babies. Clearly, they seemed to be doing much more than they were aware of, as illustrated by the following anecdote:

> We asked the mother whether she would mind, and what she would think, whether we could interrupt the feeding a couple of times. And she had no idea. And so she says, "wait and I'll try." And then she comes the next day and says "Oh, you can do it easily. I interrupted a couple of times, and with no difficulty." So we take the baby to the laboratory, and interrupt for the first time and "waaaah"—the baby is crying, you know! So you go back to the mother and ask how to do it—we tried it and it didn't function. And so she was looking at us and said "Well that really surprises me, you know, that he objects and he didn't object when I did it." So she then said, "Well, I'll try again, and I don't know what I can tell you, but I'll try to find out." And the next day then she comes and tells you that she has no idea. But again, she could interrupt feeding with no difficulty. So you go, and you *observe*. And we found out that she was obviously using a rule. That means, when there is a pause in sucking, she interrupts. She *never* does it as long as the baby is sucking firmly. And it was not easy for me to notice, you know! But it was interesting to see how little she knew about it, and how unable she was to detect the rule she was using. So you know, I was sort of pre-primed in Prague to do the observations, but then when I was filming the families (in Munich), I noticed more and more of it. And it occurred to me that there is a system in it. And that's a very interesting system. Because most of those interventions had to do with the development of communication, so we then studied intuitive parenting. (Papoušek Interview, July 15–16, 1998)

Another key experience occurred when Papoušek became interested in infant cognition at the Center for Cognitive Studies at Harvard and engaged in efforts to examine the infant's ability to imitate and follow parental affective models responding to an unfamiliar object or toy. As reported in chapter 5, the results were startling: When the models and their reactions were reversed, it appeared that parents who exhibited pleasure or approach first were then able to transform the infant's behavior (during the next exposure) into fear almost immediately. By contrast, those who modeled fear first and then pleasure had a much more difficult time "convincing" the baby to take a more positive approach to the strange toy (Papoušek, unpublished manuscript). The role of parental behaviors in the developing infant's emotional regulation therefore became a focus of concern for his future studies.

Beyond these specific incidents, a number of other insights before coming to Munich influenced the development of the Papoušeks' thinking as well. One of these was the general process for conducting new research that Papoušek had found useful in Prague when he and his colleagues first embarked on the study of infants. Referring to his first studies, he liked to point out that the state of knowledge about infant behaviors at the time was so minimal that scientists found it necessary first to elucidate the most fundamental forms of early human learning. What proved invaluable was that he and his colleagues were able to bring in the different perspectives of pediatricians, developmental psychologists, and biologists who were able to help him analyze various aspects of the infant's mental development and physical state. An interdisciplinary team could become aware of the inadequacies in each of their individual approaches, and exchange views across boundaries of knowledge in an effort to help bridge gaps.

The Papoušeks followed this same approach in beginning the study of the mental and physical aspects of caregiving and parenting, engaging in ongoing dialogues and exchange of ideas with a wide range of experts—including biologists, physiologists, psychologists, psychiatrists, parent educators, social workers, and physical therapists. Also playing a role was the influence on Hanuš Papoušek of the more dialectically oriented intellectual traditions of Central Europe, which he felt facilitated the search for commonalities and helped avoid rigidly dichotomous views such as those typically separating physicians from psychologists, or biologists from sociologists and linguists. These interdisciplinary and dialectical approaches, together with writings of a general systems theorist such as von Bertalanffy (1968), helped to inform the Papoušeks' analyses of the observations that laid the foundation for looking at emotional and communicative cues in infants and parents (H. Papoušek & M. Papoušek, 1987). Although the term *dialectical* is not commonly found in North American psychological literature (perhaps due to its association with Marx's theory of *dialectical materialism*), its influence can be seen in more contemporary *transactional* approaches to parent–child interactions as articulated by Sameroff (e.g., Sameroff & Fiese, 1990).

Other influences derived from the fact that the Institute for the Care of Mother and Child was essentially a "lying-in unit" where infants and mothers remained for as long as 6 months postpartum. This gave the professional team of caregivers an opportunity to become acutely aware of infant signals and infant needs, not just nutritional, health, and emotional needs, and led to an understanding that infants expressed needs to acquire and integrate experience (i.e., cognitive needs), as well as to engage in interactions with other human beings (i.e., social and communicative needs). In addition, the researchers began to be aware that vocalizations, facial displays, and hand gestures were being used systematically by the infants as social and communicative signals that influenced caregiving responses—all of which became invaluable background knowledge for commencing to observe either the parent alone, or both the parent and infant interacting at the same time (H. Papoušek & M. Papoušek, 1978).

Most importantly for the development of a theory of parenting, it had also become evident in Prague that caregivers were capable of reading sufficient information regarding infant needs from physical behaviors so as to predict discomfort in the infant and to respond appropriately even before the infant began crying. Other nondistress behaviors by the infant often appeared to be interpreted by parents or caregivers as indications of cognitive processing, problem solving, or signs that the infant already understood what the parent was saying. It should be remembered that this revelation came at a time (i.e., during the 1950s) when scientific knowledge of the cognitive capacities of young infants was still minimal. From these observations, Papoušek determined that caregivers can learn how to influence favorably the infants' behavioral/emotional states, prevent risks of deprivation (particularly in group-care settings), and ensure that the infant is able to thrive on a daily basis—knowledge that would also prove to be important for parents.

Another aspect of the Prague research was that fathers could only visit their infants intermittently, and mothers were sometimes available only part of the time, due to work or study schedules. Therefore, nurses and male coworkers from the research team were specially trained to serve as "substitute parents." Many pilot studies of behavioral regulation in infants were undertaken that included detailed analyses of feedback cues indicating the effectiveness of caregiving strategies. However, adequate child-rearing information regarding the most relevant features of parental behaviors, particularly with infants, was virtually impossible to find.

His work in Prague had sensitized Papoušek to the subtleties of communication between caregivers and preverbal infants. In Munich this led to a search for comparable learning situations in more naturalistic home environments, and ultimately to the realization that opportunities for infant learning are found most strikingly in the social environment and during exchanges with caregivers.

New Technologies

In the late 1960s and early 1970s, the introduction of new technologies became an important factor in the way it changed the observational methods of researchers in developmental psychology. Like most developmentalists, infancy researchers were heavily reliant on observational methods, but a number of new technologies made it possible for observations of early behavioral processes to become increasingly objective and quantifiable as compared to the previous maternal self-report methods. In particular, the introduction of video-recording techniques gradually allowed more microscopic examinations of parent–infant interactions, making it possible to reveal previously undetected patterns of social interchanges during the first year of life. As data began replacing impressions and speculations, collaboration with biologists and neuroscientists was also enhanced. In Osofky's *Handbook of Infant Development* (1987), the Papoušek's chapter discussed these technological and interdisciplinary advances in some detail:

The introduction of modern technology, making possible the unobtrusive audiovisual documentation of observed events, has brought about significant consequences. It has substantially improved behavioral analyses in several scientific disciplines. It has also contributed to better cooperation among disciplines since it has made it possible to look at the observed events again and again for additional analyses and to exchange documentation with related disciplines. The Center for Cognitive Studies at Harvard University, directed by Jerome Bruner until 1972, was an outstanding example of a breeding site for infancy research where such an interchange among disciplines flourished. Not only did Bruner point out that infancy studies might lead to solutions of some general problems in psychology, he also brought together developmentalists from zoology, anthropology, psychology, linguistics, pediatrics, and other disciplines, and provided all the modern tools for effective sharing of experience and theories. (H. Papoušek & M. Papoušek, 1987, pp. 677–678)

In this regard, it should be noted that Papoušek personally was a strong proponent of new technology throughout his life. In Prague, he had the reputation of being "a progressive," acquiring or constructing new lab equipment whenever possible. He continued this tradition in Munich, where he was among the first behavioral researchers in Germany to introduce videotaping, split-screen devices, and frame-by-frame analysis, thus greatly enhancing his capability to conduct fine-grained microanalyses of parent–infant interactions.

With the help of these advances, the Papoušeks were able to challenge traditional notions that the human infant's prolonged inability to walk or talk implies total incompetence, or "blooming, buzzing confusion," as once characterized by James (1890). In actuality, most human newborns cope successfully with the dramatic transition from a protective *intra*uterine environment to an *extra*uterine one in which the protection must come primarily from the social (i.e., caregiving) world. This transition involves the infant's synchronization of day–night cycles, regulation of hunger and affective responses, and adaptation of their immune systems to new environmental exposures; these processes barely leave enough waking time for engagement in social interactions during the first one or two postpartum months. The Papoušeks knew that the ability of caregivers to perceive and interpret cues in the neonate's behavior is of utmost importance during this time, regardless of whether or not the newborn is responding with intentionality. Caregivers typically go to great efforts to establish a dialogue, and tend to interpret even the most subtle nonvocal aspects of the infant's behavior as communicative feedback (H. Papoušek & M. Papoušek, 1987).

For example, in their early studies together, the Papoušeks saw that parents are both motivated and predisposed to interpret infant vocal utterances, facial and gestural displays, and changes in general motility or muscle tone as indicators of infant communication. However, as indicated previously, these aspects of parental competence remained largely unexplored prior to the introduction of audiovisual recording systems and computer-aided voice analyses. Because such behaviors escape conscious awareness by caregivers (H. Papoušek & M. Papoušek, 1978, 1987), they had not been previously revealed through the questionnaires or interviews that dominated earlier research on parenting behaviors.

Also important for their studies was an awareness of the optimal conditions required for demonstrating infant learning: an alert waking state in the infant, a simple structuring of stimuli and learning trials, frequent repetitions, gradual ordering of the learning tasks in terms of complexity, the use of adequate rewards, and sensitivity to feedback from the infant indicating thresholds of tolerance (H. Papoušek & M. Papoušek, 1987, 1989). In their early analyses of parental behavior, the Papoušeks realized that during interactions with infants, parents unknowingly apply these same principles, particularly during interchanges that foster the infant's integrative and communicative capacities. Furthermore, this repertoire of caregiving behaviors was evident not only in mothers, but appeared to be universal across gender, age, and culture (H. Papoušek & M. Papoušek, 1987).

To explore another aspect of Intuitive Parenting, recall the Prague studies demonstrating the infant capacity to detect and conceptualize contingency rules between their own behavior and environmental consequences. The experimenter would introduce a situation in which a 4-month-old turned on an attractive visual display through three consecutive headturns to the left in one case, or four consecutive headturns to the right in another (H. Papoušek & Bernstein, 1969). With the use of polygraph records, the researchers demonstrated that infants not only solve the problems, but also exhibit interesting temporal and affective patterns along the way. That is, as the learning of goal-directed movements increases over the first few months, facial displays during problem-solving experiences become even more expressive (H. Papoušek, 1967b). During interactions, caregivers can therefore more easily read feedback cues in facial expressions and hand gestures, indicating the extent to which the infant has processed the experience. The caregivers' own comments during this time indicate that they have begun to view the infant as a competent social partner. Infants who were previously (i.e., shortly after the birth) imitating only oral activities and facial expressions, now start imitating vocal sounds as well. As a result, interactions between caregivers and infants increasingly acquire a reciprocal character (Papoušek, 1995).

Developments in the Field

Coinciding with the Papoušeks' work, the field of infancy research was blossoming. It became clear that for the first few months after birth, the infant invests a great deal of energy into the organization and coordination of central nervous system functions, basic perceptual and cognitive operations, and the process of becoming a participating partner in social relationships. To Hanuš and Mechthild Papoušek, it was also becoming particularly clear that throughout this early period, the infant requires carefully attuned support, protection, stimulation, and reinforcement from caregivers in order to nurture emerging capabilities. Many investigative efforts (including his own in Prague) had elucidated the competencies and inherent adaptiveness of the human *infant*, whereas few had examined how parents, caregivers, or the social environment support and enhance these qualities in newborns. By accumulating evidence in support of the Intuitive Parenting concept, the Papoušeks attempted to provide both empirical evidence and a theoretical framework for exploring and interpreting early social interactions from a new perspective.

By the late 1970s, other researchers had established that the human newborn possesses integrative and communicative competencies early in ontogeny, such as those skills that predispose the infant to recognize and respond to social stimuli (e.g., the human voice, the human face, etc.) (DeCasper & Fifer, 1980; Fagan, 1979; Schaffer, 1979). In terms of optimizing the chances for survival of a so-called helpless being, these are highly adaptive behaviors that help to establish the newborn as a reciprocating member of a social group. But the Papoušeks also recognized the importance of understanding the characteristics of the ecological support system that allow these competencies to emerge and blossom, rather than to disappear or become nonfunctional like many of the early reflexes in humans. Thus, these nonconscious parental behaviors, highly adapted to serve the best interests of the infant, became the focus of the model of Intuitive Parenting (Koester, H. Papoušek, & M. Papoušek, 1987; H. Papoušek & M. Papoušek, 1979, 1982a, 1987).

Viewing the parent–infant dyad as prototypical of a teacher–learner partnership, the Papoušeks observed one particularly striking feature contributing to its uniqueness: Its inherent heterogeneity is even more extreme than usual due to the wider discrepancy in levels of maturity, communication, and experience of the dyad's two members. Obviously, the newborn has no prior experience of communicating with another human being. The question then became, how does a "naive" parent accomplish the task of establishing an effective means of communicating with one so inexperienced as the newborn child?

A Vygotskian approach to the interrelations between social and cognitive functioning (as elaborated in Rogoff & Wertsch, 1984) emphasizes that the child brings to an interaction skills that are in the process of developing, plus interests in exploration and gaining knowledge, and then participates with the adult partner in setting the direction and pace of the interaction. The adult takes responsibility for modifying the task, through simplification, redundancy, and so forth, to make it more manageable for the child's emerging competency level. Thus, whereas parents of infants may have no *conscious* curriculum in the sense of the instructional scripts and goals that a teacher has in mind for a larger group, they frequently function in similar ways by providing this early support for the infant's developmental progress.

By the late 1970s, other research teams (e.g., Fogel, 1977; Stern, Beebe, Jaffe, & Bennett, 1977; Stern & Gibbon, 1979) were also demonstrating that parents do, in fact, respond to the infant's limited repertoire by adjusting their own levels of communication and methods of eliciting and maintaining attention, in much the same ways in which experimenters had optimized their conditions to demonstrate infant learning (H. Papoušek & M. Papoušek, 1982a). For example, the adult modulates the complexity of communicative and didactic strategies according to the development of the infant's capacities, so that the newly emerging skills receive the most supportive attention.

THEORETICAL AND METHODOLOGICAL CONCERNS

Throughout his years in Munich, Hanuš Papoušek was keenly aware of the theoretical disagreements that often arose between experimental psychologists and ethologists, or even between American and European traditions in terms of preferences for laboratory experiments over field observations. He had a unique understanding and appreciation of the value of each. Experimental laboratory analyses had previously allowed him to concentrate on specific aspects of complex phenomena related to infant learning; he used these methods to develop techniques for measuring well-defined events under carefully controlled conditions. Conversely, he was also drawn to naturalistic observations—perhaps influenced here by his perspective as a pediatrician—and saw that they could also reveal very relevant aspects of spontaneous behavior in more anecdotal forms, and yet contribute in important ways to our understanding of developmental processes. His first few years in Munich turned out to be a transitional opportunity during which he observed naturalistic parent–infant interactions in advance of designing ways of systematizing these for use in his laboratory-based observations. Papoušek became convinced of the advantages of combining these two approaches in the search for greater understanding of human infancy and parental support. This theme can be followed throughout his professional life, from his dual role in Prague as pediatrician and researcher, to filming at the San Diego Zoo (during a sabbatical at NIH) in search of Intuitive Parenting behaviors in nonhuman primates.

Once established in their Munich laboratory, the Papoušeks were able to use filmed observations of parent–infant interactions to demonstrate that some parental behaviors occur with a high degree of regularity, and are interpretable as ways of sharing knowledge, conveying information about the environment, or in other ways enhancing both learning and cognition in infants. However, they also noticed that parents are not consciously aware of these behaviors, typically cannot recall or report them when questioned immediately afterward, cannot predict how they would solve certain learning situations again, and are in many cases unaware of the corresponding level of competence of their infants (Koester et al., 1987; H. Papoušek & M. Papoušek, 1983; Stern, 1985). Furthermore, most parents had difficulty modifying these intuitive behaviors in response to the researchers' instructions, even after being made aware of their own patterns of interactions (H. Papoušek & M. Papoušek, 1982a, 1982b, 1984) This is illustrated by the following description of the early filming Hanuš undertook after joining the Max Planck Institute in Munich:

> While being with the mothers in their homes, and while doing filming, I sometimes tried to sort of test my findings, test my hypotheses. I just, for instance, wanted to find out whether they really are unable to control those intuitive, nonconscious behaviors. So, here and there, I was filming for my purposes and then when I was ready I made a short film for the family, and gave it to the family; which was of course a very nice reinforcer for some of them.
>
> But I noticed for instance that the mothers regularly do the *greeting response* when the baby looks at them—as a response to the achievement of visual contact. So I asked the mother to allow me to make a close shot of her face and the baby's face, and I told her "but it's going to be a very close shot—actually for you, because you look so nice, and the baby looks so nice." So I told her "I am only filming this part of your face and this part of the baby's face, so please don't move." And when she makes this movement, I'd say "Ohh! We have to do it once more—you moved the head!" (*Laughter*) And I told her, I told her what she did with the head. And so she promised, not to do it any more. After a while, in the middle of the talk, the baby looks at her, and I'd say "Jesus Christ, you did it again!" So you know, I had actually evidence, *documentation* of how difficult it is for us to control those behaviors. And so then, as you can imagine, it opened a lot of small projects where we had to test this, you know. (Papoušek Interview, July 15–16, 1998)

It seemed evident that these behaviors are not consciously controlled, but it was more difficult to prove whether or not certain human predispositions for communicating with their offspring are innate. Many experimental manipulations, such as postpartum social isolation, are not possible in research with human neonates. Instead, one must rely on *indirect* evidence of innateness, such as indications that the behavior of interest has proved adaptive during the species' evolution. "Universal appearance across age, sex, and cultures, striking involvement of affective components, early functioning during ontogeny, relation to species-specific means of adaptation, and lack of conscious control indicate innateness in intuitive behaviors and distinguish them from newly learned and automated skills" (H. Papoušek, M. Papoušek, & Kestermann, 2000, p. 92). Neurophysiologically, intuitive behaviors are faster and less demanding than are rationally controlled behaviors. Their response latencies are usually within from 200 to 400 ms— longer than those of simple reflexes (with latencies closer to 40–60 ms), but shorter than those of rational decisions. Although it is difficult to test experimentally whether or not a given human behavior is innate or learned, the fact that many important parental responses seem to fall within this intermediate latency range lends important support to the Intuitive Parenting theory.

Again in their chapter for the *Handbook of Infant Development* (Osofsky, 1987), the Papoušeks describe the emergence of these concepts:

> We started paying more attention to behaviors that parents carry out unknowingly when we realized how little parents are consciously aware of the infant's integrative competence and of the possibilities of fostering its proper development. The repertoire of human behaviors occurring mostly without conscious awareness is rich and interesting but has been neglected in research. One reason for this neglect may be the view of intuitive behaviors as being undesired relics of animal instincts, although our health and survival would hardly be thinkable without certain sets of autonomic, reflexive, and intuitive responses. The difficulties in studying them may be another reason, since intuitive behaviors cannot be easily separated from rational, culturally determined ones, nor can they be readily classified according to the didactic potential that they may hold in interactions with infants. (p. 686)

COMPONENTS OF INTUITIVE BEHAVIORS: EMPIRICAL STUDIES

In a series of studies conducted in the 1970s and 1980s in collaboration with other members of their Munich research team, the Papoušeks focused their attention on a broad repertoire of intuitive behaviors that manifest themselves when parents interact with human infants. Based on these studies, five general categories of such behaviors were identified: "motherese" (infant-directed speech), imitation, temporal patterns, testing the infant's state of alertness, and visual distance regulation.

"Motherese"

The earliest human social interchange begins with a compelling desire for dialogue on the part of the adult, and with what appears to be a willingness to accept any response in the newborn as a potential contribution to that dialogue. Certainly, the adult does not expect verbal reciprocation in this case; nevertheless, the adjustments adults make in their vocalizations to infants provide an excellent example of the ways in which parental behaviors may be very precisely tuned to the needs and abilities of their young (Fernald & Simon, 1984; M. Papoušek, 1989). During the 1980s, at the Max Planck Institute, this became the primary focus of attention for Mechthild Papoušek, who made an important contribution to the relatively new documentation in support of an Intuitive Parenting model. With postdoctoral colleague Marc Bornstein, the Papoušeks explored the homogeneity as well as variability in parents' vocal communication to infants, noting that both melodic contours and temporal patterns are influenced by the infant's own state and the interactional context (e.g., whether soothing is called for as opposed to playfulness, etc.) (H. Papoušek, M. Papoušek, & Bornstein, 1985).

As the Papoušeks and Anne Fernald noted, infant-directed speech is typically slower and modified for intelligibility, prototypical melodies occur frequently, its vocabulary is restricted and concrete, and its pitch is higher and more variable than in other kinds of dialogues. It was easy to compare this form of vocalization to that directed to other members of society: The researchers needed only to observe the speed and facility with which parents switched into and out of the "babytalk" mode when speaking alternately to the newborn and to another adult or older child.

Furthermore, even before the first syllables appeared in the infant's vocalizations, parents were observed to be exaggerating their vocal input as if giving lessons to accompany their nonverbal messages. For example, they would present frequent questions (and often the answers as well), call to the infant to elicit attention, and use an astounding proportion of repetition and "theme and variation" patterns, in both verbal and nonverbal behaviors, as they sought to sustain the infant's alertness (Koester, 1986, 1988; H. Papoušek et al., 1985). The melodic contours in parental vocalizations were also shown to be tailored to the interactional context: Falling contours appeared to be associated with attempts to soothe, rising contours were paired with efforts to activate, and bell-shaped contours served to reward the infant (M. Papoušek, 1989).

Imitation

As the infant develops its own ability to modulate pitch, parents respond to the new opportunity this affords for vocal imitation. Initially, newborns' and young infants' imitative capacities were studied primarily in relation to facial or manual behaviors (e.g., Field, Woodson, Greenberg, & Cohen, 1982; Maratsos, 1973; Meltzoff & Moore, 1983). However, caregivers also imitate infants, providing models and gradual refinements in response to the infant's own efforts and functioning as a "biological mirror" for the child. (See Fig. 7.1 for examples of feeding imitation and instructions as well.) As the Papoušeks (1987) noted, vocal imitation in particular supports the development of perceptual, integrative, and communicative processes, and frequently co-occurs with pleasant, mutually rewarding emotional experiences. Between 3 and 6 months of infant age, this vocal imitation is increasingly incorporated in nursery games initiated by mothers, and in infants' vocal play.

Data from the Munich studies indicated that vocal matching is yet another part of intuitive didactic guidance. In a study published in the mid-1980s, the Papoušeks and student Monika Haekel found that mothers modify their infant-directed speech in a way that reduces the usual disparity between adult speech and infant sounds, maximizing the likelihood of infant vocal imitation (H. Papoušek, M. Papoušek, & Haekel, 1987). Thus, mothers intuitively adjust their vocal utterances to the developmental level of infant sounds, choosing the most appropriate models for the sake of culturally determined speech while following the infant's progress in vocal production.

Temporal Patterns

Parental vocalizations do not occur in a vacuum, but are typically accompanied by various forms of nonvocal stimulation. One interesting feature of the exaggerated communicative style during interchanges between infants and caregivers is that of temporal patterning, particularly the rhythms of repetitive stimulation provided to the infant in various sensory modalities. The Papoušeks' work drew attention to the notion that temporal organization plays an important role both in the internal organization of infant experience, and in the coordination of infant motor behavior (Wolff, 1991). Lynne Koester also collaborated with the Munich team to study the significance of interactional context in relation to rhythmicity in nonvocal patterns of maternal stimulation (Koester, H. Papoušek, & M. Papoušek, 1989).

Similarly, Mechthild Papoušek carried out a long-term analysis of vocal interchanges between infants and mothers, finding that rhythmical games appear in the maternal repertoire at 5 months, culminate at 7 months, and then gradually decrease in frequency toward the end of the first year. Interestingly, the peak overlaps with the beginning of reduplicated, canonical syllables in the infant; the use of rhythmical vocal games may therefore support the infant's ability to segment breath for the purpose of rhythmically chaining several syllables within one exhalation (M. Papoušek, 1994).

As if this distinct and rather striking new feature in infant vocalizations was a cue for parents to modify their infant-directed speech, parents then begin to utilize each of the infant's canonical syllables as a potential proto-

FIG. 7.1.   Three examples of intuitive behaviors related to feeding instructions: 7.1-a) Mother feeding baby 7.1-b) Sister feeding baby 7.1-c) Baby feeding Mother.

word, assigning it meaning, and teaching the infant to associate it with the corresponding referent (M. Papoušek, 1994; M. Papoušek & H. Papoušek, 1981). On the infant's side, the appearance of these reduplicated, canonical syllables occurs simultaneously with improved functioning of the speech-dominant hemisphere (de Schonen & Mathivet, 1989). On the parents' side, these vocal strategies are another indication of Intuitive Parenting, supporting the emerging linguistic competence of the child.

Testing the Infant's State of Alertness

As noted in the Prague studies, an infant's behavioral state is often all too clear to the caregiver, particularly when the infant resorts to its earliest form of communication—crying. At other times, however, the infant's level of arousal, attention, or readiness for interaction is not so apparent. As more parents participated in the Munich studies, several behaviors became apparent as ways of assisting the caregiver in evaluating the newborn's state and determining the need for additional or reduced stimulation. These consisted of subtle testing of the infant's muscle tone around the mouth, chin, hands, or legs. Differences in the infant's responses are indicative of behavioral state, which is inherently related to muscle tone; therefore, these interventions seem well designed to inform the parent of the infant's readiness for interaction, sleep, or feeding. Gunhild Kestermann, a doctoral student at the time, joined the Papoušeks' efforts to explore this idea further.

As reported in chapter 6, Kestermann became interested in a visual cue to which parents respond but are usually unable to describe, that is, the position or activity of the infant's hands. The transition from waking to sleeping in infants is characterized by a gradual decrease in muscle tone, and dropping (or extension) of the fingers, hands, and eventually arms, thus providing clear signals for interpretation of state (Kestermann, 1982). These cues facilitate appropriate responses in parents to assist the infant in making the transition from one state to another (e.g., altering position so as to increase visual alertness or to permit sleep), and may indirectly serve to protect the infant from too little or too much stimulation.

Visual Distance Regulation

Another example of intuitive parenting relates to the infant's visual perception. Although by then it was known that even newborns can see and focus quite well (Aslin, 1987; Fantz, 1973), the limited range of the newborn's visual field had also been demonstrated. In this case, Papoušek's background both in pediatrics and as a researcher at the Prague facility most likely enhanced his knowledge and his astute observations of parental responses to the infant's perceptual needs; in addition, the Munich team was joined for a time by another pediatrician, Angela Schoetzau, who assisted in the investigations of visual distance regulation by parents.

In their microanalytic studies, the Papoušeks were able to document a predominant tendency for adults to use two specific eye-to-eye distances with infants (H. Papoušek & M. Papoušek, 1984). One might be called an "observational distance," as it corresponds to most adults' optimal reading distance of about 40–50 cm (16–20″) and is normally used when watching an infant who is not attending to the adult in return. More striking, however, is the "dialogue distance"—within 20–25 cm (8–10″)—corresponding to the infant's range of accommodation (focal distance), and used as soon as the infant shows interest in communicative interaction (Schoetzau & H. Papoušek, 1977). As these two investigators noticed, this occurs even in adults who believe that the infant cannot see, and regardless of whether or not the infant is being held.

Taking this one step further, Papoušek and another student member of his team noticed that when eye contact is achieved (i.e., when the infant turns toward the caregiver's face), the parent frequently rewards this behavior with a contingent "greeting response": first, a slight retroflexion of the head, raised eyebrows, widely opened eyes, open mouth, and finally a smile or a verbal greeting to the infant (Haekel, 1985). All of these visually related behaviors ensure that the caregiver is a salient feature of the infant's perceptual world—that is, by reducing the distance to that within the infant's optimal range, by incorporating movement and exaggerated facial expressions to capture the infant's attention, and by reinforcing the infant's own responsiveness to the social partner.

Thus, within the framework of Intuitive Parenting, nonvocal forms of communication represent another lens through which to observe the subtle but skillful methods used by parents—methods that, although unconscious, appear tailor-made to facilitate the adaptive integrative processes of the human infant.

As is covered in the concluding chapter, a relatively new aspect of the Papoušeks' research lies in its potential applicability to clinical and exceptional populations. That is, more recent investigations are including efforts to better understand the variations in parenting behaviors that may stem from exceptionalities (e.g., deafness) on either side of the dyad, parent or child, but that can have important consequences regardless of the origin. By first understanding the seemingly naturally occurring parenting behaviors that are so well tuned to the needs of the infant, it has been possible to use these as a basis for comparison when such patterns are not apparent, but where programmatic or intervention decisions must be made. It is clear that interactive difficulties can result from disruptions in those subtle parenting behaviors that normally require very little thought and yet are necessary to sustain and enhance the emerging parent–infant relationship.

Throughout all of these studies, it was Hanuš Papoušek's training as a pediatrician, his keen observational skills, his technological expertise, and his ability to bring together scholars and ideas from diverse fields to enrich his concepts that all contributed to the remarkable breadth and uniqueness of this theory of Intuitive Parenting behaviors. In addition, as is discussed in the next chapter, Mechthild's extensive training in psychiatry contributed greatly to the development of these concepts and to the clinical applications that emerged later. Especially after his retirement from the Max Planck Institute in 1988, Hanuš and Mechthild Papoušek began to make frequent appearances throughout Germany, but also in Czechoslovakia, Yugoslavia, The Netherlands, and other European countries, in which they made an effort to reach wider audiences with both the overall idea and the practical applications of their theory. Especially in Germany, this work is making a significant impact on the present generation of practitioners, university students, and scholars interested in early childhood and developmental psychology.

Retirement Years, Current Applications, and Legacy

Hanuš Papoušek remained head of the Unit on Developmental Psycho-biology at the Max Planck Institute for Psychiatry in Munich until 1988, when he had no choice but to retire in accordance with the mandates of the German government. Retirement for Hanuš did not mean relaxation and a life of leisure, but rather the opportunity to freely pursue his interest in science and infancy studies. For the next decade, he continued his professional reading, writing, lecturing, mentoring, and traveling around the world. Papoušek's life continued to be influenced by major international political events, but this time in a much more positive direction. His retirement coincided with the end of the Cold War and the breakdown of political barriers between East and West, allowing him to reunite once again with his family in Czechoslovakia, to resume contacts and research collaboration with former colleagues at the Institute for the Care of Mother and Child, Charles University, and other Czech institutions of medical and pediatric sciences. Until the onset of acute leukemia in 1998, he remained a model of professional vigor and physical health, and a valued "senior mentor" for leading developmentalists in a variety of countries around the world.

With retirement also came renewed recognition for his scientific achievements. To commemorate Papoušek's work, the Max Planck Institute sponsored an international symposium in May 1989, at which he was awarded the prestigious Heinrich Hoffmann Medal of the German Society of Child and Adolescent Psychiatry. The Hoffmann Medal is granted to an outstanding scientist every 4 years in recognition of important contributions to research in child development. At about the same time, editors of *Scientific Europe* selected Hanuš and Mechthild Papoušek's work for inclusion in a volume of the most significant scientific contributions to appear throughout the history of their publication. Both professional accolades went a long way toward convincing Hanuš Papoušek that, at long last, his ideas were receiving recognition among developmentalists and psychiatrists in Germany.

The person chosen to pay tribute to Hanuš upon receipt of the Heinrich Hoffmann Medal was his longtime friend and supervisor, Detlev Ploog, founding director of the Max Planck Institute for Psychiatry. Almost identical in age, and also close to retirement, Ploog clearly delineated the significance of Hanuš' contributions to infancy, parenting, and child development research on an international level. Noting the close relationship of Hanuš' work to his own, Ploog pointed out that Hanuš had been a pediatric researcher with a major reputation in the areas of learning and information processing before moving to Germany. As noted in Ploog's *Laudatio* for Papoušek,

> No one in the late 1950s and early 1960s wanted to believe that human infants can learn or react systematically to external, especially visual stimuli. But you, dear Papoušek, proved it. You demonstrated that by simple head movements, infants respond behaviorally to an external stimulus. You presented the newborn with small stimulus–response tasks and discovered how the infant learned to perform them. What was it that was so fascinating about this discovery? To me, it was the simplicity of the scientific method, and the clarity of the results you obtained. (Ploog, 1989; translated by O. Koester)

With equal clarity, Ploog also summarized the importance of Papoušek's contributions while working in Munich:

> To be sure, in 1972 when Hanuš came to Munich, there were Piaget's profound studies about the development of the child in the realm of intelligence and thought, but we knew almost nothing about psychosocial development and the interaction and communication processes underlying it. . . . The remarkable achievement of the research conducted by Hanuš, together with Mechthild, resides in the nature of the scientific questions that he posed at a time when there was much theorizing and speculation about emotional development in infancy, and the scientific manner in which he went about trying to find answers to some of these questions. What I'm referring to are the microanalytic methods and techniques which he developed in order to document and analyze infant behavior. . . . You, dear Papoušek, were the one who discovered, among other things, the didactic elements inherent in the mother–child relationship in which certain infant behaviors evoke intuitive actions on the part of the mother, which in turn stimulate the child. Your studies of Western and Oriental cultures allow us to conclude that this is a universal phenomenon that, it would seem, is related to human evolution. (Ploog, 1989; translated by O. Koester)

After Hanuš' retirement, the Unit for Developmental Psychobiology was disbanded and Papoušek's laboratory facilities were disassembled. According to Max Planck policy, incoming directors (i.e., Ploog's successor) were free to establish their own research agendas and priorities, independent of any their predecessor might have set in place. By June 1989, Papoušek had concluded all research activities at the Institute. Concurrent with the dissolution of their laboratory, Mechthild assumed a new position at the Institute for Social Pediatrics and Youth Medicine in Munich, where Hanuš was also given office space for his research equipment. It appeared as if his writing and data analyses could continue unhindered. The Institute for Social Pediatrics and Youth Medicine provides diagnostic, intervention, and therapeutic services for children of all ages with a wide variety of disabilities. Papoušek functioned as a part-time but influential research advisor to Theodor Hellbrügge, the Institute's director.

In addition, from 1989 Hanuš held an appointment as special professor of developmental psychology at the Free University in Amsterdam. This arrangement, facilitated by fellow developmentalist Brian Hopkins, continued until 1993. Papoušek traveled regularly from Munich to Amsterdam to give lectures and work with students on a part-time basis. During this time, he collaborated with Hopkins in launching a new international journal, *Early Development and Parenting* (later renamed *Infant and Child Development*).

Yet another momentous international political event, the 1989 demise of the Soviet Union and the end of the Cold War, influenced his life. The fall of the Berlin Wall and the "Velvet Revolution" in Czechoslovakia both signaled profound changes for a person whose entire adult life had been defined by the political barriers separating East from West. A phone call from Hanuš to Lynne's office in Washington, DC, shortly after the Berlin Wall had been destroyed, expressed the impact of this event. In a voice choked with emotion, Hanuš said, "You have no idea what this means—I *never* imagined that in my lifetime I would ever be able to visit my homeland again!" (In an interview in July 2002, a former German colleague, Joest Martinius, commented on the semantic distinction between two words in the German language: *heimat,* meaning "where I come from," and *heim,* meaning "where I live." As Martinius reflected, Hanuš Papoušek lost his *heimat,* or *homeland,* when he defected to Germany. With the end of the Cold War, he regained it.)

Following what must have been his first trip back to Prague, Hanuš wrote in an e-mail message to Edna and Lew Lipsitt that "the days in Prague could not have been better. I had unexpected invitations for talks in Budapest, Warsaw, Prague, and Moscow—after 20 years of a quotation ban. . . . I hope that I shall be able to help the Czech colleagues in some way, at least with lectures. They try very much to overcome the handicaps caused by the lack of international contacts and unavailability of foreign literature" (March 1, 1990). All three of his Prague children were well-established in their careers by then, and he was especially moved by the opportunity to meet some of the Czech grandchildren whom he had never yet seen or held. It is difficult for many in the Western world to fully comprehend the profound impact of this major political change on an individual who had earlier fled an oppressive regime in his own country. In addition to affording him this long-awaited opportunity to be reunited with family and former coworkers, the fall of the Berlin Wall gave Hanuš the chance to give back to his people some of the expertise and experience he had gained during his years in the United States and in Germany. As soon as was possible, he began offering his services as guest lecturer, mentor, research consultant, or workshop organizer—usually at his own expense—not only in Czechoslovakia but also in other newly independent Eastern European countries. Together with Mechthild, Hanuš became a much soughtafter lecturer, seminar leader, and workshop presenter in Hungary, Yugoslavia, and neighboring countries where both scientists and clinicians were eager to learn more about the theory and applications of Intuitive Parenting. In addition, he was influential in persuading various international professional organizations to offer travel stipends to scholars from those countries, and in convincing publishers (e.g., Lawrence Erlbaum Associates) to donate scientific books and journals to their libraries, in order that the East Europeans could now be more fully integrated into the global infancy research community. Papoušek's dedication to promoting greater international exchange of ideas guided his activities not only during the Cold War era, but afterward as well.

In another message to the Lipsitts dated November 20, 1995, Hanuš reported that his time between then and the next ICIS meetings would be packed with lectures, seminars, and colloquia at various places. Increasingly, these were "benefit" (or *pro bono*) lectures in Eastern Europe; different people close to him interpreted this in very different ways, asking whether or not he was "growing wise," or "becoming senile." He became an Honorary Guest Professor at Charles University of Prague and Pilsen in 1997, and made numerous professional trips to the Czech Republic and other Eastern European countries.

For almost a decade, Hanuš Papoušek enjoyed the freedom that came with no longer having a full-time position, and dedicated his life to research, writing, and hard work. Year after year he gave workshops and attended international conferences around the globe, while his publications continued to appear on a wide range of topics and in numerous languages. He utilized this freedom to become an even more prolific writer than ever before. An examination of his publication list between 1989 and 2000 reveals an astounding number of articles and chapters covering a broad range of themes (see Appendix A). What makes this productivity remarkable is that he did not have any research or clerical assistance throughout these years. There were numerous articles and chapters on Intuitive Parenting, others on early vocal and nonvocal communication (including applications to the development of deaf infants), and the roles of play and musicality. In addition, he wrote extensively about clinical implications, directed toward early interventionists and pediatricians. Many of these postretirement publications were coauthored with Mechthild Papoušek, and others reflected his collaboration with researchers from the United States, Germany, the Czech Republic, the United Kingdom, Switzerland, and several other countries. Included in this list with Mechthild were collaborators such as Marc Bornstein, Jaroslavá Dittrichová, Brian Hopkins, Gunhild Kestermann, Lynne Koester, Karel Paul, Charles Rahn, Miriam Rothaug, Steve Suomi, David Symmes, and others. Publications are found in English, German, Czech, French, and Portuguese, attesting to his international research efforts, his facility with languages, as well as his enduring desire to share his research and theoretical insights with a broad audience in a variety of cultures.

Perhaps even more significant is that Papoušek began new collaborative efforts with a generation of younger scholars in Prague: Vladimir Komárek (his son-in-law) and Tomaš Rodny, both of whom are affiliated with Charles University and the medical school there. This partnership developed as a result of conversations between Papoušek and Komárek during joint family vacations in the early 1990s. Komárek began recognizing the relevance of Intuitive Parenting concepts for his own work with adolescents hospitalized following traumatic brain injury. Knowing of Hanuš and Mechthild's concepts regarding intuitive behaviors of parents with very young children, Komárek began to notice similar patterns as he watched parents interacting with their teenagers who could no longer speak or communicate easily. Informal discussions and exchange of ideas finally led to more formalized plans to study this phenomenon systematically at Motol Hospital in Prague, where Komárek was a pediatric neurologist. His colleague, Tomaš Rodny, joined this new investigation as part of his graduate research, and these efforts have continued even after the time of Hanuš' death.

Papoušek's life during retirement was full. In 1998, however, at age 75, Papoušek suddenly fell ill, and after a series of medical tests his doctors in Munich informed him that he was suffering from acute leukemia. Many rounds of chemotherapy, frequent hospitalizations, and intermittent bouts of renewed strength ensued. Prior to his struggle with leukemia, however, Hanuš had given his consent to have a "scientific biography" written about his life, research, and his experiences in the East and the West. He generously granted numerous interviews to the authors of this book, and guided them to contacts with many of his former coworkers in a variety of countries.

In an ironic connection back to his work in Prague, visitors to his hospital room were often required to wear surgical face masks to avoid exposing him to further health risks when his immunity was already perilously low. Conducting interviews under these conditions was nevertheless cause for humor, as he delighted in retelling the story of his efforts, and ultimate success, to convince the Ministry of Health authorities in Prague that the infants in his unit should not be cared for by nurses whose facial expressions were covered by masks!

Hanuš coped with the first two rounds of chemotherapy remarkably well, so that when he was again feeling stronger the nominating committee of the International Society for Infant Studies (ISIS) approached him about having his name submitted as candidate for the presidency of the organization. Optimistic that he would be able to fulfill these duties, Hanuš accepted the nomination. To serve as leader of this particular organization would be symbolic of so much that he had believed in and valued throughout his life. As mentioned earlier, ISIS had begun as a small "correspondence club" in the early 1960s, with members including such scholars as Lewis Lipsitt, Arnold Sameroff, Rachel Keen, Marshall Haith, Bob Emde, Joseph Campos, William Kessen, Jerome Kagan, Jerome Bruner, Harriet Rheingold, Peter Wolff, Heinz Prechtl, T. Berry Brazelton, and others. Initially, they had simply distributed carbon copies of typed manuscripts to each other for review and feedback; eventually, it emerged as a large and well-established professional organization. Papoušek's election served as a symbolic capstone to his long, distinguished scientific career. It represented all that he embodied in his own professional life—rigorous and creative science, international connections, and the freedom to pursue one's own ideas and to have a critical but fair review of these by one's peers. Had his illness not recurred, Hanuš would have been honored to lead this illustrious group.

By late 1999, the dreaded disease had returned full force. Lynne Koester visited him one last time at the Papoušek's home in Olympic Village, Munich, only 2 weeks before his death. It was apparent that he would not live much longer, which made it all the more astounding to her when Hanuš joined the small gathering on their balcony for "Kaffee und Kuchen" and a long conversation. He apologized at the end of this visit because he was afraid he had disappointed us. Because he desired to provide more material for this book, he *apologized* for being ill. The tone with which he apologized seemed to typify the Central European modesty that was so much a part of his personal character and style. Hanuš Papoušek died of leukemia in Munich's Klinikum Großhadern on May 5, 2000. He was buried at Forstenried Cemetery outside of Munich, Germany. Family members from both Germany and the Czech Republic were present, as were former colleagues from both countries.

PAPOUŠEK'S LEGACY

As soon as word of his death spread, tributes attesting to the importance of his scientific achievements poured in from around the world. Obituaries appeared in Germany, the Czech Republic, and the United States. The following is taken from an obituary that appeared in the Czech journal *Psychologie Dnes* and in the *Newsletter* of the Society for Research in Child Development. It summarizes the themes of many other tributes and eulogies delivered in his honor:

> Hanuš Papoušek—pediatrician, scientist, teacher, and humanitarian—has left a warm and enduring legacy. In one walk of life, Hanuš was a caring husband, father, grandfather, and always generous friend. Down another walk of life, he was a distinguished scholar, mentor, humanitarian and teacher to numerous colleagues and students he knew and to countless others he did not. Hanuš was a pioneering theoretician and researcher in his field, and scientists worldwide followed in his footsteps. To all those fortunate enough to walk life's paths together with him, Hanuš was a wise, caring and ageless citizen of the world. Few who knew him can believe Hanuš has now left this world, which has suddenly become a colder and less compassionate place without him.
>
> Beyond his professional accomplishments, Hanuš Papoušek was not only a highly principled man who invariably gained the respect of those around him, but he was also creative and multi-talented. As a painter and avid photographer, his keen observations of the natural world were always a memorable part of his travels. He was an enthusiastic swimmer, whether in the Atlantic off Cape Cod, in the Mediterranean off Corte, or in the Pacific off the Great Barrier Reef; and he was always a mountain climber—in the Tatras in his native country, the Rockies in North America, the Alps in Austria and Switzerland, and the Himalayas in Nepal. Language presented no barrier to this citizen of the world, for he spoke in native tongues to Czechs, Russians, English and Americans, Germans, French, and to scientists and lay people alike. Hanuš was an eminent and pioneering figure in the physician-psychologist nexus of developmental science, infancy studies, and infant–parent relationships in the 20th century. His ideas have had a major impact on innumerable colleagues and friends around the world. His was a life that made a difference. (Bornstein & Koester, 2000a, 2000b)

Hanuš Papoušek had a great impact on the lives and work of many individuals in the infancy field. For those considered to be the early "pioneers" in infancy research, he is viewed as an innovative researcher and a valuable colleague, who gained their respect, stimulated their ideas, and challenged preconceived notions. For a younger generation that arrived on this research scene somewhat later, he became a loyal mentor and a guiding light who was willing to challenge their ideas and assumptions, but always ready to motivate them to higher levels of inquiry.

Interestingly, despite significant continuities over the course of his re-search career, Papoušek's legacy took on a somewhat different flavor in Eu-rope than in the United States. Among the early pioneers of infancy stud-ies, Jerome Bruner was one who pointed to a central characteristic of Hanuš' impact on fellow scientists on both sides of the Atlantic. His legacy, Bruner observed, was subtle and "stylistic," having to do with a deep under-standing of the very nature of infants and their world. Papoušek's underly-ing contribution was the introduction of a whole new way of looking at in-fants, a perspective that had been virtually unknown until the 1950s. According to Bruner,

> He was the person who always came forth with an image of the child as some-how not passive, but from the start, able to cope with problems. "I have to cope with the problem of keeping warm, keeping close to my mother, keep-ing in some kind of communicative contact from the start." And that, rather than having just this kind of vegetable-like character being overwhelmed by a blooming, buzzing confusion, you had an active, plucky kid who was trying out strategies for dealing with things. . . . And I think the legacy is . . . the im-age of the infant as a concerned, motivated little human being, so to speak. (Bruner Interview, January 30, 2002)

Bruner acknowledged how much this had influenced a number of "In-fancy Correspondence Club" members at the time, including himself, Wil-liam Kessen, and others:

> I remember our talking after one of those meetings of the CIBA Foundation in London, talking about the richness of Hanuš' approach—that somehow the integration of the senses and the limited motor capacity that the child has was not just some sort of Pavlovian, associative business, but that the child was trying to put together enterprises. That to me is one hell of an important thing. You know, the funny thing about it is that some of us—Bill Kessen, me, and others—are credited with having changed that [thinking], but the fact of the matter is we got it in a very considerable degree from Hanuš' encourage-ment. Give credit where credit is due. (Bruner Interview, January 30, 2002)

Peter Wolff, with whom Hanuš also worked during his time at Harvard, made a similar observation: "Hanuš had an imagination about babies *telling* us something. In other words, he wanted to find out *what babies can do . . .*— let's find out what the repertoire of the baby is. And that always seemed to me to be the great contribution that Hanuš made" (Wolff Interview, De-cember 2, 1999). It is interesting to speculate why the introduction of such a new perspective came from a European as opposed to an American scien-tist. Did it have to do with the more philosophical approach of many Euro-pean social scientists, seeking new and intriguing questions about the nature of human existence? In contrast, were the Americans more concerned with outcomes, with "getting it right" as Kagan was later to assert? Or, does the explanation reside more in the individual talents and temperament of the man himself, of Hanuš Papoušek, pediatrician, father, scholar, and observer of human behavior?

Associated with this new view of the infant as a dynamic, motivated human being, was what other colleagues saw as Hanuš' exceptionally broad view of the world. Derived from Papoušek's background in multiple disciplines, languages, and perspectives, it was informed by both theoretical insights and a wisdom that comes from practice. He had a remarkable ability to integrate his knowledge of music, visual arts, philosophy, photography, nature, sports, technology, and science with a genuine love of children—sometimes all within one conversation. His longtime friend and Prague colleague, Jaroslavá Dittrichová, saw this as evidence of an extraordinarily open mind, citing his interest in the arts as well as sciences, and his own talents both musically and artistically. As she commented, "I think it's very rare in our time; the majority of people concentrate on one field, and are very good in this field, but are not able to see how it is connected and related. . . . Few people are able to do this, and I think Hanuš was one who could" (Dittrichová Interview, October 7, 1999).

Anne Fernald noted that Hanuš Papoušek's contributions are probably not as widely appreciated today as they should be. He was part of "that wonderful, ebullient time when people were coming from ethology and psychobiology and psychiatry and pediatrics—basically, there were few people who watched children the way Hanuš did. . . . And the richness of Hanuš' approach! To me it's immensely valuable work" (Fernald Interview, May 11, 2000). Much of this richness stems from his keen observational eye, his ability to draw insights from his knowledge of multiple disciplines, and a mind that could be both highly analytical and integrative. But Fernald joins others in her feeling that, particularly for students, Papoušek's writing style was sometimes a barrier to wider appreciation. (Given that English was his third or fourth language, his level of sophistication in both written and spoken usage was quite impressive in itself.)

In addition, Papoušek is remembered by his own generation, both in Europe and in the United States, for his unique penchant for designing research with infants—a skill for which he became known early in the history of the infancy field. Few had previously seen any benefit in trying to study the human organism before language made the research subject capable of verbal communication. Hanuš and a handful of other developmental scientists in the 1950s took up this challenge and began a tradition of creating procedures and scenarios by which even an infant could "answer the questions" posed to them by curious adult scientists. Are infants really "blind" at birth? Can they discriminate the different voices they hear? Is their behavior simply controlled by reflexes, or do newborns also exhibit intentional behaviors? The Prague conditioning studies established Papoušek in the international arena as an infancy researcher who developed ingenious equipment, methodology, and hypotheses that led to major breakthroughs in the understanding of infant behavior.

In describing Papoušek's contribution to research methodology, some spoke primarily of his original approach to conditioning. Many (again, both Europeans and Americans) commented on his special way of "being around infants," his respect for them and for their mothers, as well as his calming presence—especially with the youngest of humans. Others (members of his own cohort, as well as younger researchers) saw in all of his work the importance of careful, systematic observation. Steve Suomi, for example, described Papoušek's influence in the area of methodology and observation as follows:

> [His unique contributions] came from his ability to set up research paradigms, and his extraordinary observational skills. I mean, he noticed things that . . . everybody else was missing. And . . . once he saw something, that allowed him to put things into perspective. . . . He resisted the notion of separating things out into cognitive components, social components, emotional components, integrational components. He was much more interested in the *whole* organism and how it expressed itself in all of these domains. . . . To focus on one to the exclusion of the others . . . carries the risk of missing important interconnections in relationships. For example, he had no problem recognizing that just the act of playing, not only was a way of promoting substantial improvement of social repertoires, but also gave cognitive processes much more flexibility. Yet play very likely had biological consequences in terms of stimulating brain growth, stimulating important formation of particular synapse arrangements. (Suomi Interview, March 11, 2000)

Peter Mangione, who worked with Papoušek both in Bonn and in Munich for several years, saw in Hanuš a kind of engineer with an abundance of ideas about how one might record and analyze early social behaviors and interactions. By describing these ideas in publications, Papoušek was able to share them with others who might be in a position to make further methodological advances to benefit the field (Mangione Interview, September 17, 2000).

Most infancy researchers, as well as parents and child-care providers, can easily relate to the response of Jerome Bruner when reminded of Hanuš' ability to design and create his own research apparatus: "In this field, you have to! Because ordinary equipment doesn't work with infants. You even have to design a chair that they can sit in comfortably . . . design just exactly the right angle, and know to put a swaddling cloth across their tummy to hold them in and to make them feel comfortable. It takes a lot of patience to work with infants!" (Bruner Interview, January 30, 2002). More importantly, perhaps, Papoušek's admirers noted something special in his manner when working with infants. Again, Bruner provided an apt characterization of this quality:

> Hanuš had a way of moving around babies that was astonishing. He knew the way of moving which didn't startle the young, but made them feel as if this were a friendly figure . . . just sort of watching them and being in that soothing kind of [role]. . . . I remember one specific instance: we had a little chamber, a little thing surrounded by curtains in which the kid could be protected from distractions in the rest of the room, and then we'd present things like pictures. I remember Hanuš looking at it once and he said "I think you do not have enough places for the child to rest his eyes. Put some decorations on the screen so the child will have somewhere to look. Little babies don't know what to do if there isn't something to look at—if it's just a great white thing." And he was so right! I laugh when I tell this story, because I remember I then went down to Harvard Square to the Five and Dime, and bought some of those things that little ten-year-old girls like to wear on their dresses. And we put some of those around so that the baby would have somewhere to inspect so it wasn't a totally blank environment. And it cut down on the incidence of crying and being upset tremendously! (Bruner Interview, January 30, 2002)

Western scientists' fascination with the unusual setting and structure of the Prague Institute had grown rapidly, so that by all accounts Papoušek's work in the 1960s was at the cutting edge of the fledgling field of infancy research. Soon, others were drawn to his ideas and to him as a person. Developmentalists were increasingly convinced that it was possible to study infants; that it was possible to ask interesting research questions of this age group; and, importantly, that studies could be designed to elicit clear, interpretable "answers" even from such young Subjects. As Bruner commented, "I found his way of conceiving of the child's tasks, and the kinds of observations that he had done—how the child put things in different modalities together—that I found to be extremely interesting. It was kind of a 'holistic bias' " (Bruner Interview, January 30, 2002). This was the beginning of a new, ground-breaking generation of founders of the "infancy correspondence club" that later became ISIS. According to Marc Bornstein, the next generation (their *students*) went very far, very fast (Bornstein Interview, March 10, 2000).

Heinz Prechtl's friendship with Papoušek dated back to the early research endeavors in Prague and lasted a lifetime. It is understandable, then, that Prechtl's reflections about his friend's early research career touch not

only on methodology, but also on political and personal aspects of Papoušek's life:

> I think that Hanuš' research was outstanding at that time [in Prague]. But it
> was in the line of the classical Russian influence, I mean Communist influ-
> ence. And if I may say so, I have the feeling that he was convinced politically,
> in the early years at least. . . . And then in '68, I think, Hanuš became very un-
> happy about the whole situation. Because he was an idealist and believed that
> things could work out . . . but they did not work out. And I think for him to
> leave, was really essential. . . . His important influence was that he had this bi-
> ological touch, as a pediatrician. I think this was a very, very important impact
> Hanuš had on the field. (Prechtl Interview, April 28, 2000)

Marc Bornstein commented that Papoušek's early research paradigm
was to some extent limited by the intellectual and historical *Zeitgeist* of the
time and place (i.e., mid-20th-century Prague, as described earlier). Nevertheless, Bornstein viewed Papoušek as a forward-looking thinker and fore-
runner whose mind was such that it let him wander out into new and unexplored terrain. Apparently, these qualities were also evident to such people
as Yvonne Brackbill, Bill Kessen, and Frank Palmer, who first "discovered"
Hanuš in Prague and brought his work to the attention of important
developmentalists in the States at that time (Bornstein Interview, March 10,
2000).

The timing of Papoušek's first trips to the United States had been fortu-
itous. Dramatic changes were occurring in the field of child development,
with particularly rapid advances in the understanding of infancy. His was
one of the early voices to be heard proposing that the infant was a competent being, and that both infants and parents may have built-in responses or
inclinations that facilitate early social relationships. According to Mangione, "He wasn't the only person who was saying those things and developing that point of view. . . . But he was a leading voice and he was in a small
group of people that . . . eventually became a larger group and then became the Zeitgeist of the time in the '70s and the '80s. So in that sense he
was extremely influential" (Mangione Interview, September 17, 2000).

At the Harvard Center for Cognitive Studies, Papoušek had use of experimental facilities in which to carry out a systematic series of studies filming
babies interacting with their mothers. There he observed babies interacting
with either a video image of themselves or with a delayed image of themselves, or with the mother, again in "real time" or with the mother's image
delayed. Others in the field were beginning to do similar kinds of work as
well, designing studies reflecting a new awareness of issues such as reciprocity, synchrony, and coordination of social exchanges in which the infant was
a contributing partner (e.g., Bell, 1968; Brazelton, Koslowski, & Main, 1974;
Lewis & Rosenblum, 1974). Microanalysis allowed Hanuš and others to ex-

amine videotaped behavioral interactions on a minute scale, frame by frame, counting frequencies with improved accuracy as well as looking at durations and latencies of responses. Clearly, Hanuš' forté was in thinking about these problems and designing creative solutions (Bornstein Interview, March 10, 2000).

Nevertheless, colleagues such as Lew Lipsitt and Darwin Muir concur that Papoušek's early prominence in North America was attributable primarily to his Prague research in which he blended aspects of both classical and operant conditioning. The day before Hanuš' death, Lipsitt commented on what an ingenious and important contribution that had been, concluding that "he was the guy who came up with the very best infant conditioning work of that era" (Lipsitt Interview, May 4, 2000). But Papoušek gradually began to shift his focus from conditioning to the study of parent–infant relationships, as described in chapter 7. Although this may have been more complicated to study, it involved less experimental control, so that some of the more orthodox experimental child psychologists who had been so interested in Hanuš' early work failed to follow along this new path (Kagan Interview, November 30, 1999).

As Peter Wolff and others confirmed, Papoušek was probably best known in the United States for his studies of newborn learning. However, a somewhat different conclusion can be drawn viewing his life from a more European perspective. As indicated in previous chapters, close examination reveals more continuity across the decades of his professional life than might be apparent upon superficial review of his research or publications. Bornstein concluded that the research he did in Prague "was very formative and very powerful for him, and it carried through for everything else he did" (Bornstein Interview, March 10, 2000).

Prechtl noted that Hanuš Papoušek's conditioning studies in Prague highlight his great talent for experimental research. Nevertheless, Prechtl emphasized that Papoušek was outstanding in this accomplishment primarily because he was such an astute *observer* (Prechtl Interview, April 28, 2000). Similarly, German developmental psychologist Hellgard Rauh spoke of Hanuš' personality as one of his most impressive qualities, but also linked this to his keen observational skills:

> He's just an amazing person—in his honest, modest, consistent way. When he has an idea that he feels is important, then he stays with it—not blindly sticking to it, but he stays with it and follows it through, and tries to look at it from all perspectives. He always sees the connections between the basic and the applied. Some researchers are fascinated by their own ideas and sell only their ideas; they become somewhat blind toward other things around them. And I never have that feeling with Hanuš. He is a very fine observer of the small and fine aspects, and he is a marvelous thinker. Perhaps because he is so modest, he doesn't take his own personality as the main focus, but rather the things he

observes. . . . And therefore, I think he also is not so strong in selling his own ideas. It's more the person and his tremendous respect for the baby. I think that's also what he perhaps transmitted to me and to many others, his respect for the baby. . . . I don't know if it comes from his training in pediatrics, but that's probably one reason why he *became* a pediatrician. (Rauh Interview, April 15, 2000)

Kagan captured the contrasting elements of the two distinct phases of Papoušek's professional endeavors, the Prague years and the Munich years, with the following metaphor:

You know, we have two kinds of psychologists. For one, the sense of beauty and relevance comes from the firmness of the facts and the experimental control. For the other, the complexity of the issue, the social relevance of the problem—that is what generates the emotion, rather than the rigor or elegance of the methods and results.

I contrast it with hunters and butterfly chasers. Physicists are hunters. They want to do a study and they want to get a *fact*, bring a trophy back—and that fact you can hang up and no one's ever going to say that you didn't get it right. The joy is in getting it right!! But the butterfly hunters know that you never get it right. They are more interested in one brief moment of beauty when you *thought* you had it right.

Hanuš was a hunter in Prague and a butterfly chaser in Munich. He changed from a hunter to a butterfly chaser. I also think he changed problems on purpose. I think maybe he *wanted to* be a butterfly hunter. I suspect the infant work he did in Prague, which the experimentalists here love, was because he was in a regime where you were supposed to do that. . . .

It is easier to be a butterfly chaser in Europe because the European tradition is for wisdom, insight, understanding—not necessarily experimental control so you can get it right. And the American is pragmatic, and concerned with not getting it wrong. . . . The American posture is: don't get it wrong, don't make an error. If your posture is don't make an error, then you will be a hunter. If you get it wrong, you will be embarrassed. That means the bear will eat you. But if you are a butterfly, butterflies don't hurt anybody. You try to get it right and if you don't, you're not harmed. So it's a different orientation and I would say in Europe, that is their tradition. . . .

I think Hanuš is a very profound man, a very deep man. I think he is an introspective man. I think he is a brave man. And I think he was actually more attracted to the complex problems he studied in Munich. I think he *wanted to* do that. It isn't that studying infant conditioning isn't interesting, but it is more circumscribed. (Kagan Interview, November 30, 1999)

When asked whether or not he thought Papoušek's impact on the field stems primarily from the studies he conducted in Prague or the later concepts about Intuitive Parenting, Steve Suomi responded that it is neither one nor the other, exclusively:

Contributions are cumulative and you look to see what's happened to those ideas, for example . . . his ideas of what infants bring to the world, and how they help stimulate and generate parental behavior from those around them, and the way you go about studying it, paying attention to those early fluctuations because they may be very meaningful. There's just a lot of *wisdom* there. I mean, I've always viewed Hanuš as full of not necessarily brilliant new research initiatives, but just a very nice way of looking at developmental processes, and saying things and viewing things in ways that make an awful lot of sense. And that inspired a person like myself to go out and say, "Let's try to test this thing." . . . The notion that the interaction system early on is not just a parent behaving independent of the infant, or the infant behaving independent of the parent, but in fact what is important is they are *moving together*. . . . And of course that whole tradition continues, and it comes straight from Hanuš' observations. . . . Many of the ideas published in individual papers in those [mainstream] journals don't have a long shelf-life. Hanuš' ideas are truly amazing [in that regard]. (Suomi Interview, March 11, 2000)

Bruner also reflected on the continuities in Hanuš' life, the linkages between his own early experiences and his later interests, his conditioning studies and his efforts to understand parenting behaviors, and even Hanuš' personal connections to the social and political changes in his country of birth:

His image of the child as an active, creative [being], trying to integrate his world, is so much in keeping with the kind of spirit that eventually led to the desperately risky Czech uprising and that kind of thing! . . . A few years ago I remember going to a play by Vaclav Havel and I was struck by the fact that these guys are of the same type—Vaclav Havel, and Milan Kundera, and Hanuš Papoušek—exploring the possibilities of humanity with all of the cultural constraints with which we live. So that was where he started, and the interesting thing is that the Harvard that he came to was the same. . . . He came to the Center for Cognitive Studies where we were saying "Let's get away from this business of having a separation of philosophy, sociology, anthropology, psychology—we're all in the same business. We use somewhat different postage stamps but the message is the same. We're trying to get at the same kind of thing." And he was wonderful at that. So there was a kind of continuity. . . . He was the perpetual Prague Spring trying to happen! (Bruner Interview, January 30, 2002)

MENTORING

Another way in which Hanuš Papoušek had an impact on others in the field was through his mentoring of younger colleagues. The history of a field of study, and particularly the impact of individual scholars, is often reflected best by the "followers"—those students, coworkers, or like-minded individuals who carry a particular person's ideas further and help to perpetuate them or broaden their applications. These may be colleagues in the next generations, or they may be those of more equivalent stature who are nevertheless deeply influenced by the message of a given scholar. In the case of Hanuš Papoušek, there are clearly people whom he mentored or who worked with him at various times who have now become important leaders in the field; people such as Marc Bornstein, Anne Fernald, and Arnold Sameroff come to mind, among others (Mangione Interview, September 17, 2000). (Mechthild Papoušek, of course, played a crucial role in the development of their concepts of Intuitive Parenting and its clinical applications, a topic that warrants a section on ongoing clinical applications. Marc Bornstein described Hanuš' impact in the realm of mentoring, "In some sense he reached Erik Erikson's *generativity* with respect to the younger generation. He was incredibly and fortuitously generous with people who allowed him to be. And, you know, I don't see a lot of that" (Bornstein Interview, March 10, 2000).

Bornstein was not alone in finding something of a "father figure" in Hanuš; as Kimbrough Oller said, "Hanuš was the wisest of the people I took on as a late-in-life mentor. . . . There has been no one more influential in my career. He elevated every discussion. And if he had a great gift, it might have been that whatever was being talked about. . . . I always felt like my opinion was being honored" (Oller Interview, September 2, 2000). Darwin Muir agreed, marveling at the openness with which Papoušek greeted ideas from the younger generation of scholars: "You could go and talk to him about your ideas, he would give you some feedback, and suddenly you'd come up with this insight that you would never have come up with otherwise" (Muir Interview, June 12, 2000). A similar sentiment is voiced by Hiram Fitzgerald, who was a first-year doctoral student in Yvonne Brackbill's infant development laboratory in Denver when Hanuš arrived there as a Visiting Scientist. Fitzgerald recalled the Tuesday "Poker Parties" as the settings in which Hanuš often shared his concepts bridging the fields of psychology and biology, exposing the students to the importance of a systems theory approach. Reflecting back on that semester, Fitzgerald commented:

> Any question you asked, any issue you came up with, was worthy of discussion. It was very pleasant—his attitude, his demeanor towards graduate students, were just unbelievable. . . . Those are the things I remember about Hanuš: you could be a really good scientist, you could be very focused on the critical issues you're concerned about, but you could also be a really nice person. . . . He was a super guy. Gentleness, and a commitment to students are the things

I remember. The conversations we had about linkages between biology and psychology were very, very influential in my graduate years. (Fitzgerald Interview, November 4, 2002)

Charles Rahn was a coworker who spent time with the Papoušeks both in their lab in Munich and during their sabbatical at the National Institutes of Health in Washington, DC. His observations reflect the crucial importance of Hanuš' influence on people: "I think it's very important, I think that's exactly where his stature is. He influenced a tremendous number of people. He trained people . . . in a very particular, very meticulous way" (Rahn Interview, March 11, 2000). Another important mentoring lesson, noted by Peter Mangione, was largely motivational: Do whatever you are capable of doing, even when you are frustrated and feel you can do no more. Perhaps this was an attitude Papoušek developed as a result of his experience in the Eastern bloc, and his years of work there within a very confining system. Despite those circumstances, he was able to accomplish a great deal in terms of important research, which continues to be cited in the infancy literature today. Despite frustrations, he proceeded with single-minded determination, passion, and clarity of message, which are also important lessons for coworkers and students (Mangione Interview, September 17, 2000):

> He took us to Austria and shared . . . his life with us and opened his heart to us and I really feel that, in a sense, that was what he was about. He wanted to open up his world for people to share. I don't think he trusted many people. It was hard for him to do that with everyone, but, if you could establish that basis and that relationship with him then he really wanted to teach you about life . . . and he was very open about that and very supportive. . . . I had tremendous respect for him and really appreciated his intellect and caring for people—that was the gift that he gave to me. (Mangione Interview, September 17, 2000)

Similarly, Charles Rahn noted Hanuš' unselfish availability to his colleagues and students, and his awareness of how little time he had left to share: "Knowing Hanuš as we all did, it must [have been] very difficult and at times quite frightening to him to be aware of his condition and what it had done to his body and mind. He was always so full of energy, so ready to help, to listen, to be a part of our lives, to talk about research, to show us a new and different angle on the research we were doing. . . . I will always cherish those times we spent together" (Rahn Interview, April 2, 2000).

Kim Bard, a primatologist, first became involved with the Papoušek research group in 1988 when she was invited to participate in a conference they were organizing on the topic of nonverbal vocal communication. Following a fascinating gathering of prominent scholars held in the Ringberg Castle in the Bavarian Alps, she was invited by Hanuš to join them in Munich to assist with editing the book of proceedings resulting from the conference. Looking back on that experience, Bard commented about Hanuš as a role model:

> An example of how being supportive and nurturing and enthusiastic about not only your own work but other people's work as well can really be good for everybody. Nobody's harmed by having enthusiasm for other people's work and extending your own work in ways you didn't anticipate or might not even have done yourself, but to encourage other people to discover new things, is really rare. There aren't too many people . . . who are these true scholars and true scientists that are curious about the world. . . . He was never unkind as well. He would find a way sometimes to say not very nice things that *needed* to be said, but he was never unkind. (Bard Interview, May 10, 2000)

The effectiveness of his mentoring went beyond conceptual and methodological issues. It also included (as alluded to by Bruner) a remarkable sense of how to interact with infants as a researcher; there was a subtle communication, often simply by example, of how to achieve that optimal state of attentiveness and readiness needed in order to accomplish the goal of recording one's observations. Rahn explained,

> In this country, the name of the game is Publish or Perish. So, you have to write papers, . . . you're in a hurry to do something quick. Hanuš I think was just the opposite: he took his time to do something methodically. I think Hanuš was a great researcher. . . . His mind was so expansive, and he tried to pull in appropriate things from so many different angles. I remember one of the first things he did [in the lab]—the baby would be sitting there, and before we'd actually start filming, he'd try to get the baby's attention: he'd open his mouth, raise his eyebrows, and all that. And the baby would start paying attention! . . . I've learned a great deal about how you relate to . . . babies, from Hanuš—a tremendous amount. But not many people who do research take the time to train other people to see. (Rahn Interview, March 11, 2000)

As a contemporary of Papoušek's, Bruner clearly enjoyed the intellectual debates the two men often engaged in, sometimes over an evening glass of scotch when thinking over things they had not been able to accomplish during the day:

> He was a wonderful companion—like so many Central Europeans, he had the art of conversation fashioned to suit not only the gossip of the day, but also the world of ideas. Which is ideal—price beyond pearls. We talked endlessly. . . . He was not only a fellow research worker and occasional collabora-

tor, but a wonderful intellectual companion. I have long been convinced that the best colleagues are also good intellectual companions—not just people you sit on committees with. (Bruner Interview, January 30, 2002)

ONGOING CLINICAL APPLICATIONS

Perhaps the most significant way in which Papoušek's legacy is being continued is through the applications of many of his ideas to special populations of parents with infants (birth to 30 months of age) experiencing some type of difficulty in their early development. Clinical applications of the Papoušeks' theory of Intuitive Parenting have been described in detail in a number of publications over the last decade. Much of this work focuses on persistent crying in infants, but also includes multiple problems of behavioral regulation and dysfunctional patterns of communication. The intervention team takes a family systems approach to understanding the origins of the problem and the ways in which parental behaviors may be perpetuating it. Persistent crying has often been attributed to abdominal pain, perhaps caused by immaturity of the digestive system, or "colic." However, the lack of empirical support for this conclusion led Mechthild Papoušek and her team at the Institute for Social Pediatrics and Youth Medicine in Munich to search for other explanations, such as regulatory disorders that interfere with the organization of the infant's sleeping, waking, and/or feeding patterns.

With Hanuš' participation, the group developed interventions and assessments of parent–infant interactions based on the concept of the parents' intuitive support of an infant's integrative capacities. Thus, the Munich Interdisciplinary Research and Intervention Program for Fussy Babies was developed in 1991 with two goals in mind: to provide diagnostic and intervention services for families with chronically "fussy babies," and to do so from a multidisciplinary perspective; and to study these families and the effectiveness of the interventions by using videotaped observations and standardized diagnostic procedures.

A few details about the methodology and findings from these efforts may be helpful in understanding the connections to Papoušek's work. First, mothers are asked to keep a log of their infant's crying, fussing, and sleeping for 5 days, 24 hours each, prior to the first session with the intervention team. The first session involves a neuropediatric examination of the baby, plus semistructured interviews with the mother about the child's symptoms, biological or psychosocial risk factors, pre-and postnatal medical history, parental psychological well-being, and current family relationships. In addition, questionnaires are used to assess infant temperament, maternal depression, marital satisfaction, perceptions of social support, and so forth. Finally, evidence of Intuitive Parenting behavior is recorded by means of videotaped observations of parent–infant interactions in a face-to-face play situation. Among the infants with the greatest amount of crying, the most significant presenting factor for their mothers tends to be depression; when compared to a control group, mothers in this group have been found to be "more exhausted, more frustrated, and more anxious. They obtained lower scores on self-esteem and self-efficacy, and higher scores on marital dissatisfaction. Failures of mother–infant communication in contexts of face-to-face interactions in the laboratory were found in one half of the mother–infant pairs in the Wessel [highest amount of crying] group" (M. Papoušek & H. Papoušek, 1996, p. 25).

Others have found psychophysiological effects on parents as a result of inconsolable infant crying (e.g., see Boukydis & Burgess, 1982), and the effects have been shown to diminish parental feelings of self-efficacy and lead to increased irritability, helplessness, and of course depression. As a result, parents' ability to rely on their intuitive competencies to guide their responses to the infant may be seriously compromised. Both physical and psychological reserves may be drained quickly when parents are unable to soothe an infant who is excessively fussy, especially if other risk factors are also present. As described by the Papoušeks, this inhibition of intuitive behaviors may lead to a variety of interactional failures within the parent–infant dyad: "Uncontrollable and unexplainable crying elicits maternal feelings of inefficacy or incompetence in soothing, feeding, or otherwise satisfying her baby. If several or all interactional domains are affected, maternal feelings of helplessness and loss of control often become pervasive and promote reliance on rational advice rather than on intuitive competence" (M. Papoušek & H. Papoušek, 1996, p. 26).

It is easy to imagine how vicious cycles of unsatisfying interactions might develop in such situations. In fact, many parents of these excessively crying infants seem to perceive their baby as requiring intense vestibular stimulation or other intense forms of distraction in order to avoid a buildup to inconsolable bouts of crying. Opportunities for stress-free, playful, and spontaneous social interactions are rare. As a result, both parents and infants may have difficulty "reading" each others' signals and establishing mutually rewarding, reciprocal and responsive relationships. However, the infant is learning something important in the process: The predominant message is that maternal behaviors are contingent on infant crying, such that instrumental crying may be promoted at an early age. Again, knowledge of infant learning from the early Prague studies is helpful even now, as seen in the realm of clinical applications. In this case, infants are also missing opportunities for developing self-soothing strategies, and continue instead to elicit tense and irritable reactions from their caregivers. When an infant is already overtired or in a state of hyperarousal, highly stimulating and intense efforts to soothe may be counterproductive; and when parental interventions fail, the effect may be felt in the entire family system. "Thus, interaction with an inconsolable infant often leads to vicious cycles of reciprocal spirals of hyperarousal, hyperstimulation, and exhaustion. . . . The keys to successful intervention . . . seem to lie in the encouragement of mutually rewarding parent-infant interchanges and in the disinhibition and reactivation of intuitive competencies in parents" (M. Papoušek & H. Papoušek, 1996, pp. 27–28).

These clinical experiences and findings may seem to contradict the notion that if intuitive forms of parenting are biologically determined, then they must somehow be resistant to disturbance. In fact, according to the Papoušeks, these behaviors may be relatively fragile and adversely influenced by many contemporary sociocultural conditions in Western societies: families with young children being isolated from extended family supports; increasing numbers of single-parent families, especially when this is the result of marital conflict or divorce; and inadequate family leave policies that diminish the amount of time parents can take to be home with their infants before returning to a workplace outside the home.

The current flood of unsubstantiated childrearing recommendations (i.e., an abundance of advice books for parents) probably does more to exacerbate than to remedy the situation. But the strategy used by Mechthild's team is quite different, because the feedback to the mother is based on actual videotapes of her interactions with the baby—not on a hypothetical, idealized parent–infant dyad. To see this in action is quite impressive: Often without even previewing the videotape herself, she will play it back to the parents and watch carefully with them. As soon as she notices something positive in the interactions, she will replay it for the parents, saying something like "Now look at how wonderfully the baby is making eye contact with you there!" or "Look at what you were doing here—see how effective that was, how much he liked that?" Step by step, she points out numerous incidents when the parents are doing something right, something barely noticeable that the child enjoyed and responded to positively—because these are parents who feel like failures.

Mechthild firmly believes that every parent has a certain level of Intuitive Parenting skills within their repertoire. The job of the "Fussy Baby Team" is to find where that level is and to build on it, to help the parents gradually, incrementally expand on the abilities they already have. The important process for these parents is to help them perceive the examples of positive feedback from the baby that signal, "Yes, you're doing something right. I like that. Continue this. Stop doing that." The parents, as well as the infants, are equally in need of positive outcomes of their interactive efforts, and this can be a powerful antidote to the downward spiral that frequently occurs with persistently crying babies.

Crying is, of course, an inevitable behavior in infants and may for some time be their primary means of communicating distress. Although this is a normal expectation and one that parents are typically able to cope with, in more extreme cases the possibility of an escalation to abuse or neglect may need to be considered. In addressing this concern, Mechthild Papoušek (2000) described the feelings often expressed by parents participating in the clinical intervention program in Munich:

> All mothers of infants with persistent crying admitted that prolonged exposure to the piercing perceptual quality of intense crying together with the infant's back arching, squirming, and resistance to close body contact elicited both feelings of being rejected by their infant and aversive feelings of frustration, anger, rejection, or even powerless rage with aggressive or escape fantasies. The same mothers felt both ashamed of and appalled by their unexpected negative feelings toward their infant. With few exceptions, they had never physically abused their infant, but they expressed their empathy with abusing parents. (M. Papoušek, 2000, p. 437)

Darwin Muir described these recent developments as the "marriage of clinical training and experimental work," and commented about the unbelievable insights one can gain by putting the two together. Muir elaborated, "It really is basically learning how to push the baby's buttons. Babies have buttons and you can push them, but boy you have to be sensitive about how to do it. Even parents can miss it" (Muir Interview, June 12, 2000).

Marc Bornstein also emphasized the value of translating the earlier microanalytic observations, combined with Mechthild's clinical skills, into a practical and applied therapeutic model. Once this had been accomplished, the Papoušeks began traveling around Europe (particularly the former Soviet bloc countries) providing training for practitioners and interventionists. This training consists of a comprehensive curriculum for professionals in the field of infant mental health, and covers a wide range of infant regulatory disorders and disturbances in parent–infant relationships.

The result has been a dedicated following, as well as innumerable invitations to contribute book chapters and additional workshops on a global level (Bornstein Interview, March 10, 2000). In 1998, Hanuš and Mechthild together were awarded the Arnold Lucius Gesell Prize in Germany, in recognition of their work and its important contributions toward improving infant mental health. In many European countries, this early intervention model has now caught on within therapeutic circles, and practitioners are eager to develop the skills for applying the concepts of Intuitive Parenting to their clinical work with infants and toddlers.

REMEMBERING HANUŠ: LESSONS FROM HIS LIFE

What, then, are some of the important lessons that Hanuš' friends, students, and coworkers have drawn from his life? There is a sense of humor that almost invariably comes through as people talk about their times with Hanuš—a memory of his often ironic laughter, the wildness of his driving, and of his ability to reflect somewhat philosophically even on the most distressing of circumstances. But there is also the image of a man who was very private, modest, and in some ways inscrutable. Lew Lipsitt reflected,

> Hanuš has always been sort of a man of mystery, you know. He is reticent to talk about some things, and that was especially noticeable during those early years. . . . I was never exactly sure what he was permitted to do, what he couldn't do; I was never exactly sure the extent to which he was being harassed by his own government, because he was very discrete. And, you know, he would say, "Well, I'll go there if I can, and maybe I'll see you, maybe I won't. . . ." Besides being a wonderful man, he was also a man of mystery to an extent, and seemed to remain so even after he was free not to be. . . . It never affected our personal relationship, . . . it was just part of the mystery of Hanuš. (Lipsitt Interview, May 4, 2000)

Hanuš was a person who could tease and be playful, even when he himself was the subject of the joke. In a 1995 message to Lew and Edna Lipsitt, this was apparent in comments about his frustrations with advanced computer technology: "The reason I have been so slow in using Internet is a lack of surfer-experience: I am unable to locate and download <SPARE TIME> in Internet menus . . ." During a previous visit to the United States, he purchased a CD of American recipes to add to his growing collection of cookbooks, but was astounded when he returned home to discover that the contents included 1,094,579 entries! As he noted in the same message, "It is a shock to search for Tiramisu and get a message '56 recipes available.' Just a simple estimate of the rest of my lifetime indicates how inexperienced I shall be dying one day even if I calculate 5 rich meals a day."

Kimbrough Oller reported another humorous incident when Hanuš was visiting him and his wife, Rebecca Eilers, at their home in Florida. Having loaned Hanuš a car, Kim gave him the key ring with three keys, each identified in a very specific way. Kim then carefully explained the strategy by which Hanuš could best remember which was the correct key. On the third day, Hanuš came home and announced, "Kim, I've figured out how to remember this precisely: it's always the *third* key!" (Oller Interview, September 2, 2000).

Other Americans recalled European car trips with the Papoušeks in later years, with particular memories related to Hanuš' love of nature and of photography. Marc and Helen Bornstein, for example, described a sequence in which Hanuš would see a flower along the side of the road, stop the car, pull over, take some photographs of this flower, get back in the car, and drive another 100 yards. Then he would see another flower, pull over, and so forth, until they were beginning to wonder if they were ever going to reach their destination. Marc commented about this incident, "But you know, he had this *passion* for photography, and for the natural world, and for wildlife—and that all just fits together" (Bornstein Interview, March 10, 2000). Thus, another lesson from Hanuš Papoušek's story becomes evident: Maintain a passion for life, an enthusiasm for learning, an inquisitiveness about nature, and strive to combine them all in an effort to create a more nurturing world for children.

According to Steve Suomi, Hanuš' love of the outdoors, his exuberance about something as simple as hiking to a beautiful place, and his extraordinary curiosity were all consistent with his scientific achievements. Suomi was in a position to know that Hanuš Papoušek was "capable of being quite critical," but Suomi also respected the fact that Hanuš was selective about the targets of his criticism (Suomi Interview, March 11, 2000).

Papoušek's passion for photography was evident to those in the family's large network of friends around the world, people who knew to anticipate a delightful annual photo of Hanuš and Mechthild, Tanja and Silvia, in the form of a seasonal greeting card accompanied by a handwritten, personalized note. Often these portrayed their family vacations, and his passion for skiing or hiking in the Alps with his family. (Several months after the onset of Hanuš' illness, Lew Lipsitt wrote to the Papoušeks about looking forward to the next holiday card, imagining that the picture that year might be Sisyphus pushing the hospital bed up a snowy hill.) In April 1997, Hanuš described their celebration of daughter Tanja's 22nd birthday, at which he had given her 250 well-organized pictures documenting her preschool years: "a kind of photographic/scientific heritage on the principles of family rearing." Silvia would receive a similar collection on her 20th birthday that June.

Hanuš Papoušek will also be remembered by many for his personal integrity, and his insistence on honesty and high standards even in the face of an authoritarian government during much of his young adulthood. A former Prague colleague who had been active in the Unitarian Church there recalled one poignant illustration. Her first awareness that Hanuš had been involved in any way came after the fall of Communism, when employees began to have access to their Secret Service files. Her personnel records indicated that she had been labeled a "rabid fundamentalist, a religious bigot" as a result of her Unitarian affiliation. Not being a Party member, this label could have easily cost her the research job she held at the Institute for the Care of Mother and Child. As it turned out, Hanuš had actively but quietly protected her, so that her position remained secure. When she finally discovered the risks he had taken to defend her, she wrote him a letter of deep appreciation, acknowledging for the first time that she surely would have lost her job had he not intervened. Hanuš apparently wrote back and said something to the effect of "Thank God the silence is broken."

Other examples of his courage have to do more with his own insights during World War II. Darwin Muir, on behalf of the History Committee of the Society for Research in Child Development, interviewed Papoušek and recalled the following:

> I asked him how he ever got involved in this [infancy research]. He said that during the war . . . they were bombing all around him. Things . . . were shattering and he was sure he was going to die, and he really wondered what made people do this sort of thing, and that kind of drove him. That was the theme. That one incident made him want to study human behavior and ask these questions about why people act the way they do. . . . That was revealing because it's what he spent his entire life doing. He really did look at the origins of social behavior. . . . The other part is that he never quit. He went literally on his dying bed, still engaged in trying to solve problems and contribute. . . . He's an inspiration. He's the kind of person you want to tell people about. Here's the life of a person that was meaningful, and here's how they did it; they went through terrible traumas and hard times. . . . He's an example, I would say, of the resilient person. His life was "high risk" and he made it. He's a great model. (Muir Interview, June 12, 2000)

It has been mentioned previously that Papoušek held his fellow countryman, philosopher, and educator Jan Comenius in high esteem. In 1992, Hanuš and Mechthild presented their concepts of Intuitive Parenting at a conference on "Comenius' Heritage and Education of Man for the 21st Century" held at Charles University in Prague. Their introductory statement seems appropriate when considered in light of Hanuš' legacy and further lessons from his life: respect for wisdom, continuities with our past, the value of intuition, and the profound importance of caring for the next generations of children:

> In his heritage, Jan Amos Comenius not only shares his enormous wisdom with us, but also expects us to continue his work and develop his ideas wherever they have been based upon beliefs or intuitive assumptions. Comenius assumed that humans learn from the very beginning of life, although he could not prove it. He also assumed that infants found spontaneous teachers in their mothers or caregivers, although he gave no detailed information on maternal capacities for teaching. Comenius knew very much about how to teach foreign languages, but left the question open how infants acquire the first language—the mother-tongue. However, the way in which Comenius

stressed the significance of these developmental phenomena compels us to pay full attention to them. (H. Papoušek & M. Papoušek, 1992, p. 84)

The Papoušeks then proceeded to review scientific evidence of infant competence, the importance of emotional regulation, parental capacities to support optimal infant development particularly in the realm of language acquisition, and the role of playfulness in the young child's life. Of course, much of this evidence was generated by Papoušek's own early experimental studies, or through his later collaborative efforts with Mechthild as they substantiated their theory of Intuitive Parenting.

Six months before Hanuš' death, Lew Lipsitt shared his pride over the dedication of Volume 7, *Advances in Infancy Research*, with his close friend and colleague: *This volume* "was dedicated to you and your enormous contributions to the behavioral study of human infants. There isn't any award in our field that would adequately acknowledge the creative foresight and instrumental ingenuity that you have had in designing and executing some of the most innovative and informative studies in the history of our field" (Lipsitt e-mail, October 25, 1999).

Following Comenius' lead, Hanuš Papoušek made impressive strides in filling in the many gaps that once existed in the understanding of the human infant. The courage he displayed in an unending quest for knowledge, despite political oppression and personal risk, also stands as a lesson for those who follow. Now, his legacy compels the next generation of scholars to expand on this knowledge, and to find appropriate applications for the betterment of humanity and for the improvement of parenting and child-rearing conditions around the world. Hanuš would have been terribly disappointed had some good for the future of children *not* come from his life's work: "I thought, no matter what you do, if you do something for the younger generation it's good for mankind" (Papoušek Interview, July 12, 1998).

References

Aslin, R. (1987). Visual and auditory development in infancy. In J. D. Osofsky (Ed.), *Handbook of infant development* (2nd ed., pp. 5–97). New York: Wiley.

Bell, R. Q. (1968). A reinterpretation of the direction of effects in studies of socialization. *Psychological Review, 75,* 81–95.

Bornstein, M. H. (Ed.). (1995). *Handbook of parenting: Vol. 2. Biology and ecology of parenting.* Hillsdale, NJ: Lawrence Erlbaum Associates.

Bornstein, M., & Koester, L. S. (2000a). Odešel Hanuš Papoušek. *Psychologie Dnes: Psychologie, Psychotherapie, Žvotní Styl, 7,* 6–7.

Bornstein, M., & Koester, L. S. (2000b). On Hanuš. *Newsletter of the Society for Research in Child Development, XI*(1), 3–4.

Boukydis, C. F. Z., & Burgess, R. L. (1982). Adult physiological response to infant cries: Effects of temperament of infant, parental status, and gender. *Child Development, 53,* 1291–1298.

Brazelton, T. B., Koslowski, B., & Main, M. (1974). The origins of reciprocity: The early mother–infant interaction. In M. Lewis & L. Rosenblum (Eds.), *The effect of the infant on its caregiver. The origins of behavior* (Vol. 1, pp. 49–77). New York: Wiley.

Bruner, J. S. (1983). *In search of mind: Essays in autobiography.* New York: Harper & Row.

Connelly, J. (1999). The foundations of diversity: Communist higher education policies in Eastern Europe, 1945–1955. In K. Macrakis & D. Hoffmann (Eds.), *Science under socialism: East Germany in comparative perspective* (pp. 125–139). Cambridge, MA: Harvard University Press.

DeCasper, A. J., & Fifer, W. P. (1980). Of human bonding: Newborns prefer their mothers' voices. *Science, 208,* 1174–1176.

de Schonen, S., & Mathivet, E. (1989). First come, first served: A scenario about development of hemispheric specialization in face recognition during infancy. *Cahiers de Psychologie Cognitive, 9,* 3–44.

Denisová, M. P., & Figurin, N. L. (1929). K voprosu a pervykh sotshetatelnykh pishtshevykh refleksakh u grudnykh detey [The question of the first conditioned alimentary reflexes in infants]. *Voprosy genetitsheskoy refleksologiyi i pedologiyi, 1,* 811–888.

185

Emde, R. (1994). Individual meaning and increasing complexity: Contributions of Sigmund Freud and René Spitz to developmental psychology. In R. Parke, P. Ornstein, J. Rieser, & C. Zahn-Waxler (Eds.), *A century of developmental psychology* (pp. 203–231). Washington, DC: American Psychological Association.

Fagan, J. F. (1979). The origins of facial pattern recognition. In M. H. Bornstein & W. Kessen (Eds.), *Psychological development from infancy: Image to intention* (pp. 616–649). Hillsdale, NJ: Lawrence Erlbaum Associates.

Fantz, R. L. (1973). Visual perception from birth as shown by pattern selectivity. In L. J. Stone, H. T. Smith, & L. B. Murphy (Eds.), *The competent infant: Research and commentary* (pp. 622–630). New York: Basic Books.

Fernald, A., & Simon, T. (1984). Expanded intonation contours in mothers' speech to newborns. *Developmental Psychology, 20,* 104–113.

Fernald, A., Taeschner, T., Dunn, J., Papoušek, M., DeBoysson-Bardis, B., & Fukui, I. (1989). A cross-language study of prosodic modifications in mothers' and fathers' speech to preverbal infants. *Journal of Child Language, 16,* 477–501.

Field, T. M., Woodson, R., Greenberg, R., & Cohen, D. (1982). Discrimination and imitation of facial expressions by neonates. *Science, 218,* 179–181.

Fogel, A. (1977). Temporal organization in mother–infant face-to-face interaction. In H. R. Schaffer (Ed.), *Studies in mother–infant interaction* (pp. 119–152). London: Academic Press.

Haekel, M. (1985, July). *Greeting behavior in 3-month-old infants during mother–infant interaction.* Paper presented at the eighth biennial meetings of the International Society for the Study of Behavioural Development, Tours, France. Abstracted in *Cahiers de Psychologie Cognitive, 5,* 275–276.

Institute for the Care of Mother and Child. (1961). *Five-year report.* Prague: Podolí.

Institute for the Care of Mother and Child. (1967). *Survey of research work, 1962–1966.* Prague: Podolí.

James, W. (1890). *Principles of psychology.* New York: Holt.

Kasatkin, N. I. (1969). The origin and development of conditioned reflexes in early childhood. In M. Cole & I. Maltzman (Eds.), *A handbook of contemporary Soviet psychology* (pp. 71–85). New York: Basic Books.

Kasatkin, N. I., & Leviková, A. M. (1935). On the development of early conditioned reflexes and differentiation of auditory stimuli in infants. *Journal of Experimental Psychology, 18*(1), 1–19.

Kestermann, G. (1982). *Gestik von Säuglingen: Ihre kommunikative Bedeutung für erfahrene und unerfahrene Bezugspersonen* [Gesticulation in infants: Their communicative significance for experienced and inexperienced caregivers]. Unpublished doctoral dissertation, University of Bielefeld, Germany.

Klímová, H. (1963a). Jako míšeňské jablíčko, jako z růže květ . . . [Like a Meisener apple, like a rose . . .]. *Literární Noviny, 7,* 1 & 6.

Klímová, H. (1963b). Děti a denní jesle: Hovoří odborníci [Children and day care: The professionals are talking]. *Literární Noviny, 7,* 18.

Klímová, H. (1966). Symposium o jeslích [Symposium on day care for infants and toddlers]. *Literární Noviny, 45,* 7.

Koester, L. S. (1986, April). *Rhythms and repetitions in parent–infant interactions.* Paper presented at the fifth international Conference on Infant Studies, Los Angeles, CA. Abstracted in *Infant Behavior and Development, 9,* 203.

Koester, L. S. (1988). Rhythmicity in parental stimulation of infants. In P. G. Fedor-Freybergh (Ed.), *Prenatal and perinatal psychology and medicine* (pp. 143–152). Lancashire, England: Parthenon.

Koester, L. S. (1992). Intuitive parenting as a model for understanding parent–infant interactions when one partner is deaf. *American Annals of the Deaf, 137*(4), 362–369.

Koester, L. S. (1994). Early interactions and the socioemotional development of deaf infants. *Early Development and Parenting* (Special Edition), *3*(1), 51–60.

Koester, L. S., Papoušek, H., & Papoušek, M. (1987). Psychobiological models of infant development: Influences on the concept of intuitive parenting. In H. Rauh & H.-C. Steinhausen (Eds.), *Advances in psychology: Vol. 46. Psychobiology and early development* (pp. 275–287). North Holland: Elsevier.

Koester, L. S., Papoušek, H., & Papoušek, M. (1989). Patterns of rhythmic stimulation by mothers with three-month-olds: A cross-modal comparison. *International Journal of Behavioural Development, 12,* 143–154.

Koester, L. S., Papoušek, H., & Smith-Gray, S. (2000). Intuitive parenting, communication, and interaction with deaf infants. In P. E. Spencer, C. J. Erting, & M. Marschark (Eds.), *The deaf child in the family and at school: Essays in honor of Kathryn P. Meadow-Orlans* (pp. 55–71). Mahwah, NJ: Lawrence Erlbaum Associates.

Korbel, J. (1977). *Twentieth century Czechoslovakia: The meaning of its history.* New York: Columbia University Press.

Krasnogorskii, N. I. (1967). The formation of conditioned reflexes in the young child. In Y. Brackbill & G. G. Thompson (Eds.), *Behavior in infancy and early childhood* (pp. 237–238). New York: The Free Press. (Original work published 1907)

Kubát, K., Papoušek, H., & Štolová, O. (1963). On some comments to the problems of child rearing in family and in institutions. *Československá Pediatrie, 18,* 468.

Lewis, M., & Rosenblum, L. (Eds.). (1974). *The effect of the infant on its caregiver. The origins of behavior* (Vol. 1). New York: Wiley.

Littell, R. (1969). *The Czech black book.* New York: Praeger.

Maratos, O. (1973). *The origin and development of imitation in the first six months of life.* Unpublished doctoral dissertation, University of Geneva, Switzerland.

Marquis, D. P. (1931). Can conditioned responses be established in the newborn infant? *Journal of Genetic Psychology, 39,* 479–492.

Meadow-Orlans, K. P., Spencer, P. E., & Koester, L. S. (Eds.). (2004). *The world of deaf infants: A longitudinal study.* New York: Oxford University Press.

Meltzoff, A. N., & Moore, M. K. (1983). Newborn infants imitate adult facial gestures. *Child Development, 54,* 702–709.

Mussen, P. (Ed.). (1965). *European research in cognitive development. SRCD Monograph.* Chicago: Society for Research in Child Development.

Osofsky, J. D. (Ed.). (1987). *Handbook of infant development* (2nd ed.). New York: Wiley & Sons.

Papoušek, H. (1954). Krvácivost v průběhu kojeneckých toxikos [Hemorrhagic diathesis in toxic diarrhoea in infants]. *Pediatrické Listy, 9,* 95–96.

Papoušek, H. (1955). Pavlovské koncepty nemoci v pediatrii [The Pavlovian concept of disease in pediatrics]. *Československá Pediatrie, 10,* 641–649.

Papoušek, H. (1963). A pediatrician looks at some ideological problems in bringing up children (in Czech). *Československá Pediatrie, 18,* 636–639.

Papoušek, H. (1964). Několik problémů dětských zařízení [Some problems of child care institutions]. *Československá Pediatrie, 19,* 1117.

Papoušek, H. (1965). The development of higher nervous activity in the first half-year of life. In P. H. Mussen (Ed.), *European research in cognitive development: Report of the International Conference on Cognitive Development. Monographs of the Society for Research in Child Development, 30*(2, Serial No. 100), 102–111.

Papoušek, H. (1967a). Conditioning during early postnatal development. In Y. Brackbill & G. G. Thompson (Eds.), *Behavior in infancy and early childhood* (pp. 259–274). New York: The Free Press.

Papoušek, H. (1967b). Experimental studies of appetitional behavior in human newborns and infants. In H. Stevenson, E. Hess, & H. Rheingold (Eds.), *Early behavior: Comparative and developmental approaches* (pp. 249–277). New York: Wiley.

Papoušek, H. (1977). Entwicklung der Lernfähigkeit im Säuglingsalter [The development of learning ability in infancy]. In G. Nissen (Ed.), *Intelligenz, lernen und lernstörungen* (pp. 75–93). Berlin: Springer-Verlag.

Papoušek, H. (1979). From adaptive responses to social cognition: The learning view of development. In M. H. Bornstein & W. Kessen (Eds.), *Psychological development from infancy: Image to intention* (pp. 251–267). Hillsdale, NJ: Lawrence Erlbaum Associates.

Papoušek, H. (1995). Frühe Angstmanifestationen im Säuglings- und Kleinkindsalter. In G. Nissen (Hrsg.), *Angsterkrankungen. Prävention und Therapie* (pp. 109–117). Bern, Stuttgart, Wien: Verlag Hans Huber.

Papoušek, H., & Bernstein, P. (1969). The functions of conditioning stimulation in human neonates and infants. In A. Ambrose (Ed.), *Stimulation in early infancy* (pp. 229–252). London: Academic Press.

Papoušek, H., & Janele, J. (1956). Hemokoagulační faktory v pathogenese traumatismu ústřední nervové soustavy u donošených novorozenců [The factors of hemocoagulation in the pathogenesis of birth injury of the central nervous system in fullterm newborns]. *Sborník vědeckých prací, 8 (Neonatal Birth Injury),* 379–392. Prague: Státní Zdravotnické Nakladatelství.

Papoušek, H., & Papoušek, M. (1974). Mirror image and self-recognition in young human infants: A new method of experimental analysis. *Developmental Psychobiology, 7,* 149–157.

Papoušek, H., & Papoušek, M. (1975). Cognitive aspects of preverbal social interaction between human infants and adults. In CIBA Foundation Symposium, *Parent–infant interaction* (pp. 241–260). Amsterdam: Elsevier.

Papoušek, H., & Papoušek, M. (1978). Interdisciplinary parallels in studies of early human behavior: From physical to cognitive needs, from attachment to dyadic education. *International Journal of Behavioral Development, 1,* 37–49.

Papoušek, H., & Papoušek, M. (1979). The infant's fundamental adaptive response system in social interaction. In E. B. Thoman (Ed.), *Origins of the infant's social responsiveness* (pp. 175–208). Hillsdale, NJ: Lawrence Erlbaum Associates.

Papoušek, H., & Papoušek, M. (1981). How human is the newborn, and what else is to be done? In K. Bloom (Ed.), *Prospective issues in infancy research* (pp. 137–155). Hillsdale, NJ: Lawrence Erlbaum Associates.

Papoušek, H., & Papoušek, M. (1982a). Infant–adult social interactions, their origins, dimensions, and failures. In T. M. Field, A. Huston, H. C. Quay, L. Troll, & G. A. Finley (Eds.), *Review of developmental psychology* (pp. 148–163). New York: Wiley.

Papoušek, H., & Papoušek, M. (1982b). Integration into the social world: Survey of research. In P. M. Stratton (Ed.), *Psychobiology of the human newborn* (pp. 367–390). London: Wiley.

Papoušek, H., & Papoušek, M. (1983). The psychobiology of the first didactical programs and toys in human infants. In A. Oliverio & M. Zappella (Eds.), *The behaviour of human infants* (pp. 219–239). New York: Plenum.

Papoušek, H., & Papoušek, M. (1984). Qualitative transitions in integrative processes during the first trimester of human postpartum life. In H. F. R. Prechtl (Ed.), *Continuity of neural functions from prenatal to postnatal life* (pp. 220–244). Spastics International Medical Publications. Oxford, England: Blackwell Scientific.

Papoušek, H., & Papoušek, M. (1987). Intuitive parenting: A dialectic counterpart to the infant's precocity in integrative capacities. In J. D. Osofsky (Ed.), *Handbook of infant development* (2nd ed., pp. 669–720). New York: Wiley.

Papoušek, H., & Papoušek, M. (1989). Intuitive parenting: Aspects related to educational psychology. In B. Hopkins, M.-G. Pecheux, & H. Papoušek (Eds.), *Infancy and education: Psychological considerations. European Journal of Psychology of Education, 4*(2, Special Issue), 201–210.

Papoušek, H., & Papoušek, M. (1992). Preverbal infants, their primary teachers and primary toys. In V. Mišurcová (Ed.), *Comenius' heritage and early childhood education* (pp. 84–92). Prague: Charles University.

Papoušek, H., & Papoušek, M. (1995). Intuitive parenting. In M. H. Bornstein (Ed.), *Handbook of parenting: Vol. 2. Ecology and biology of parenting* (pp. 117–136). Hillsdale, NJ: Lawrence Erlbaum Associates.

Papoušek, H., & Papoušek, M. (1997). Fragile parts of early social integration. In L. Murray & P. J. Cooper (Eds.), *Postpartum depression and child development* (pp. 35–53). New York: Guilford.

Papoušek, H., Papoušek, M., & Bornstein, M. H. (1985). The naturalistic vocal environment of young infants: On the significance of homogeneity and variability in parental speech. In T. Field & N. Fox (Eds.), *Social perception in infants* (pp. 269–297). Norwood, NJ: Ablex.

Papoušek, H., Papoušek, M., & Haekel, M. (1985). Der Vater und sein Säugling: Anfänge einer Beziehung [Fathers and infants: The beginnings of a relationship]. In C. Mühlfeld, H. Oppl, H. Weber, & W. R. Wendt (Eds.), *Brennpunkte sozialer Arbeit* (pp. 48–63). Frankfurt: Diesterweg.

Papoušek, H., Papoušek, M., & Kestermann, G. (2000). Preverbal communication: Emergence of representative symbols. In N. Budwig, I. C. Uzgiris, & J. V. Wertsch (Eds.), *Communication: An arena of development* (pp. 81–107). Norwood, NJ: Ablex.

Papoušek, H., Papoušek, M., & Koester, L. S. (1986). Sharing emotionality and sharing knowledge: A microanalytic approach to parent–infant communication. In C. E. Izard & P. Read (Eds.), *Measuring emotions in infants and children* (Vol. 2, pp. 93–123). Cambridge, UK: Cambridge University Press.

Papoušek, H., Papoušek, M., & Koester, L. S. (1999). Early integration of experience: The interplay of nature and culture. In A. F. Kalverboer, B. Hopkins, & L. Genta (Eds.), *Current issues in developmental psychology. Biopsychological perspectives* (pp. 27–51). Amsterdam: Kluwer.

Papoušek, H., Papoušek, M., Suomi, S., & Rahn, C. (1991). Preverbal communication and attachment: Comparative views. In J. L. Gewirtz & W. M. Kurtines (Eds.), *Intersections with attachment* (pp. 97–122). Hillsdale, NJ: Lawrence Erlbaum Associates.

Papoušek, M. (1989). Determinants of responsiveness to infant vocal expression of emotional state. *Infant Behavior and Development, 12,* 505–522.

Papoušek, M. (1994). *Vom ersten Schrei zum ersten Wort: Anfänge der Sprachentwicklung in der vorsprachlichen Kommunikation* [From first cry to first word: The onset of speech development in preverbal communication]. Bern: Huber.

Papoušek, M. (2000). Persistent crying, parenting, and infant mental health. In J. D. Osofsky & H. E. Fitzgerald (Eds.), *WAIMH handbook of infant mental health: Vol. 4. Infant mental health in groups at high risk* (pp. 417–453). New York: Wiley.

Papoušek, M., Bornstein, M. H., Nuzzo, C., Papoušek, H., & Symmes, D. (1990). Infant responses to prototypical melodic contours in parental speech. *Infant Behavior and Development, 13,* 539–545.

Papoušek, M., & Papoušek, H. (1981). Musical elements in the infant's vocalizations: Their significance for communication, cognition and creativity. In L. P. Lipsitt (Ed.), *Advances in infancy research* (Vol. 1, pp. 163–224). Norwood, NJ: Ablex.

Papoušek, M., & Papoušek, H. (1989). Forms and functions of vocal matching in precanonical mother–infant interactions. *First Language, 9,* 137–158.

Papoušek, M., & Papoušek, H. (1996). Infantile persistent crying, state regulation, and interaction with parents: A systems view. In M. H. Bornstein & J. L. Genevro (Eds.), *Child development and behavioral pediatrics* (pp. 11–33). Mahwah, NJ: Lawrence Erlbaum Associates.

Papoušek, M., Papoušek, H., & Bornstein, M. H. (1985). The naturalistic vocal environment of young infants: On the significance of homogeneity and variability in parental speech. In T. Field & N. Fox (Eds.), *Social perception in infants* (pp. 269–297). Norwood, NJ: Ablex.

Papoušek, M., Papoušek, H., & Haekel, M. (1987). Didactic adjustments in fathers' and mothers' speech to their three-month-old infants. *Journal of Psycholinguistic Research, 16,* 491–516.

Papoušek, M., Papoušek, H., & Harris, B. J. (1987). The emergence of play in parent–infant interactions. In D. Görlitz & J. F. Wohlwill (Eds.), *Curiosity, imagination, and play: On the devel-*

opment of spontaneous cognitive and motivational processes (pp. 214–246). Hillsdale, NJ: Lawrence Erlbaum Associates.

Ploog, D. (1989, May). Laudatio for Hanuš Papoušek. Presented at the XXI. Wissenschaftliche Tagung der Deutschen Gesselschaft für Kinder- und Jugendpsychiatrie, München.

Ripin, R., & Hetzer, H. (1930). Frühestes Lernen des Säuglings in der Ernährungssituation [Early infant learning in feeding situations]. *Zeitschrift für Psychologie, 118*, 1–3, 82–127.

Rogoff, B., & Wertsch, J. V. (Eds.). (1984). Children's learning in the "zone of proximal development." *New directions for child development* (No. 23). San Francisco: Jossey-Bass.

Sameroff, A. J., & Fiese, B. H. (1990). Transactional regulation and early intervention. In S. J. Meisels & J. P. Shonkoff (Eds.), *Handbook of early childhood intervention* (pp. 119–149). Cambridge: Cambridge University Press.

Schaffer, H. R. (1979). Acquiring the concept of the dialogue. In M. H. Bornstein & W. Kessen (Eds.), *Psychological development from infancy* (pp. 279–305). Hillsdale, NJ: Lawrence Erlbaum Associates.

Schoetzau, A., & Papoušek, H. (1977). Mütterliches Verhalten bei der Aufnahme von Blickkontakt mit dem Neugeborenen [Maternal behavior in response to eye contact with newborns]. *Zeitschrift für Entwicklungspsychologie und pädagogische Psychologie, 9*, 231–239.

Stern, D. N. (1985). *The interpersonal world of the infant: A view from psychoanalysis and developmental psychology.* New York: Basic Books.

Stern, D. N., Beebe, B., Jaffe, J., & Bennett, S. L. (1977). The infant's stimulus world during social interaction: A study of caregiver behaviours with particular reference to repetition and timing. In H. R. Schaffer (Ed.), *Studies in mother–infant interaction* (pp. 177–194). London: Academic.

Stern, D. N., & Gibbon, J. (1979). Temporal expectancies of social behaviors in mother–infant play. In E. B. Thoman (Ed.), *Origins of the infant's social responsiveness* (pp. 409–430). Hillsdale, NJ: Lawrence Erlbaum Associates.

Street, W. (1994). *A chronology of noteworthy events in American psychology.* Washington, DC: American Psychological Association.

Traci, M. A., & Koester, L. S. (2003). Parent–infant interactions: A transactional approach to understanding the development of deaf infants. In M. Marschark & P. Spencer (Eds.), *The Oxford handbook of deaf studies, language and education* (pp. 190–202). Oxford: Oxford University Press.

Valsiner, J. (1988). *Developmental psychology in the Soviet Union.* Bloomington, IN: Indiana University.

von Bertalanffy, L. (1968). *Organismic psychology theory.* Barre, MA: Clark University Press.

Wenger, M. A. (1936). An investigation of conditioned responses in human infants. *University of Iowa Studies in Child Welfare, 12*, 9–90.

Wenger, M. A. (1943). Conditioned responses in human infants. In R. G. Barker, J. S. Kounin, & H. F. Wright (Eds.), *Child behavior and development: A course of representative studies* (pp. 67–86). New York: McGraw-Hill.

Wolff, P. H. (1991). Endogenous motor rhythms in young infants. In J. Fagard & P. H. Wolff (Eds.), *The development of timing control and temporal organization in coordinated action: Invariant relative timing, rhythms and coordination* (pp. 119–133). Amsterdam: North Holland.

Appendix A:
List of Publications

1. Papoušek, H. (1954). Hemorrhagic diathesis in toxic diarrhoea in infants. *Pediatrické Listy*, *9*, 95–96.

2. Papoušek, H. (1955). The Pavlovian concept of disease in pediatrics. *Československá Pediatrie*, *10*, 641–649.

3. Papoušek, H. (1955). The Pavlovian concept of disease and its application in pediatrics. In *The textbooks of the Medical Institute for Postdoctoral Training* (pp. 1–34). Prague: Medical Institute for Postdoctoral Training.

4. Trapl, J., Vojta, M., et al. (1955). *The textbook of obstetrics* (3rd ed.). Prague: Státní Zdravotnické Nakladatelství.

5. Papoušek, H. (1956). Activity recording in small infants. *Československá Pediatrie*, *11*, 850–854.

6. Papoušek, H., Brachfeld, K., Svatý, J., & Rousarová, J. (1956). The care for injured newborns. *Sborník vědeckých prací*, *8*, 335–353.

7. Papoušek, H., & Janele, J. (1956). The factors of hemocoagulation in the pathogenesis of birth injury of the central nervous system in fullterm newborns. *Sborník vědeckých prací*, *8*, 379–392.

8. Papoušek, H. (1957). The conference on the problems of the physiology of the human and animal infancy. *Československá Pediatrie*, *12*, 375–392.

9. Papoušek, H., & Janovský, M. (1957). Infant nutrition. In K. Kubát (Ed.), *The principles of the care for newborns* (pp. 93–122). Prague: Státní Zdravotnické Nakladatelství.

10. Papoušek, H. (1959). Method of studying conditioned food reflexes in infants during the first six months of their life. *Zhurnal Vysshey Nervnoy Deyatelnosti*, *9*, 143–148.

11. Papoušek, H. (1959). New methods for studying the higher nervous functions in early human infancy. *Activitas Nervosa Superior*, *1*, 130–131.

191

12. Papoušek, H. (1959). The group rearing of children below three years in the USSR. *Československá Pediatrie, 14,* 183–186.

13. Papoušek, H. (1959). Studies of the higher nervous activity in the early childhood in the USSR. *Československá Pediatrie, 14,* 275–280.

14. Papoušek, H. (1959). Research in human neonatology in the USSR. *Československá Pediatrie, 14,* 471–476.

15. Papoušek, H. (1960). *Conditioned alimentary motor reflexes in infants.* Unpublished dissertation for the degree of Candidate of Sciences, 1959, the Charles University, Prague.

16. Papoušek, H. (1960). Conditioned motor alimentary reflexes in infants: I. Experimental conditioned sucking reflexes. *Československá Pediatrie, 15,* 861–872.

17. Papoušek, H. (1960). Conditioned motor alimentary reflexes in infants: II. A new experimental method of investigation. *Československá Pediatrie, 15,* 981–988.

18. Papoušek, H. (1960). Conditioned alimentary motor reflexes in infants: III. Experimental conditioned rotation reflexes of the head. *Československá Pediatrie, 15,* 1057–1065.

19. Papoušek, H. (1960, September). *Physiological aspects of the early ontogenesis of the so-called voluntary activity.* In Proceedings of the I. International Symposium on Development of Functions and Metabolism in the Higher Sections of the Central Nervous System, Pilsen.

20. Papoušek, H. (1961). Conditioned alimentary motor responses in infants. *Thomayerova Sbírka Přednásek* (Vol. 409). Prague: Státní Zdravotnické Nakladatelství.

21. Papoušek, H. (1961). Über die Beziehungen einiger Formen des Hospitalismus bei Säuglingen zur Ontogenesis der Nahrungsreflexe. In H. Schwarz (Ed.), *Das milieugeschädigte Kind* (pp. 37–39). Sammlung zwangloser Abhandlungen aus dem Gebiete der Psychiatrie und Neurologie, H. 21. Jena: G. Fischer.

22. Papoušek, H. (1961). Conditioned head rotation reflexes in infants in the first month of life. *Acta Pediatrica* (Uppsala), *50,* 565–576.

23. Papoušek, H. (1961). A physiological view of early ontogenesis of so-called voluntary movements. *Plzeňský lékařský Sborník* (Suppl. 3), 195–198.

24. Janos, O., Dittrichova, J., Koch, J., & Papoušek, H. (1961). The higher nervous functions in early infancy. In M. Vojta (Ed.), *10 years of the care for the health of the youngest generation* (pp. 20–23). Prague: Research Institute for the Care of Mother and Child.

25. Cibulec, A., & Papoušek, H. (1961). Electro-acoustical metronom. *Activitas Nervosa Superior, 3,* 448–452.

26. Papoušek, H. (1962). On the development of the so-called voluntary movements in the earliest stages of the child's development. *Československá Pediatrie, 17,* 588–591.

27. Papoušek, H. (1962). Physiological aspects of "voluntary movements" in early ontogeny. *Acta Universitatis Carolinae Medicinae* (Prague), *8,* 665–680.

28. Dittrichová, J., Janos, O., & Papoušek, H. (1962). Higher nervous activity in newborn infants. In *100 years of the Czechoslovak Medical Society of J. E. Purkinje* (p. 243). Prague: Czechoslovak Medical Society of J. E. Purkinje.

29. Janos, O., Papoušek, H., & Dittrichová, J. (1962). The influence of age upon some manifestations of higher nervous activity in infants in the first months of life. In *100 years of the Czechoslovak Medical Society of J. E. Purkinje* (pp. 306–307). Prague: Czechoslovak Medical Society of J. E. Purkinje.

30. Papoušek, H. (1963). A pediatrician looks at some ideological problems in bringing up children. *Československá Pediatrie, 18,* 636–639.

31. Papoušek, H. (1963). Paediatric care in Great Britain. *Československá Pediatrie, 18,* 568–571.

32. Papoušek, H. (1963). The education of pre-school children in Great Britain. *Československá Pediatrie, 18,* 757–760.

33. Papoušek, H., Janos, O., & Dittrichová, J. (1963). Development of higher nervous activity of infant in the first months of life. In *Proceedings of the 6th Congress of Developmental Morphology, Physiology, Biochemistry* (pp. 435–436). Moscow: Akademiya Pedagogizheskykh Nauk.

34. Dittrichová, J., Janos, O., & Papoušek, H. (1963). Methods and criteria in research work concerning the development of infants during the first year of life. In *Handbook of efficiency criteria. Proceedings of the 1963 Conference of the Czechoslovac Academy of Science at Liblice* (pp. 199–204). Prague: Czechoslovac Academy of Science.

35. Janos, O., Papoušek, H., & Dittrichová, J. (1963). The influence of age upon some manifestations of higher nervous activity in the first months of life. *Activitas Nervosa Superior, 5,* 407–410.

36. Kubát, K., Papoušek, H., & Štolová, O. (1963). On some comments to the problems of child rearing in family and in institutions. *Československá Pediatrie, 18,* 468.

37. Papoušek, H. (1964). Some problems of child care institutions. *Československá Pediatrie, 19,* 1117.

38. Papoušek, H. (1964). Conditioned reflectory movements of the head in the human newborn. *Activitas Nervosa Superior, 6,* 83–84.

39. Papoušek, H. (1965). The development of higher nervous activity in children in the first half-year of life. In European Research in Cognitive Development. *Monographs of the Society for Research in Child Development, 30*(2, Serial No. 100), 102–111.

40. Papoušek, H. (1965). Manifestation of genetic differences in the behavior of man. Wenner-Gren Foundation Symposium in Wartenstein 1964. *Activitas Nervosa Superior, 7,* 92–94.

41. Papoušek, H. (1965). Individual differences in conditioned food-seeking reflexes in newborns. *Activitas Nervosa Superior, 7,* 140–141.

42. Janos, O., Dittrichová, J., Koch, J., Papoušek, H., Tautermannová, M., & Melichar, V. (1966). Early development of higher nervous activity in premature infants with respiratory distress syndrome. *Activitas Nervosa Superior, 8,* 201.

43. Janos, O., & Papoušek, H. (1966). Comparison of appetitional and aversive conditioning in the same infants. *Activitas Nervosa Superior, 8,* 203–204.

44. Papoušek, H. (1967). Experimental studies of appetitional behavior in human newborns and infants. In H. W. Stevenson, E. H. Hess, & H. L. Rheingold

(Eds.), *Early behavior: Comparative and developmental approaches* (pp. 249–277). New York: Wiley.

45. Papoušek, H. (1967). Conditioning during early post-natal development. In Y. Brackbill & G. G. Thompson (Eds.), *Behavior in infancy and early childhood* (pp. 259–274). New York: The Free Press.

46. Papoušek, H. (1967). Genetics and child development. In J. N. Spuhler (Ed.), *Genetic diversity and human behavior* (pp. 171–186). Chicago: Aldine.

47. Papoušek, H. (1967). When longitudinal inquiry is essential. In J. L. Fearing & G. T. Kowitz (Eds.), *Some views of longitudinal inquiry* (pp. 108–120). Houston: Research and Services Series No. 321.

48. Papoušek, H. (1967). Experimental studies of the development of learning abilities in human infants during the first months of life. *Pediatria Internazionale* (Roma), *17*, 199–206.

49. Papoušek, H. (1967). Studies on early mental development, their social importance, and needs of international cooperation. *Materialy i Prace Antropologiczne* (75), 26–27.

50. Papoušek, H., & Jungmannová, C. (1967). Nutrition. In K. Kubát (Ed.), *Care of the newborn infant* (pp. 50–83). Prague: Státní Zdravotnické Nakladatelství.

51. Papoušek, H., Kubát, K., Štolová, O., & Šamánková, L. (1967). Symposion on nurseries. Prague, 24–26 Oct., 1966. *Československá Pediatrie, 22*, 1036–1042.

52. Kubát, K., Štolová, O., Syrovátka, A., & Papoušek, H. (1969). Sociologic aspects of modern pediatrics. *Demografie, 11*, 30–36.

53. Papoušek, H., & Bernstein, P. (1969). Basic cognitive functions in the pre-verbal period of infancy. *Activitas Nervosa Superior, 11*, 285–286.

54. Papoušek, H., & Bernstein, P. (1969). The functions of conditioning stimulation in human neonates and infants. In A. Ambrose (Ed.), *Stimulation in early infancy* (pp. 229–252). London: Academic Press.

55. Papoušek, H. (1969). Individual variability in learned responses in human infants. In R. J. Robinson (Ed.), *Brain and early behaviour development in the fetus and infant* (pp. 251–266). London: Academic Press.

56. Martinius, J. W., & Papoušek, H. (1970). Responses to optic and exteroceptive stimuli in relation to state in the human newborn: Habituation of the blink reflex. *Neuropädiatrie, 1*, 452–460.

57. Papoušek, H. (1970). Effects of group rearing conditions during the preschool years of life. In V. H. Denenberg (Ed.), *Education of the infant and young child* (pp. 51–59). New York: Academic Press.

58. Papoušek, H. (1973). Group rearing in day care centers and mental health: Potential advantages and risks. In J. I. Nurnberger (Ed.), *Biological and environmental determinants of early development*. Research Publications of the Association of Nervous and Mental Diseases (Vol. 51, pp. 398–411). Baltimore: Williams & Wilkins.

59. Papoušek, H., & Papoušek, M. (1974). Mirror image and self-recognition in young human infants: I. A new method of experimental analysis. *Developmental Psychobiology, 7*, 149–157.

60. Papoušek, H., & Papoušek, M. (1974). Die Mutter-Kind-Beziehung und die kognitive Entwicklung des Kindes. In R. Nissen & P. Strunck (Eds.), *Seelische Fehlentwicklung im Kindesalter und Gesellschaftsstruktur* (pp. 83–100). Neuwied: Luchterhand Verlag.

61. Papoušek, H. (1975). Soziale Interaktion als Grundlage der kognitiven Frühentwicklung. In T. Hellbrügge (Ed.), *Kindliche Sozialisation und Sozialentwicklung* (pp. 117–141). Fortschritte der Sozialpädiatrie, Vol. 2. München: Urban & Schwarzenberg.

62. Papoušek, H. (1975). Der Säugling und seine soziale Umwelt: Heutige Forschung und gesellschaftliche Trends. In H. Heinemann & H. Wichterich (Eds.), *Kind und Gesellschaft* (pp. 28–41). Neuburgweier: Schindele.

63. Papoušek, H. (1975). Early human ontogeny of the regulation of behavioral states in relation to information processing and adaptation organizing. In P. Levin & W. P. Koella (Eds.), *Sleep 1974. 2nd European Congress of Sleep Research, Rome 1974* (pp. 384–387). Basel: Karger.

64. Papoušek, H., & Papoušek, M. (1975). Cognitive aspects of preverbal social interaction between human infants and adults. In *Parent–infant interaction*. Ciba Foundation Symposium 33 (New Series) (pp. 241–260). Amsterdam: Elsevier.

65. Papoušek, H. (1976). Die Entwicklung früher Lernprozesse im Säuglingsalter. *Der Kinderarzt, 6*(10), 1077–1081; *6*(11), 1205–1207; *6*(12), 1331–1334.

66. Papoušek, H. (1976). Food and psychological development. In D. N. Walcher, N. Kretchmer, & H. L. Barnett (Eds.), *Food, man, and society* (pp. 244–254). New York: Plenum.

67. Papoušek, H., & Papoušek, M. (1977). Das Spiel in der Frühentwicklung des Kindes. *Pädiatrische Praxis, 18*(Suppl.), 17–32.

68. Papoušek, H., & Papoušek, M. (1977). Mothering and cognitive head-start: Psychobiological considerations. In H. R. Schaffer (Ed.), *Studies in mother–infant interaction* (pp. 63–85). London: Academic Press.

69. Papoušek, H. (1977). Entwicklung der Lernfähigkeit im Säuglingsalter. In G. Nissen (Ed.), *Intelligenz, Lernen und Lernstörungen* (pp. 89–107). Berlin: Springer.

70. Papoušek, H., & Papoušek, M. (1977). Die ersten sozialen Beziehungen: Entwicklungschance oder pathogene Situation? *Praxis der Psychotherapie, 22,* 97–108.

71. Janos, O., & Papoušek, H. (1977). Acquisition of appetitional and palpebral conditioned reflexes by same infants. *Early Human Development, 1,* 91–97.

72. Papoušek, H. (1977). Individual differences in adaptive processes of infants. In A. Oliverio (Ed.), *Genetics, environment and intelligence* (pp. 269–283). Amsterdam: Elsevier.

73. Schoetzau, A., & Papoušek, H. (1977). Mütterliches Verhalten bei der Aufnahme von Blickkontakt mit dem Neugeborenen. *Zeitschrift für Entwicklungspsychologie und pädagogische Psychologie, 9,* 231–239.

74. Papoušek, H., & Papoušek, M. (1977). Die Entwicklung kognitiver Prozesse im Säuglingsalter. *Der Kinderarzt, 8*(8), 1071–1077; *8*(9), 1088–1089.

75. Papoušek, H. (1977). Entwicklung der Lernfähigkeit im Säuglingsalter. In G. Nissen (Ed.), *Intelligenz, Lernen und Lernstörungen: Theorie, Praxis und Therapie* (pp. 75–93). Berlin: Springer-Verlag.

76. Simons, G., & Papoušek, H. (1978). Methoden der Kleinkindforschung: Beobachtung und Experiment. In R. Dollase (Ed.), *Handbuch der Früh- und Vorschulpädagogik* (Vol. 2, pp. 93–110). Düsseldorf: Pädagogischer Verlag Schwann.

77. Papoušek, H., & Papoušek, M. (1978). Interdisciplinary parallels in studies of early human behavior: From physical to cognitive needs, from attachment to dyadic education. *International Journal of Behavioral Development, 1*, 37–49.

78. Papoušek, H. (1979). From adaptive responses to social cognition: The learning view of development. In M. H. Bornstein & W. Kessen (Eds.), *Psychological development from infancy: Image to intention* (pp. 251–267). Hillsdale, NJ: Lawrence Erlbaum Associates.

79. Papoušek, H. (1979). Verhaltensweisen der Mutter und des Neugeborenen unmittelbar nach der Geburt. *Archives of Gynecology, 228* (42.Gynäkologen-Bericht), 26–32.

80. Papoušek, H., & Papoušek, M. (1979). Lernen im ersten Lebensjahr. In L. Montada (Ed.), *Brennpunkte der Entwicklungspsychologie* (pp. 194–212). Stuttgart: Kohlhammer.

81. Papoušek, H., & Papoušek, M. (1979). The infant's fundamental adaptive response system in social interaction. In E. B. Thoman (Ed.), *Origins of the infant's social responsiveness* (pp. 175–208). Hillsdale, NJ: Lawrence Erlbaum Associates.

82. Papoušek, H., & Papoušek, M. (1979). Early ontogeny of human social interaction: Its biological roots and social dimensions. In M. von Cranach, K. Foppa, W. Lepenies, & D. Ploog (Eds.), *Human ethology: Claims and limits of a new discipline* (pp. 456–478). Cambridge, England: Cambridge University Press.

83. Papoušek, H., & Papoušek, M. (1979). Care of the normal and high risk newborn: A psychobiological view of parental behavior. In S. Harel (Ed.), *The at risk infant* (pp. 368–371). International Congress Series No. 492. Amsterdam: Excerpta Medica.

84. Papoušek, H. (1980). Diskussionsbeitrag zur Frage von Kontinuität und Diskontinuität in der Verhaltensbiologie von Depression. In H. Heimann & H. Giedke (Eds.), *Neue Perspektiven in der Depressionsforschung* (pp. 48–52). Bern: Huber.

85. Papoušek, H. (1980). Diskussionsbeitrag zur Bedeutung der Kontingenz in der Verhaltensbiologie von Depression. In H. Heimann & H. Giedke (Eds.), *Neue Perspektiven in der Depressionsforschung* (pp. 188–190). Bern/Stuttgart/Wien: H. Huber.

86. Papoušek, H., & Mangione, P. (1980). A comment to Keogh, B. K. & Glover, A. T., "Research needs in the study of early identification of children with learning disabilities." *Thalamus, 1*, 21–22.

87. Papoušek, H., & Papoušek, M. (1981). Die frühe Eltern-Kind-Beziehung und ihre Störungen aus psychobiologischer Sicht. In O. Hövels, E. Halberstadt, V. v. Loewenich, & I. Eckert (Eds.), *Geburtshilfe und Kinderheilkunde: Gemeinsame aktuelle, praktische Probleme.* Symposium in Bad Kreuznach 1979 (pp. 72–79). Stuttgart/New York: Thieme.

88. Papoušek, H. (1981). The common in the uncommon child: Comments on the child's integrative capacities and on intuitive parenting. In M. Lewis & L. A. Rosenblum (Eds.), *The uncommon child* (pp. 317–328). New York: Plenum.

89. Papoušek, H. (1981). Audiovisuelle Verhaltensregistrierung mit Hilfe von Film- und Fernsehtechnik. In H. Remschmidt & M. Schmidt (Eds.), *Neuropsychologie des Kindesalters* (pp. 49–57). Stuttgart: Enke.

90. Papoušek, H., & Papoušek, M. (1981). Frühentwicklung des Sozialverhaltens und der Kommunikation. In H. Remschmidt & M. Schmidt (Eds.), *Neuropsychologie des Kindesalters* (pp. 182–190). Stuttgart: Enke.

91. Papoušek, M., & Papoušek, H. (1981). Neue Wege der Verhaltensbeobachtung und Verhaltensmikroanalyse. *Sozialpädiatrie in Praxis und Klinik, 3*, 20–22.

92. Papoušek, M., & Papoušek, H. (1981). Verhaltensmikroanalyse mit Hilfe der Filmtechnik. *Sozialpädiatrie in Praxis und Klinik, 3*, 60–64.

93. Papoušek, M., & Papoušek, H. (1981). Verhaltensmikroanalyse mit Hilfe der Fernsehtechnik. *Sozialpädiatrie in Praxis und Klinik, 3*, 137–141.

94. Papoušek, M., & Papoušek, H. (1981). Intuitives elterliches Verhalten im Zwiegespräch mit dem Neugeborenen. *Sozialpädiatrie in Praxis und Klinik, 3*, 229–238.

95. Papoušek, M., & Papoušek, H. (1981). Musikalische Ausdruckselemente der Sprache und ihre Modifikation in der "Ammensprache." *Sozialpädiatrie in Praxis und Klinik, 3*, 294–296.

96. Papoušek, H., & Papoušek, M. (1981). How human is the newborn, and what else is to be done? In K. Bloom (Ed.), *Prospective issues in infancy research* (pp. 137–155). Hillsdale, NJ: Lawrence Erlbaum Associates.

97. Papoušek, H., & Papoušek, M. (1981). Lernpsychologische Grundlagen der normalen psychischen Entwicklung. *Der Kassenarzt, 21*, 1832–1838.

98. Papoušek, M., & Papoušek, H. (1981). Musical elements: Their significance for communication, cognition, and creativity. In L. P. Lipsitt (Ed.), *Advances in infancy research* (Vol. 1, pp. 163–224). Norwood, NJ: Ablex.

99. Papoušek, H., & Papoušek, M. (1982). Vocal imitations in mother–infant dialogues. *Infant Behavior and Development* (Special ICIS Issue), *5*, 176.

100. Papoušek, H., & Papoušek, M. (1982). Integration into the social world: Survey of research. In P. M. Stratton (Ed.), *Psychobiology of the human newborn* (pp. 367–390). London: Wiley.

101. Papoušek, H., & Papoušek, M. (1982). Infant–adult social interactions, their origins, dimensions, and failures. In T. M. Field, A. Huston, H. C. Quay, L. Troll, & G. A. Finley (Eds.), *Review of developmental psychology* (pp. 148–163). New York: Wiley.

102. Papoušek, H., & Papoušek, M. (1982). Zur Frühentwicklung der Kommunikation. In K. R. Scherer (Ed.), *Vokale Kommunikation* (pp. 78–84). Weinheim/Basel: Beltz.

103. Papoušek, H., & Papoušek, M. (1982). Die Rolle der sozialen Interaktionen in der psychischen Entwicklung und Pathogenese von Entwicklungsstörungen

im Säuglingsalter. In G. Nissen (Ed.), *Psychiatrie des Säuglings- und des frühen Kleinkindalters* (pp. 69–74). Bern: Huber.

104. Papoušek, H., & Papoušek, M. (1983). Interactional failures: Their origins and significance in infant psychiatry. In J. D. Call, E. Galenson, & R. L. Tyson (Eds.), *Frontiers of infant psychiatry* (pp. 31–37). New York: Basic Books.

105. Papoušek, H., & Papoušek, M. (1983). Biological basis of social interactions: Implications of research for an understanding of behavioural deviance. *Journal of Child Psychology and Psychiatry* (Special Issue No. 1), *24*, 117–129.

106. Papoušek, H., & Papoušek, M. (1983). The psychobiology of the first didactic programs and toys in human infants. In A. Oliverio & M. Zappella (Eds.), *The behavior of human infants* (pp. 219–239). New York: Plenum.

107. Papoušek, H., & Papoušek, M. (1984). Learning and cognition in the everyday life of human infants. In J. S. Rosenblatt (Ed.), *Advances in the study of behavior* (Vol. 14, pp. 127–163). New York: Academic Press.

108. Papoušek, H., Papoušek, M., & Giese, R. (1984). Die Anfänge der Eltern-Kind-Beziehung. In V. Frick-Bruder & P. Platz (Eds.), *Psychosomatische Probleme in der Gynäkologie und Geburtshilfe* (pp. 187–204). Berlin: Springer.

109. Papoušek, H., & Papoušek, M. (1984). Qualitative transitions in integrative processes during the first trimester of human postpartum life. In H. F. R. Prechtl (Ed.), *Continuity of neural functions from prenatal to postnatal life* (pp. 220–244). Spastics International Medical Publications. Oxford: Blackwell Scientific.

110. Papoušek, M., & Papoušek, H. (1984). Categorical vocal cues in parental communication with presyllabic infants (Abstract). *Infant Behavior and Development* (Special ICIS Issue), *7*, 283.

111. Papoušek, H., & Papoušek, M. (1984). The evolution of parent–infant attachment: New psychobiological perspectives. In J. D. Call, E. Galenson, & R. L. Tyson (Eds.), *Frontiers of infant psychiatry* (Vol. 2, pp. 276–283). New York: Basic Books.

112. Papoušek, H., Papoušek, M., & Bornstein, M. H. (1985). The naturalistic vocal environment of young infants: On the significance of homogeneity and variability in parental speech. In T. Field & N. Fox (Eds.), *Social perception in infants* (pp. 269–297). Norwood, NJ: Ablex.

113. Papoušek, H., & Papoušek, M. (1985). Der Beginn der sozialen Integration nach der Geburt: Krisen oder Kontinuitäten? *Monatsschrift der Kinderheilkunde, 133*, 425–429.

114. Koester, L. S., Papoušek, H., & Papoušek, M. (1985). Patterns of rhythmic stimulation by mothers with young infants: A comparison of multiple modalities (Abstract). *Cahiers de Psychologie Cognitive, 5*, 270–271.

115. Papoušek, H., Papoušek, M., & Haekel, M. (1985). Der Vater und sein Säugling: Anfänge einer Beziehung. In C. Mühlfeld, H. Oppl, H. Weber, & W. R. Wendt (Eds.), *Brennpunkte sozialer Arbeit* (pp. 48–63). Frankfurt: Diesterweg.

116. Papoušek, H. (1985). Biologische Wurzeln der ersten Kommunikation im menschlichen Leben. In W. Böhme (Ed.), *Evolution der Sprache: Über Entstehung und Wesen der Sprache* (pp. 33–47). Herrenalber Texte, No. 66. Karlsruhe:

Evangelische Akademie. Also published in W. Böhme, H. Greifenstein, E. Lohse, G. Ruhbach, K. Schmidt-Clausen, & M. Seitz (Eds.), *Zeitwende, 57*, 1–16.

117. Papoušek, M., & Papoušek, H. (1986). Didactic adjustment in parental speech to three-month-old infants: Age-specificity, and universality across sex of parent (Abstract). *Infant Behavior and Development* (Special Issue), *9*, 285.

118. Papoušek, H., Papoušek, M., & Giese, R. (1986). Neue wissenschaftliche Ansätze zum Verständnis der Mutter-Kind-Beziehung. In J. Stork (Ed.), *Zur Psychologie und Psychopathologie des Säuglings: Neue Ergebnisse in der psychoanalytischen Reflektion* (pp. 53–71). Problemata, 112. Stuttgart/Bad Cannstatt: Frommata-Holzboog.

119. Papoušek, H., Papoušek, M., & Koester, L. S. (1986). Sharing emotionality and sharing knowledge: A microanalytic approach to parent–infant communication. In C. E. Izard & P. Read (Eds.), *Measuring emotions in infants and children* (Vol. 2, pp. 93–123). Cambridge, England: Cambridge University Press.

120. Papoušek, H., & Papoušek, M. (1986). Structure and dynamics of human communication at the beginning of life. *European Archives of Psychiatry and Neurological Sciences, 236*, 21–25.

121. Papoušek, M., Papoušek, H., & Harris, B. J. (1987). The emergence of play in parent–infant interactions. In D. Görlitz & J. F. Wohlwill (Eds.), *Curiosity, imagination, and play: On the development of spontaneous cognitive and motivational processes* (pp. 214–246). Hillsdale, NJ: Lawrence Erlbaum Associates.

122. Papoušek, H., & Papoušek, M. (1987). Intuitive parenting: A dialectic counterpart to the infant's integrative competence. In J. D. Osofsky (Ed.), *Handbook of infant development* (2nd ed., pp. 669–720). New York: Wiley.

123. Papoušek, H., Papoušek, M., & Harris, B. J. (1987). Intuitive parenting behaviors: An early support for the infant's mental health development. In H. Galjaard, H. F. R. Prechtl, & M. Velickovic (Eds.), *Early detection and management of cerebral palsy* (pp. 121–136). Dordrecht: Martinus Nijhoff.

124. Koester, L. S., Papoušek, H., & Papoušek, M. (1987). Psychobiological models of infant development: Influences on the concept of intuitive parenting. In H. Rauh & H.-C. Steinhausen (Eds.), *Advances in psychology: Vol. 46. Psychobiology and early development* (pp. 275–287). North Holland: Elsevier.

125. Papoušek, H., & Papoušek, M. (1987). *The structure and dynamics of early parental interventions: A potential contribution to evolution and ontogeny of speech.* Urbana: Clearing House on Early Childhood Education. (ERIC Document Reproduction Service No. 276528)

126. Papoušek, M., Papoušek, H., & Haekel, M. (1987). Didactic adjustments in fathers' and mothers' speech to their three-month-old infants. *Journal of Psycholinguistic Research, 16*, 491–516.

127. Papoušek, H., & Papoušek, M. (1988). Musikalität am Anfang des Lebens. *Üben und Musizieren, 5*(1), 25–30.

128. Papoušek, H. (1988). The Middle European contribution to infancy research. In *Research and Clinical Center for Child Development Annual Report No. 10* (pp. 9–20). Sapporo, Japan: Hokkaido University.

129. Papoušek, H., & Papoušek, M. (1989). Frühe Kommunikationsentwicklung und körperliche Beeinträchtigung. In A. Fröhlich (Ed.), *Kommunikation und*

Sprache körperbehinderter Kinder (pp. 29–44). Dortmund: Verlag Modernes Lernen.

130. Papoušek, H. (1989). Coevolution of supportive counterparts in caretakers: A potential contribution to the hemispheric specialization during early infancy. *Cahiers de Psychologie Cognitive, 9*, 113–117.

131. Koester, L. S., Papoušek, H., & Papoušek, M. (1989). Patterns of rhythmic stimulation by mothers with three-month-olds: A cross-modal comparison. *International Journal of Behavioural Development, 12*, 143–154.

132a. Papoušek, H., & Papoušek, M. (1989). Intuitive parenting: Aspects related to psychology. In B. Hopkins, M.-G. Pecheux, & H. Papoušek (Eds.), Infancy and education: Psychological considerations. *European Journal of Psychology of Education, 4*(2, Special Issue), 201–210.

132b. Hopkins, B., Pecheux, M.-G., & Papoušek, H. (Eds.). (1989). Infancy and education: Psychological considerations. *European Journal of Psychology of Education, 4*(2, Special Issue).

133. Papoušek, M., & Papoušek H. (1989). Stimmliche Kommunikation im frühen Säuglingsalter als Wegbereiter der Sprachentwicklung. In H. Keller (Ed.), *Handbuch der Kleinkindforschung* (pp. 465–489). Berlin: Springer-Verlag.

134. Papoušek, H., & Papoušek, M. (1989). Ontogeny of social interactions in newborn infants. In C. von Euler, H. Forssberg, & H. Lagercrantz (Eds.), *Neurobiology of early infant behaviour* (pp. 217–225). Proceedings of an International Wallenberg Symposium at the Wenner-Gren Centre, Stockholm, August 28–September 1, 1988. Vol. 55. London: Macmillan.

135. Papoušek, H. (1989). A remedy for Stendhal's syndrome. Review of J. B. Lancaster, J. Altmann, A. S. Rossi, & L. R. Sherrod (Eds.), Parenting across the life span: Biosocial dimensions. (New York: de Gruyter, 1987). *Contemporary Psychology, 34*, 688–689.

136. Papoušek, M., & Papoušek, H. (1989). Wie wird die unbekannte Welt vertraut? Ein Blick in die frühe Erfahrungswelt des Kindes. *Welt des Kindes, 5*, 31–36.

137. Papoušek, M., & Papoušek, H. (1989). Forms and functions of vocal matching in interactions between mothers and their precanonical infants. *First Language, 9*(Special Issue on "Precursors to speech"), 137–158.

138. Papoušek, H. (1989). Kinderärzte und Früherziehung. *Der Kinderarzt, 20*, 1605–1610.

139. Papoušek, H. (1990). Frühe Eltern-Kind-Interaktion in ihrer Bedeutung für die kindliche Entwicklung. *Der Kinderarzt, 21*(2), 191–194.

140. Papoušek, H., & Papoušek, M. (1990). Frühe Kommunikation, soziale Integration. *Beschäftigungstherapie und Rehabilitation, 29*, 189–194.

141. Papoušek, M., & Papoušek, H. (1990). Intuitive elterliche Früherziehung in der vorsprachlichen Kommunikation: I. Grundlagen und Verhaltensrepertoire. *Sozialpädiatrie in Praxis und Klinik, 12*(7), 521–527.

142. Papoušek, M., & Papoušek, H. (1990). Intuitive elterliche Früherziehung in der vorsprachlichen Kommunikation: II. Früherkennung von Störungen und therapeutische Ansätze. *Sozialpädiatrie in Praxis und Klinik, 12*(8), 579–583.

143. Papoušek, H., & Papoušek, M. (1990). Die Kunst der Mutterliebe. In Foundation Scientific Europe (Ed.), *Wissenschaft und Technik in Europa* (pp. 382–387). Heidelberg: Spektrum der Wissenschaften.

144. Papoušek, M., Bornstein, M. H., Nuzzo, C., Papoušek, H., & Symmes, D. (1990). Infant responses to prototypical melodic contours in parental speech. *Infant Behavior and Development, 13,* 539–545.

145. Papoušek, M., & Papoušek, H. (1990). Excessive infant crying and intuitive parental care: Buffering support and its failures in parent–infant interaction [Special issue]. *Early Child Development and Care, 65,* 117–126.

146. Papoušek, H., & Papoušek, M. (1990). The art of motherhood. In N. Calder (Ed.), *Scientific Europe: Research and technology in 20 countries* (pp. 382–387). Maastricht, Holland: Scientific Publishers.

147. Papoušek, H., & Papoušek, M. (1991). Innate and cultural guidance of infants' integrative competencies: China, the United States, and Germany. In M. H. Bornstein (Ed.), *Cultural approaches to parenting* (pp. 23–44). Hillsdale, NJ: Lawrence Erlbaum Associates.

148. Papoušek, H. (1991). Frühe menschliche Kommunikation: Biologisches Erbe und Entwicklungspotential. In H. Viebrock & U. Holste (Eds.), *Therapie. Anspruch und Widerspruch* (pp. 70–83). Bremen: Bremische Evangelische Kirche.

149. Papoušek, H., Papoušek, M., Suomi, S., & Rahn, C. (1991). Preverbal communication and attachment: Comparative views. In J. L. Gewirtz & W. M. Kurtines (Eds.), *Intersections with attachment* (pp. 97–122). Hillsdale, NJ: Lawrence Erlbaum Associates.

150. Papoušek, H. (1991). Toward hemispheric specialization during infancy: Manual skills versus acquisition of speech. In H. E. Fitzgerald, B. M. Lester, & M. W. Yogman (Eds.), *Theory and research in behavioral pediatrics* (Vol. 5, pp. 209–215). New York: Plenum.

151. Papoušek, M., & Papoušek, H. (1991). Early verbalizations as precursors of language development. In M. E. Lamb & H. Keller (Eds.), *Infant development: Perspectives from German-speaking countries* (pp. 299–328). Hillsdale, NJ: Lawrence Erlbaum Associates.

152. Papoušek, M., Papoušek, H., & Symmes, D. (1991). The meanings of melodies in motherese in tone and stress languages. *Infant Behavior and Development, 14,* 415–440.

153. Papoušek, H., & Papoušek, M. (1992). Early integrative and communicative development: Pointers to humanity. In H. M. Emrich & M. Wiegand (Eds.), *Integrative biological psychiatry* (pp. 45–60). Berlin: Springer-Verlag.

154. Papoušek, H., Jürgens, U., & Papoušek, M. (Eds.). (1992). *Nonverbal vocal communication: Comparative and developmental aspects.* New York: Cambridge University Press.

155. Papoušek, H., & Bornstein, M. H. (1992). Didactic interactions: Intuitive parental support of vocal and verbal development in humans. In H. Papoušek, U. Jürgens, & M. Papoušek (Eds.), *Nonverbal vocal communication: Comparative and developmental aspects* (pp. 209–229). Cambridge, England: Cambridge University Press.

156. Papoušek, H., & Papoušek, M. (1992). Beyond emotional bonding: The role of preverbal communication in mental growth and health. *Infant Mental Health Journal, 13*, 42–52.

157. Papoušek, H. (1992). Láska rodice pod mikroskopem [Microscopic view of parental love]. *Efeta, 2*(1), 11–14.

158. Beek, Y. van, Papoušek, H., & Hopkins, B. (1992). Beweging en vroege communicatie bij prematuren [Movement and early communication in prematures]. In B. Hopkins & A. Vermeer (Eds.), *Kinderen in beweging* (pp. 63–77). Amsterdam: Free University Press.

159. Papoušek, H., & Papoušek, M. (1992). Vorsprachliche Kommunikation: Anfänge, Formen, Störungen und psychotherapeutische Ansätze. *Integrative Therapie, 18*(1–2), 139–155. Also in H. G. Petzold (Ed.), *Die Kraft liebevoller Blicke. Psychotherapie & Babyforschung: Vol. 2. Säuglingsbeobachtungen revolutionisieren die Psychotherapie* (pp. 123–141). Paderborn, Germany: Junfermann Verlag, 1995.

160. Papoušek, H., & Papoušek, M. (1993). Early interactional signalling: The role of facial movements. In A. F. Kalverboer, B. Hopkins, & R. H. Geuze (Eds.), *A longitudinal approach to the study of motor development in early and later childhood* (pp. 136–152). Cambridge, England: Cambridge University Press.

161. Papoušek, H. (1992). Contemporary approaches to individual differences in infants (Review of J. Colombo and J. Fagen (Eds.), *Individual differences in infancy: Reliability, stability, prediction.* Hillsdale, NJ: Lawrence Erlbaum Associates, 1990). *Contemporary Psychology, 37*(7), 712–713.

162. Papoušek, H., & Papoušek, M. (1992). Koevolution von spezifisch menschlichen Prädispositionen zur Sprachentwicklung [Coevolution of specific human predispositions in the development of language]. In H. Gundermann & S. Markner (Eds.), *Wissenschaftliche Zeitschrift der Humboldt-Universität zu Berlin, Reihe Medizin, 41*(2), 25–30.

163. Papoušek, H., & Papoušek, M. (1993). Apprentissage chez le nourrisson: un point de vue synthétique [Learning and memory in infants: A bird's-eye view]. In V. Pouthas & F. Jouen (Eds.), *Les comportements du bebe: Expressions de son savoir?* (pp. 123–137). Liège: P. Mardaga.

164a. Papoušek, H. (1993). Emergence of musicality and its adaptive significance in humans. *European Society for the Cognitive Sciences of Music Newsletter*, No. 3 (April), E 2–6.

164b. Papoušek, H. (1993). Emergence de la musicalité et sa signification adaptive chez l'humain. *European Society for the Cognitive Sciences of Music Bulletin d'Information*, No. 3 (April), F 2–6.

165. Papoušek, H., & Papoušek, M. (1993). Beyond emotional bonding: Preverbal communication and mental health in children. In J. E. de Boer (Ed.), *Infant psychiatry II* (pp. 94–102). Assen, Holland: Van Gorcum & Comp.

166. Papoušek, H. (1993). *Frühe Kommunikation: Anfang und Störungen. Bewegung und Entwicklung* (No. 25, pp. 2–7). Bremen: Vereinigung der Bobath-Therapeuten Deutschlands.

167. Papoušek, H. (1993). Transmission of the communicative competence: Genetic, cultural, when, and how? In F. Winnykamen & J. Beaudichon (Eds.),

Gestion socio-cognitive du traitement de l'information chez l'enfant [Socio-cognitive management of information processing in children] (Special issue). *International Journal of Psychology, 28*(5), 709–717.

168. Papoušek, H., & Papoušek, M. (1994). Language and thought in children: A look behind curtains. In A. Vyt, H. Bloch, & M. H. Bornstein (Eds.), *Early child development in the French tradition: Perspectives from current research* (pp. 241–243). Hillsdale, NJ: Lawrence Erlbaum Associates.

169. Papoušek, H. (1994). Emergence of musicality and its adaptive significance. In C. Faienza (Ed.), *Music, speech and the developing brain* (pp. 111–135). Milano: Guerini e Associati.

170. Papoušek, H. (1994). Intuitive parenting: Arguments for comparative approaches. *Early Development and Parenting, 3*(1, Thematic Issue), 1–3.

171. Papoušek, H. (Ed.). (1994). Intuitive parenting: Comparative and clinical approaches. *Early Development and Parenting, 3*(1, Thematic Issue).

172. Papoušek, H. (1994, April). *Infant psychiatry and infancy research: Contributions to concepts and therapeutical applications.* Invited paper at the Japanese Regional Meeting of the World Association of Infant Mental Health, Tokyo.

173. Papoušek, H., & Papoušek, M. (1995). Beginning of human musicality. In R. Steinberg (Ed.), *Music and the mind machine. The psychophysiology and psychopathology of the sense of music* (pp. 27–34). Berlin: Springer-Verlag.

174. Papoušek, H., Rothaug, M., & Flehmig, I. (1995, April). *The role of bodily (tactile, proprioceptive, and vestibular) communication in preverbal caregiver–infant/child interactions.* Paper presented at the biennial meeting of the Society for Research in Child Development, Indianapolis, IN.

175. Koester, L. S., Papoušek, H., & Brooks, L. (1995, April). *The role of tactile contact in deaf and hearing mother–infant dyads.* Paper presented at the biennial meeting of the Society for Research in Child Development, Indianapolis, IN.

176. Papoušek, H. (1995). Frühe Angstmanifestationen im Säuglings- und Kleinkindsalter. In G. Nissen (Hrsg.), *Angsterkrankungen. Prävention und Therapie* (pp. 109–117). Bern: Verlag Hans Huber.

177. Papoušek, H. (1995, Mai). *Bedeutung der Frühentwicklung für die Psychiatrie des Säuglings und Kleinkindes.* Vorgetragem an dem Kongreß der Schweizerischen Gesellschaft für Kinder- und Jugendpsychiatrie und VI. Genfer Symposium über Kinder- und Jugendpsychiatrie in Genf, am 11.–13. Mai.

178. Papoušek, H., & Papoušek, M. (1995). Intuitive parenting. In M. H. Bornstein (Ed.), *Handbook of parenting: Vol. 2. Ecology and biology of parenting* (pp. 117–136). Hillsdale, NJ: Lawrence Erlbaum Associates.

179. Papoušek, H. (1995). Musicalité et petite enfance. Origines biologiques et culturelles de la précocité. In I. Deliège & J. A. Sloboda (Eds.), *Naissance et développement de sens musical* (pp. 41–62). Croissance de l'enfant, genèse de l'homme (No. 27, ed. R. Zazzo). Paris: Presses Universitaires de France.

180. Papoušek, H., & Papoušek, M. (1995). No princípio é uma palavra—uma palavra melodiosa. In J. Gomes-Pedro & M. F. Patrício (Eds.), *Bebé XXI. Crianca e família na viragem do século* (pp. 171–175). Lisbon: Fundacao Calouste Gulbenkian.

181. Papoušek, H., Papoušek, M., & Rothaug, M. (1996). Frühförderung der sozialen Integration des Kindes: Der Zukunft wegen ein Blick in die Vergangenheit. In G. Opp & F. Peterander (Hrsg.), *Focus Heilpädagogik—"Projekt Zukunft"* (pp. 234–242). München: Ernst Reinhardt.

182. Papoušek, H. (1996). Musicality in infancy research: Biological and cultural origins of early musicality. In I. Deliege & J. Sloboda (Eds.), *Musical beginnings: Origins and development of musical competence* (pp. 37–55). Oxford, England: Oxford University Press.

183. Papoušek, H. (1996). In eigener Sache: Die Entwicklungspsychologie der frühen Kindheit. In K. U. Ettrich & M. Fries (Eds.), *Lebenslange Entwicklung in sich wandelnden Zeiten* (pp. 17–22). Landau: Verlag Empirische Pädagogik.

184. Papoušek, H. (1996). Das Spiel des menschlichen Säuglings: Ursprung und Bedeutung. In K. U. Ettrich & M. Fries (Eds.), *Lebenslange Entwicklung in sich wandelnden Zeiten* (pp. 17–22, 37–41). Landau: Verlag Empirische Pädagogik.

185. Papoušek, H., Papoušek, M., & Rothaug, M. (1996). Ein transkultureller Blick auf den Anfang der menschlichen Kommunikation und seine medizinische Bedeutung. In C. E. Gottschalk-Batschkus & J. Schuler (Hrsg.), *Ethnomedizinische Perspektiven zur frühen Kindheit* (pp. 301–310). Berlin: VWB.

186. Papoušek, H., & Papoušek, M. (1996). Environmental support to infants' mental development and health. In S. Harel & J. P. Shonkoff (Eds.), *Early childhood intervention and family support programs: Accomplishments and challenges* (pp. 91–109). Jerusalem: JDC-Brookdale Institute of Gerontology and Human Development.

187. Papoušek, M., & Papoušek, H. (1996). Infantile persistent crying, state regulation, and interaction with parents: A systems view. In M. H. Bornstein & J. L. Genevro (Eds.), *Child development and behavioral pediatrics* (pp. 11–33). Mahwah, NJ: Lawrence Erlbaum Associates.

188. Papoušek, H., & Papoušek, M. (1992). Nemluvnata, jejich prvotní ucitelé a prvotní hracky [Preverbal infants, their primary teachers and primary toys]. In J. Misurcová (Ed.), *Komensky, dedictví a vychova cloveka v 21. století* (pp. 93–101). Prague: Charles University, Comenius Institute of Education.

189. Papoušek, H., & Papoušek, M. (1992). Preverbal infants, their primary teachers and primary toys. In J. Misurcová (Ed.), *Comenius, heritage and education of man for the 21st century* (pp. 84–92). Prague: Charles University, Comenius Institute of Education.

190. Paul, K., Papoušek, H., & Dittrichová, J. (1996). Infant feeding behavior: Development in patterns and motivation. *Developmental Psychobiology, 29*(7), 563–576.

191. Papoušek, H. (1996). Importance du développement précoce pour la psychiatrie du nourrisson et de l'enfant en bas âge. In J. Manzano (Ed.), *Les relations précoces parents–enfants et leurs troubles* (pp. 57–79). Chêne-Bourg, Switzerland: Editions Médecine et Hygiène.

192. Papoušek, H., & Papoušek, M. (1997). Preverbal communication in humans and the genesis of culture. In U. Segerstrale & P. Molnár (Eds.), *Nonverbal communication: Where nature meets culture* (pp. 87–107). Mahwah, NJ: Lawrence Erlbaum Associates.

193. Papoušek, H., & Papoušek, M. (1997). Fragile parts of early social integration. In L. Murray & P. J. Cooper (Eds.), *Postpartum depression and child development* (pp. 35–53). New York: Guilford.

194. Papoušek, H. (1997). Anfang und Bedeutung der menschlichen Musikalität. In H. Keller (Hrsg.), *Handbuch der Kleinkindforschung.* 2. Aufl. (S. 565–585). Bern: Verlag H. Huber.

195. Papoušek, H., & Papoušek, M. (1997). Stimmliche Kommunikation im Säuglingsalter als Wegbereiter der Sprachentwicklung. In H. Keller (Hrsg.), *Handbuch der Kleinkindforschung.* 2. Aufl. (S. 535–562). Bern: Verlag H. Huber.

196. Papoušek, H., Papoušek, M., Kestermann, G., Kiesling, U., & Rothaug, M. (1997). Dialogische Formen der Therapie, pädagogisches Potential und objektive Analyse. In H. Viebrock & U. Brandl (Hrsg.), *Neurophysiologie cerebraler Bewegungsstörungen und Bobath-Therapie* (S. 199–211). Berlin: ProduServ/ Springer Verlag.

197. Paul, K., Dittrichová, J., & Papoušek, H. (1997). Potravové chování kojencu [Feeding behavior in infants]. *Neonatologické Listy, 3*(1), 5–18.

198. Papoušek, H., & Papoušek, M. (1999). Symbolbildung, Emotionsregulation und soziale Interaktion. In W. Friedlmeier & M. Holodynski (Eds.), *Emotionale Entwicklung. Funktion, Regulation und soziokultureller Kontext von Emotionen* (pp. 135–155). Heidelberg: Spektrum Akademischer Verlag.

199. Papoušek, H., Papoušek, M., & Koester, L. S. (1999). Early integration of experience: The interplay of nature and culture. In A. F. Kalverboer, B. Hopkins, & L. Genta (Eds.), *Current issues in developmental neuropsychology* (pp. 27–51). Amsterdam: Kluwer Academic.

200. Papoušek, H. (1999). Die Frühentwicklung des kindlichen orofazialen Systems. In V. Hahn, Ch. Schneider, & H. Hahn (Hrsg.), *Schauplatz Mund. Das orofaziale System als sensomotorische Einheit. Berichte vom 11. Europäischen Kongress für Myofunktionelle Therapie* (pp. 117–125). München: Arbeitskreis für Myofunktionelle Therapie e. V.

201. Papoušek, M., & Papoušek, H. (1999). Intuitive elterliche Früherziehung in der vorsprachlichen Kommunikation. In Th. Hellbrügge (Hrsg.), *Kindliche Sozialisation und Sozialentwicklung* (S. 113–123). Lübeck: Hansisches Verlagskontor.

202. Papoušek, M., & Papoušek, H. (1999). Kritische Belastungen der intuitiven elterlichen Früherziehung. In Th. Hellbrügge (Hrsg.), *Kindliche Sozialisation und Sozialentwicklung* (S. 124–135). Lübeck: Hansisches Verlagskontor.

203. Papoušek, H., Papoušek, M., & Bornstein, M. H. (2000). Spiel und biologische Anpassung. In S. Hoppe-Graff & R. Oerter (Eds.), *Spielen und Fernsehen. Über die Zusammenhänge von Spiel und Medien in der Welt des Kindes* (pp. 21–45). Weinheim: Juventa.

204. Papoušek, H. (2000). Intuitive parenting. In H. E. Fitzgerald & J. D. Osofsky (Eds.), *Handbook of infant mental health* (Vol. 3, pp. 299–322). New York: Wiley.

205. Papoušek, H. (2001). Signalling in early social interaction and communication. In A. F. Kalverboer & A. Gramsbergen (Eds.), *Handbook of brain and behaviour in human development* (pp. 883–900). Dordrecht: Kluwer Academic.

206. Papoušek, H., Papoušek, M., & Kestermann, G. (2000). Preverbal communication: Emergence of representative symbols. In N. Budwig, I. Č. Užgiris, & J. V. Wertsch (Eds.), *Communication: An arena of development. Advances in applied developmental psychology* (pp. 81–107). Norwood, NJ: Ablex.

207. Papoušek, H., & Papoušek, M. (2002). Intuitive parenting. In M. Bornstein (Ed.), *Handbook of parenting: Vol. 2. Biology and ecology of parenting* (pp. 183–203). Mahwah, NJ: Lawrence Erlbaum Associates.

208. Papoušek, H. (2003). Spiel in der Wiege der Menschheit. In M. Papoušek & A. von Gontard (Eds.), *Spiel und Kreativität in der frühen Kindheit* (pp. 17–55). Stuttgart: Pfeiffer bei Klett-Cotta.

209. Koester, L. S., Papoušek, H., & Smith-Gray, S. (2000). Intuitive parenting, communication, and interaction with deaf infants. In P. Spencer, C. Erting, & M. Marschark (Eds.), *The deaf child in the family and at school: Essays in honor of Kathryn P. Meadow-Orlans* (pp. 55–71). Mahwah, NJ: Lawrence Erlbaum Associates.

Author Index

Subject Index

Note. Page number followed by *f* indicates photograph; page number followed by *t* indicates table.